THROUGH MY EYES

THROUGH MY EYES

Tim Tebow with Nathan Whitaker

HarperCollins*Publishers*

Unless otherwise noted, scripture quotations are taken from the
New American Standard Bible®. © Copyright the Lockman Foundation 1960,
1962, 1963, 1968, 1971, 1972, 1973, 1975, 1977, 1995. Used by permission.

Scripture quotations marked (NIV) are taken from the Holy Bible,
New International Version®, NIV®. Copyright © 1973, 1978, 1984, 2010 by
Biblica Inc.™ All rights reserved worldwide.

FIRST EDITION

Library of Congress Cataloging-in-Publication Data is available.

ISBN 978–006–200728–5

11 12 13 14 15 RRD(H) 10 9 8 7 6 5 4 3 2 1

To all those who have been told that they couldn't achieve their dreams . . .

Contents

Preface

Since I first started playing high school football, a lot has been written about me. Some true, some not so true. Some positive, some not so positive. And some of it claiming to even know my mind-set and motivation.

It's not always the easiest thing to be the center of so much spilled ink. You read glowing things, and it doesn't feel deserved. You read things that are critical, and it cuts you to the bone. It's because of both those extremes of others' opinions that I felt it the natural thing to do to tell my story, written from my perspective. It also seemed like the right thing to do—perhaps in many instances to simply set the record straight—sharing my story as I see it, as I remember it, including my actual mind-set and motivation. Sharing it all—what is true and actually happened. Some of it positive, and some perhaps, still, not so positive. That's the nature of truth. But all of it is my story.

Through my eyes.

In addition, the sheer amount that has been written about me also seems to indicate that, for whatever reason, a great number of people have a significant interest in me. In some respects that is very flattering. I'd guess that any one of us would be flattered by that level of interest. However, my parents always told me, from an early age, that we *all* have the ability to influence others, whether through our words or actions, or both. They always added that, besides possessing the ability, we also have the responsibility to use it in a positive, encouraging, and uplifting way—a platform. Who knows? Maybe my platform will be the same in five years; maybe not. One thing I'm confident of is that the Lord already knows the answer to that, and He has a plan for it all. That is something I've learned to have the utmost assurance of and faith in—His daily, weekly, monthly, total and eternal plan for our lives.

Therefore I have learned that, though God is in control of the big picture, I am responsible for how I use my platform, whatever its size—at this moment in time—to influence others. Or whatever my age. Or wherever I am, or no matter what is going on in my life at any time. I have a platform that He can use for His good purposes and perhaps even the good of others—today.

We all know of people who thought they could do it (whatever "it" is) tomorrow. We have all procrastinated in such a way, and often to our personal regret. It happens time and again, putting off things that we convince ourselves might be better, more meaningful, more appropriate for another time. So often that better time either never comes or really isn't better or more appropriate after all. And then, sadly, the window of opportunity—to do something great—closes. Here's something else that I haven't always grasped but which in the last few years I have come to understand in my own life, and which now burns in my heart for others to also recognize and realize: we all have stories to share. We all have life experiences that can bless the lives of others. Whoever we are. Wherever we find ourselves. Whatever we are involved in, no matter our age or station in life. Stories that, when shared with others, can make a positive difference in the world.

As I tell my story, I hope that you will see that its true focus is on God and on those eternal values that He holds before us as beacons and benchmarks, to help us live lives of abundance that will ultimately glorify Him, while also lifting and bettering the lives of His children everywhere.

What it all boils down to is that if there's one kid who keeps pushing to attain his dreams, or . . .

if there's one dad who accepts the saving grace of Christ and changes his whole family, or . . .

if there's one person who sees my mistakes, realizes that we all fall short, and keeps pressing on, or . . .

if there's someone who agrees that Christians don't have to be weak, either in mind, body, or soul, then undertaking this project was the right thing to do, regardless of what the world thinks is the "right time" to write a memoir.

God challenges us to change the world. And to accomplish this, He asks us to change it *one life at a time*.

I appreciate that you are taking this journey alongside me, and I pray that as we take this journey together, you will feel the Lord's presence along the way and that you will let Him cover you with His grace and power.

I also pray that in this journey you and I may discover that not only our lives but the lives of others are better because they were touched by something we have shared together.

Through my eyes.

Chapter One

HEADACHE

The LORD *is my shepherd; I shall not want.*
—PSALM 23:1

My head was killing me.

It had been a full day already, but as if that weren't enough, now my head was splitting in two. The timing could have been better. I was in New York City for the presentation of the Heisman Trophy and I'd spent most of the day exploring New York with my family and friends. But it had taken its toll. A migraine had set in; I guess the travel and schedule had brought it on. I had been traveling non-stop, it seemed, since the conclusion of the regular season a week earlier. I had been blessed enough to win several awards already, including the ones that I was the most proud of, several first-team Academic All-American teams.

The ceremony took place on the periphery of Times Square, at the Nokia Theater, as it was then called. There were about twenty of the 2,100 in attendance on December 10, 2008, who were pretty nervous for me. Those twenty—my parents, siblings and spouses, close friends, Coach Urban Meyer and Coach Mickey Marotti from the University of Florida—had been on hand to support me throughout the entire season, as always, in good times and bad.

Statistically, there had been more good than bad that season. I'd thrown for over 2,500 yards with 28 touchdowns and 2 interceptions. I'd also rushed for 564 yards and had 12 touchdowns. But more important, as a team, we'd seen far more good than bad as well. We were 12–1 and had only had one close game in the last two months—all of them wins.

Of course, Colt McCoy and Sam Bradford, both of whom were invited by the Downtown Athletic Club and were seated beside me on the front row, also had great seasons.

We hadn't played either team, yet. We would be facing Oklahoma and Sam Bradford in the BCS National Championship game a month after the ceremony.

Finally, the moment arrived, and none too soon. As the ceremony unfolded, my head was hurting more and more, and I was feeling nauseated.

The announcement came from the podium, in a moment that none of us would ever forget.

"The Downtown Athletic Club presents the 2008 Heisman Trophy to . . .

Sam Bradford, University of Oklahoma."

My phone began vibrating and wouldn't stop for hours. Texts and voicemails from teammates and coaches, all to the effect that we would take it to Oklahoma in the championship game. I wasn't paying attention to the phone, though, as Sam accepted the award—the pounding in my head had continued to intensify.

Finally, at a break, I headed out to the bathroom to run cold water over my face. On the way, I passed Coach Meyer and Coach Marotti, and I could feel the intensity of their disappointment and anger as I approached. They were obviously biased in my favor, and were two of my biggest advocates.

I caught their eye and mouthed two words.

"Game on."

Chapter Two

GIVEN A CHANCE

*We know that God causes all things to work together for
good to those who love God, to those who are called
according to His purpose.*
—ROMANS 8:28

My dad was preaching in a remote village in the Philippines in 1986. As
The Jesus Film played on a large, homemade screen hanging between
two coconut trees, he became heavily burdened by the millions of
babies being aborted in America. While weeping over the gigan-
tic loss of human life, my dad began to pray, "Father, if you want
another preacher in this world, you give him to me. You give me
Timmy, and I will raise him to be a preacher."

Dad returned home to Mindanao, Philippines where our family
was living, and the next morning at breakfast he told our family
about his prayer and invited them to join him in praying for Timmy.
At first, Mom was not as excited as my four siblings, but after a few
days, she began praying along with the rest of my family—for me—
Timothy, which means, "honoring God."

From the start, it was a difficult pregnancy with a great deal of pain and bleeding. A number of times they were certain they had lost me. Mom and Dad went to the best doctor in their area of Mindanao and listened to her lay out their options—in her opinion—for how to save my mom's life.

After examining my mother, the doctor spoke in a slow monotone. "An abortion is the only way to save your life."

According to her, the "mass of fetal tissue" or "a tumor"—me— had to go.

That is how the doctor viewed me, simply a mass of fetal tissue. It was not an isolated view then, and it isn't an isolated or novel view today. Or maybe she just called me that to toughen us up for the names I would be called the first time I played at LSU.

My parents walked out of her office, shocked and a bit numb, but resolute in what course they would take. My mom's strongest recollection of those moments, which must have been overwhelming for her, was an unexpected and indescribable peace. God's peace, she later told me, is what sustained her through the pain, bleeding, and uncertainty of the next eight months of her pregnancy.

Miraculously, later on in the pregnancy, a surprise blessing occurred. The bleeding subsided, leaving her able to fly, along with my siblings, to Manila. There, at the Makati Medical Center, she met with an American trained doctor. It was the first time she'd seen a doctor since the "mass of fetal tissue" consultation.

In the delivery room, my parents tell me that I entered the world without much fanfare, followed immediately by a blood clot that was bigger than I was.

The attending physician spoke first to my dad, "Mr. Tebow, your child is a miracle baby. I can't explain how it happened, but despite all odds, he beat them. Only a small part of the placenta was attached, but it was just enough to keep your baby nourished all these months."

My mom, dad, and family were so grateful for my safe arrival and thanked the Lord for His protection of both my mom and me. But the drama was not over yet—for either of us.

That first week, I lost weight instead of gaining it and had to remain in the hospital. My parents asked our friends and family in America to pray that I would grow big and strong. I guess their prayers were answered.

Mom also struggled physically and needed ongoing care. The staff at Makati Medical Center provided the expert care both of us needed. Mom had surgery when I was a week old, and she finally began to recover after the health challenges of many months. The doctor told my parents that if we had not come to Manila, Mom probably would not have survived my birth.

We are all grateful Mom survived the pregnancy and childbirth. We have met families whose mothers gave their lives in childbirth for the lives of their children. We also know of children who went through normal pregnancies as well as difficult ones and did not end up thriving or even surviving the birth process at all. My parents knew that Mom might not survive, but they trusted God with her pregnancy. Trusting God is how they started their marriage, and how they have continued to this day. My dad always tells us that faith is like a muscle. You trust God for the small things and when He comes through, your muscle grows. This enables you to trust God for the bigger things, in fact, all things.

And while they waited for me to be born, my mom and brothers and sisters would sing Bible verses together. Mom always believed that putting verses to tunes helped us to learn and retain them. Later, they taught me these verses as well:

Wait for the Lord, be strong and let your heart take courage. Wait for the Lord, wait for the Lord. I wait for the Lord, my soul does wait. And in His Word do I hope.

—PSALM 27:14; 130:5

My unusual birth story has been important to our family for many reasons. Of course, we are so grateful that God's plan included Mom's and my survival. It also provided a deeper connection to one another, since all my family prayed specifically for me. The story has also given us a platform to share with others a variety of spiritual applications, including the faithfulness of God. And the fact that it all occurred in the Philippines made the land and its people all the more meaningful to us.

My story really began when my parents met at the University of Florida. They got married after they graduated and headed off to grad school to prepare for ministry. In 1976, they moved back to Jacksonville, Florida, where Dad had several ministry positions, and Mom had four children. While Dad was pastoring a church, he went on a mission trip to the Philippines, and he fell in love with the Filipino people. Not long after he returned, both Mom and Dad sensed a clear calling from the Lord to return there as missionaries.

In October of 1985, Dad, Mom, and my siblings (Christy, Katie, Robby, and Peter, who were nine, seven, four, and one respectively) left Florida for the Philippines. God had not even put the smallest of thought in my dad's or mom's mind about me. After living in Manila for a month, my family moved to General Santos City, on the more primitive southern island of Mindanao. It was tough for my mom when they first arrived, with the many challenges of a new culture, very little contact with friends and family, and homeschooling four young children, while Dad immersed himself in ministry, traveling throughout the islands preaching and planting churches.

My first couple of years living in the Philippines were much more uneventful than the circumstances and events surrounding my birth. At least they were for me, anyway. I guess that my sister Katie was responsible for some of that as she was acting as my second mom even though she was only eight. She insisted on carrying me everywhere I went. At the time, I was growing and gaining weight quickly, which was probably a result of all those prayers on my behalf. Poor Katie. She ended up having to have surgery for a double hernia before we returned to the States, which everyone, to this day, blames me for.

Chapter Three

THE EARLY YEARS

Let another praise you, and not your own mouth;
a stranger, and not your own lips.

—PROVERBS 27:2

My memories of my life and surroundings—at least those I myself can remember—really begin in Jacksonville. We returned from the Philippines in October of 1990 and moved back into the house on Sheri Lane that my parents owned since 1977.

I was three when we returned to Jacksonville; that's when I met Uncle Dick.

Uncle Dick was our next-door neighbor and an important part of our lives. Known to the rest of the world as Richard Fowler, I really thought he was my uncle. He was close to all the children in the Tebow family, probably in no small part because he'd never been married and therefore never had children of his own.

As a family, we children spent a great deal of time with him, including almost every Saturday morning. A partial explanation for spending Saturday mornings at Uncle Dick's might be the fact that he owned a television and we didn't. My parents would let us watch cartoons over there with him on Saturday mornings, but the reasons for letting us hang out there went much deeper than that.

No, I don't mean the small bottles of Coke that he always had on hand in the refrigerator and popsicles that he kept in the freezer. Although he gave us plenty of those, too. I'm sure that he told us no, or that we had too much of one thing or another, on occasion. I'm sure he told us that too much Coke or popsicles, or whatever, wasn't that good for you. Actually, now that I think about it, I'm not sure he ever did say no to any request any of us made for anything in his refrigerator, freezer, or pantry.

It's funny. My folks always preferred that we bring our friends over to our house whenever possible, since they wanted to be the parents of influence, not necessarily allowing us to be influenced by whoever's house we were headed to. Not that the influence would be bad elsewhere, but they just felt more comfortable when they knew exactly what the influence was to which we were being exposed. And so for that reason, and the simple fact that they loved kids, anyone and everyone was always welcome to hang out with us, at all sorts of crazy hours.

But with Uncle Dick, they relaxed some of the rules—at least on the television we could watch and the snacks we were allowed to eat. Even on weekdays we were there; you might have found us watching old Westerns or *Flipper* or whatever he'd let us watch. He was pretty strict about the kind of things we could see. Maybe that's why Mom and Dad let us go over so much—they trusted him and were assured of the influence we were getting through his guidance.

Robby would often dress up, before we headed next door, in his little Western outfit with fake six-shooter and holster, especially for those movie times where a Western would be the highlight show at Uncle Dick's. In fact, those movies were a part of the inspiration that caused Robby to break his arm.

It happened a year and a half later, when my parents decided to move us from the house on Sheri Lane to a farm—but only because my parents were desperate for more room and the farm was being sold at a government auction at an incredible price. One of the additional pluses to life on the farm, besides having more room, was that we were able to keep some horses. Now, keeping and boarding horses may sound glamorous to some, for riding purposes, but as anyone who has kept horses knows, the work required in making sure they get the care and feeding they need and deserve is never ending.

And so the stage was set for the broken arm inspired by one of Uncle Dick's Western movies.

As I remember it, at the time one of our horses was in its stall—and Robby was hanging from the barn rafters, above the stall door—waiting for me to open it. It was a scene Robby envisioned straight out of the movies. Of course, right on cue as Robby had orchestrated, I opened the door, the horse came out, and Robby dropped onto the horse's bare back, just like in the movies we watched at Uncle Dick's house. Robby may have held on to his seat on the horse for maybe one of the horse's strides out of the barn before he slid off and fell to the ground, landing on his arm extended to brace his fall. His arm broke. By the time Robby was twelve, he had broken his arm three times.

Our parents have told us on numerous occasions, both then and now, that Uncle Dick loved our visits. I have no doubt he did—I mean, after all, who wouldn't have loved five brothers and sisters descending upon your house and food supply on a regular basis? But as a kid, all I knew was that we loved going over there. He was truly a member of our family. In fact, he spent every Thanksgiving and Christmas with us.

The relationship with Uncle Dick and our family, though, began long before I was born. In 1982, my dad left the staff of Southside Baptist Church in Jacksonville and began a church out of our house. The total attendance that first Sunday in the living room, of those who didn't have a name ending in "Tebow"?

One.

Uncle Dick.

Dad preached that Sunday, Uncle Dick accepted Christ, and the church and relationship with Uncle Dick was off and running, for the church and for Uncle Dick. Uncle Dick then became the treasurer of the church, Cornerstone Community Church, and later became the treasurer of the Bob Tebow Evangelical Association (BTEA), when we moved to the Philippines. Richard Fowler was faithful and meticulous with the ledgers of the church and BTEA, and even when the rest of the world started migrating to computers and accounting software methods in the 1980s, Uncle Dick continued to keep the books by hand—the long way—and my parents found it incredible that he never made a single mistake.

When we arrived back in the States, Uncle Dick made sure I also came over as much as possible, along with my four older brothers and sisters whom he already knew and loved. After all, I was his namesake, Timothy Richard Tebow. He wanted to give to all of us at every turn in every way; he was a giver and a great influence in that way and in so many others.

He truly was almost like a third parent, albeit one who played big-band music all the time. I mean, all the time. I remember once when Dad was out of town and a couple of us spent the night at Uncle Dick's. The next day, he took us to Peter's baseball game. While we were there at his house, he was—as always—continually working through and listening to all of his big-band collection.

In order. From the beginning. To the very last one in the collection.

He had a routine and followed it day after day. Over the course of the year he would follow his order of music, picking up the next day where he had stopped the previous day. Must have been the meticulous bookkeeper in him that served others, including the Cornerstone Community Church and BTEA, so well.

It was great growing up with two older brothers always around to play with. Actually, all of us were very competitive, including my parents and all my siblings. It didn't matter if it was Monopoly or chess inside with my sisters or baseball or basketball outside with my brothers—or if I was only four and the rest of them were far older. They took no prisoners—the rules applied equally to all. There was no "letting someone win" because he was younger, or to cheer her up or encourage her to keep playing. The first time I won any of those games or contests, I earned it.

It was something I remembered.

Most of my first clear memories seem to revolve around sports and all the crazy stuff that I did trying to be just like Robby and Peter, and to do everything they did, despite the fact that they were nine and six years old when we returned from the Philippines and I was three. We were in constant motion, always playing whatever game was in season or, if for some reason one of those didn't interest us, then just the ones that we made up ourselves.

My dad says that I wasn't much fun to throw with, even at age four. Apparently, even then I was a bit too intense and threw pretty hard. A lot of my competitiveness was probably just how I was wired, but part of it was because I looked up to my brothers and wanted to be just like them. For example, I had started working out, even then. I wanted to be as strong as my brothers, so when I was a bit older, I used surgical tubing that was attached to the top of the door—only because my dad wouldn't let me use any weights. He didn't feel they were safe enough for my development at that age or would provide anything more beneficial at that point than the rubber tubing could provide. While my brothers and I were sitting or standing around talking or doing whatever we were doing—and it was always something— I wasted no time and would stand in front of the door and pull against the tubing, working each shoulder. For thirty minutes or so. Looking back, I'm not sure why I didn't tire of it, but I didn't and simply kept pulling on the tubing, working each shoulder. Over and over.

When it came time to play T-ball at age five, I had already played so much actual player pitch with my brothers that the idea of hitting off of a tee didn't interest me. So instead of my using a tee for my at bats, my coach at Normandy Athletic Association would toss the ball to me underhand, while my brothers took great pride—maybe even more than I did—in watching me hit ball after ball over the fence during the course of the baseball season. Peter claims I hit thirty-six home runs that year. Then again, he was eight at the time and maybe not the best and most unbiased source of information for keeping the records. I know, though, that I finished second in the league in home runs to a kid who was two years older. I made a commitment to myself right then and there that that would be my last year of finishing second.

Apparently I had such a good year that my dad even claims that one of the parents from that team said he was saving my baseball card (the league had a photographer come out and take photos of all the kids) for the future. He was kind to say that, and it certainly made me feel good at the time, but I'm somewhat doubtful that he ended up saving it, since I doubt that even *my parents* saved one of my cards—part of the family plan, I'm sure, to keep me and the rest of us humble.

I do know that I didn't enjoy little league baseball for the fun of playing. I can't help it—but that's true. When I hear parents tell their kids today, "It doesn't matter if you win or lose, as long as you have fun," I'm puzzled. That's just not how I'm wired. Bottom line, losing simply isn't any fun. Oh sure, in thinking back on plays and moments, I knew I was loving every minute of playing the game. But if there's a score, then there's a purpose to the game beyond having fun—it's having a greater score. Of course, there is intrinsic value in playing the game itself and how well you play it, and always playing to the best of your ability, but at some point the actual competition has to be a piece of the analysis as well. After all, there'd be no point to the rules or to keeping score if it were simply and only about having fun.

Just like in life. For better or worse, we don't all end up getting patted on the back. "Hey, Bill, you didn't come close to hitting your sales numbers, but it looked like you really enjoyed the interaction with the customers, so we're giving you a raise." Maybe, but I don't think so.

I had two brothers who beat me at everything, at every turn, as badly as they could. So when I played anything else with them, I wanted to win. When our coach would say, "I just wanted to make sure you're having fun," I didn't understand. And when my teammates seemed more interested in ice cream or snow cones after the game, especially if it was a game we lost, I was baffled and upset. I couldn't understand why they bothered to play. Just go get dessert without bothering to be on the team, I figured. What's the point?

The preseason Home Run Derby was like that as well. Every year that I played baseball, the league conducted a Home Run Derby before the regular season began. I knew it was an exhibition contest and had no bearing on the outcome of the season or anything else. I knew it was supposed to be "fun." But I couldn't see the point of entering the contest unless you were going to do all you could to win. And so each year, I entered with that goal in mind—to win. Not to simply compete. Not to simply enjoy myself. But to win. And sometimes I did, and sometimes I didn't, and that was okay. But what mattered to me was the mind-set that I entered the Home Run Derby contest with. I really think, looking back, that it made me perform better and at least closer to the fullest extent of my ability. And I believe this approach served me well later in life when the competition got tougher.

That outlook may have had an impact on my ability as a teammate back then. In T-ball, I was friends with the other players, and I remember very few of them then who could catch or throw. Early in the games I would tolerate this, but as it got later and more critical to the outcome, I found myself wanting the ball in my hands.

Once, in the last inning of a close game, the ball was hit to me at shortstop. I fielded it and ran down the runner, who was breaking from third to score, for the final out. After the game, the coach asked me why I didn't throw it to the catcher. The question puzzled me because I thought the answer would have been obvious to him.

"Because he can't catch."

"Well, he's the catcher. You're supposed to throw it to him for him to try and catch it to get the runner out. That's how you do it."

I was sure—no I was positive—that wasn't how you do it. I wasn't interested in someone's "trying to catch" it with the game on the line. I also wasn't interested in someone's trying to remember if he was supposed to tag the base or the runner. If he didn't know what to do, I would do it myself. I would let him try to catch early on, but I wanted to win, and when the game was on the line, I would do whatever I had to—within the rules—to win the game.

My parents decided that, with three boys around the house who were as competitive as we were, we had to institute a new rule. I was still young, and they were already concerned about the bragging that we were doing among ourselves. Here was the rule: we were forbidden from talking about our own accomplishments, unless asked first by someone else. If someone specifically asked us how the game went or how we played, we could answer, but we couldn't volunteer the information. They based this new rule on the admonition found in Proverbs 27:2:

> Let another praise you, and not your own mouth;
> a stranger, and not your own lips.

It was a great lesson for us toward living our lives with a humble spirit, a lesson we needed to learn and continue to work on. Our parents certainly have always lived their lives with humility.

We did, though, have family friends who knew the rule, and before long, they'd help us out, asking us on a Sunday morning at church, "Any of you boys had any games lately? Anything happen?" And so we would fill them in.

But at the same time, we began to realize that it was nicer to not hear ourselves brag, and so over time, we all just began talking about ourselves less and less.

Plus, we were given a dollar if someone complimented us on our character to Mom or Dad. We quickly became focused on those matters—such as character and humility—rather than on trying to impress someone with our exploits on or off the field.

Life on the farm, like anything, had its pros and cons.

The good news? There was plenty of room to take batting practice without losing a ball in a neighbor's yard or worrying about a nearby window, and to play whatever other games we wanted to play.

The bad news? My dad made it perfectly clear that ours was a working family farm, and he and Mom were thrilled to have three healthy boys available every day for all the manual labor life on a farm required.

Actually, even that was good news, as I look back on it. Shortly after we moved, I became "farmer strong," simply from lifting hay bales or chopping wood or chasing down cows.

Dad used to throw us batting practice in one corner of the yard, and we dented the fence more than once from pitches that he threw to us or we threw to each other while working on our pitching technique. My parents are now having to replace the fence to keep their grandchildren safe around the pool—I guess we left too many dents behind. We would hit balls—for hours on end—toward the tree line on the other side of the pasture. Even with all the extra farm chores we had to do, living on the farm was tremendous. On one occasion, we had a visit from a former White Sox pitcher, Joel Davis, who met my dad through the Fellowship of Christian Athletes. He wasn't going to be able to care for his dog any longer, so he dropped him at our house. The dog, named White Sox because of his white feet, became a family fixture. As did the stories of the balls that Joel hit, before he left that day, well into the tree line across the pasture.

Dad finally wised up before he threw so much that he tore up his shoulder. So he drove up to Fernandina Beach, north of Jacksonville, to buy some fishnet to make a batting cage. With a number of four-by-four posts, we built what turned out to be a pretty sturdy and functional structure, and then we put a pitching machine in it. From that point forward we were set. We could pitch to each other to our hearts' content, without fear of losing baseballs to the surrounding woods. All with no further wear and tear on Dad's shoulder.

Somewhere in there, in all the time spent with the stretchy surgical bands or the competitive streak in T-ball or the endless hours of batting practice, I realized that I never wanted to "fit in." I mean, I was only five, so that exact phrase, "fit in," never occurred to me. But as I look back now, it was clear that very early on the seeds of that concept began taking root and sprouting within me in everything I did. As I got older and heard kids talk about wanting to "fit in," or wanting to be "normal," I never quite understood why they felt that way. What's the point of being "normal"? That sounds average to me, and I never felt like I was created to be average.

I remember reading Coach Tony Dungy's book *Uncommon* and in it his challenge to so many, especially those of us within the younger generation, to not be "common." From lessons in his own life, he encouraged us to always strive to be "uncommon" and align our lives with the ways of the Lord.

So if everybody was doing the same thing, the normal and usual thing, I looked for a different way. The crowd, by definition, gravitates toward average, which could tend toward middle of the road or toward mediocrity. If we're all special *in the same way*, then nobody really is. A view of that kind of life, I believe, discounts the belief that God created each of us special, each with gifts and abilities like no one else's. He created each of us different, fully intending that we would use our unique gifts and abilities to do what He created us to do.

You and I were created by God to be so much more than normal. My parents always told us that was true of each of my siblings and me.

Following the crowd is not a winning approach to life. In the end it's a loser's game, because we never become who God created us to be by trying to be like everybody else. I figured that out when I was five, but I couldn't have expressed it then. I just knew that I wanted to be different in those areas that excited me. I wanted to be me—and then I began to understand that I wanted to be who God created me to be.

The most important thing that has occurred in my life happened in those early years. When I was six, I knew I was ready to accept Jesus into my heart, to accept what He had done for me to allow me to go to heaven.

I tried to bring it up with my dad. After all, we talked about Bible verses every day as a family, and I'd heard him preach somewhere around a million times by then. Here I was, the last one in the family to trust Christ. I knew I was ready and that I wanted to. Every time I tried to bring it up with Dad and told him I was ready, he would question me on my understanding of the gospel message to make sure I was not taking this decision lightly. The first couple of times I talked with him, his questions frustrated me. Remember, I was only six years old.

There came a time during which, for several nights in a row, I went to bed, thinking, *What if I'm in a car accident or something else happens tomorrow? I want to end up in heaven.*

When I was five, friends took Peter and me to Jacksonville Beach. I was wading near the shore, when I was suddenly caught up in a rip tide and pulled quickly out to sea. Eight-year-old Peter ran into the water to save me. Even though he was immediately caught up in the dangerous tide too, he managed to swim out to me and hold me up long enough to get us both rescued by the lifeguard. A close call.

So one morning after breakfast, after Robby and Peter went out to work with Dad, I went straight to Mom. "I want to ask Jesus to come into my heart. I'm ready to be saved. I tried with Dad, but he's just too hard."

Mom and I went over to the couch, and I prayed for Jesus to come into my heart. Since then, I've known that I am headed to heaven and have tried to live in a way that pleases Jesus.

We all laugh about it now, but Dad will tell you that he is very glad I went to Mom that morning.

And that afternoon we went to Epcot to celebrate.

Chapter Four

PREPARING A FOUNDATION

*For I am not ashamed of the gospel, for it is the
power of God for salvation to everyone who believes,
to the Jew first and also to the Greek.*

—ROMANS 1:16

Every year, whatever sport was in season, we played it—my brothers and I. Since there were only three of us, we set up certain rotations in order to maintain fairness while still being competitive.

For example, every time it would rain, we'd head out to play football in the yard. There's something fun about football and mud. One of us would play quarterback, while the other two would face off against each other, with one as a receiver and the other the defensive back assigned to cover him. The receiver would have "four hard," meaning four downs to score a touchdown. After those four downs, we'd rotate positions so that each of us would play each of the three positions at least one time through. If we played longer, we made sure we each played each position an equal number of times to fairly determine the winner. You'd get a point for scoring whether you were playing as the receiver or quarterback, while the defensive back would get a point for stopping you from scoring. In those early days, when we were still fairly small and our bones pretty resilient, we would also play tackle. It may just have been that my brothers only wanted to play tackle until I got bigger.

We didn't have a set score that we played to, but rather played until we got called to school, to work or eat, until someone got hurt, until we got into a fight with one another, or it got so dark that we finally could not see well enough to play.

We played basketball in the rain as well, with puddles to navigate through and around as we tried to dribble. And forget hanging on to the ball when shooting. You simply tried to keep your hand as close as possible to the ball—as it began slipping out of your control from being so wet—and long enough to give one last guided push toward the basket with the hopes that somehow it would find its way there. We didn't play in those conditions to make shooting difficult, but I'm convinced those years of informal "wet ball drills" probably helped my skills in both football and basketball.

We weren't always outside, although my mom probably wished we were. We had a version of the old "Oklahoma" drill that every football coach has run at practice at one time or another. We'd play in one of our rooms—usually the room of whoever hadn't been in trouble lately. Two of us would stand at opposite sides of the room, one of us with a football. The third one would watch for Mom, since she had a strict no playing ball in the house rule, and do a bit of refereeing or breaking up a fight, if necessary, while waiting his turn.

On a signal, we'd begin to run at each other, with the idea being that the defender would have to tackle the ball carrier before he reached the other side of the room. Our rooms weren't all that big, so there was quite a lot of wrestling each other down to the floor before the guy with the ball reached the other side of the room.

So we'd play until something was broken or Mom came and kicked us outside. But it was never as good a game outside as inside, where you were in a confined space with very little room for escape or maneuvering to get by. It was definitely a power game inside.

Someone was always getting hurt when we played—regardless of the game. And it was usually Peter. Once we were playing a three-way game of catch in the yard. We were each a pretty good distance apart, forming the three points of a rough triangle, and instead of following the pattern that we had followed all that day, where Robby was throwing to me, Robby decided to switch things up. Thinking that Peter was looking, Robby crow hopped and wound up to put his full weight into the throw. Of course, Peter wasn't looking, fully expecting that Robby would be throwing to me, as had been the pattern that day; and so we ended up having to take him into Mom with a bloody nose and bruised face for some patching up.

Another time, we were playing baseball but decided to use a basketball instead of a baseball just to see what would happen. Nothing good, as it turned out, at least as far as Peter was concerned. I was pitching, and the bat richocheted with Peter—swinging as hard as he could to see how far he could hit the basketball—right into his face.

More blood. More bruises. Back to see Mom.

Our favorite Peter injury, however, was less about sports and more about one of his moments of pretending he was a superhero. Funny that a kid who is so smart could have done something so crazy. I was about eight when he climbed a rope which had been attached to the ceiling in the barn, and decided to swing from one end of the barn all the way to the other. All went well until his shin discovered, at a high rate of speed, the post-hole digger that hadn't been put away and was sitting sideways in the barn, causing his shin to split wide open. Blood was everywhere.

Enter Mom, once again, on the scene.

Living on a farm, there was always a certain amount of excitement around the house, and if it wasn't one of us getting injured, it was the realities of farm life that kept things interesting. On one occasion, my dad decided, this being a working farm and all, to have a controlled burn to get the weeds out of the pasture. Controlled burns were normal but occasional occurrences, and completely necessary in settings such as ours. Apparently "controlled" is in the eye of the fire starter, especially when you don't call the forestry department to forewarn them.

The first indication we had that things were no longer under control was when Dad ran into the house frantically to get our help. As it turned out, the pasture was ablaze, and the fire was moving rapidly toward the woods. If it had reached the woods, it would have been devastating not only to us but to the families around us as well. All of us—Mom, my sisters, my brothers—struck out to help Dad contain the fire.

The fire hadn't yet reached the woods, but we all noticed that it had jumped into our neighbor's pasture. The good thing was that our neighbor would no longer have a weed problem. Hopefully he would still have a house.

For the next few hours, we used shovels to beat on the edges of the fire. All of us did, although Christy got out of working early. She had a piano audition that day but was worried about leaving us. We all insisted she go, however, and she focused well enough to earn a college scholarship. The rest of us followed in her footsteps, earning scholarships to college, and it's pretty funny that it started that day, during the fire. Even Otis, our dog, was pawing at the flames. Finally, through what had to be God's grace and our collective efforts, we won out.

From that point on, Dad has always called the forestry department for a burn permit ahead of time for a number of good reasons, one of which no doubt is that he doesn't have a bunch of kids on hand to help put out any more "controlled" burns. Afterward, Dad took us all inside and used a teachable moment to have a brief Bible study on James 3:1–12. With the smell of the fire still on our clothes, Dad got us glasses of water, sat us down, and picked up his Bible. "Just like a small spark can cause a big fire," Dad said, "the smallest part of the body, the tongue, can cause great damage when we do not control it. A wrongly chosen word can hurt a reputation, alienate a friend, or break a heart," he continued, and had us each name a word that could hurt someone. A memorable lesson.

In general, all these activities—"controlled burns" and sports— served to toughen us up, usually because no matter what, we wouldn't stop working or playing. Looking back, my injuries were numerous but much less serious than either Robby's or Peter's. I was never as much of a daredevil. But whether we twisted an ankle or cut a chin (my brothers, my dad and I all have chin scars), the competition and winning was what mattered, so we played through everything. Anything not to quit.

And just as the farm made us tough, it also helped make us smart. As we were growing up, it was the backdrop for much of the learning we did—starting when we were toddlers and continuing until we were packing our bags for college. From the moment I was born, homeschooling was our way of life.

It's funny how, because I enjoyed homeschooling so much, it seemed like such an obvious choice for our family, but back when my parents first did it, it was far from common. My parents made the decision to homeschool their children long before I came into this world. It happened at some point after my older sister, Christy, was born, but before she'd started school. Dad was seeking direction and was struck by this passage in Deuteronomy 6:4–7:

> *Hear, O Israel! The LORD is our God, the LORD is one!*
> *You shall love the LORD your God with all your heart and with all your soul and with all your might.*
> *These words, which I am commanding you today, shall be on your heart.*
> *You shall teach them diligently to your sons and shall talk of them when you sit in your house and when you walk by the way and when you lie down and when you rise up.*

After reading and studying that passage, he knew he wanted us to homeschool. That way, they could focus on the curriculum and character lessons that they thought were most important, while emphasizing the best teachings for their children on a daily basis.

Mom thought he was crazy, but she'd gotten used to his ability to follow wild ideas to some logical conclusion—regardless of what the crowd thought. It was the early 1980s, and she didn't know anyone who was homeschooling. She didn't know if it would be a good idea for her or for our family in general. In fact, people told her that her children would never be able to play sports or even go to college if she homeschooled. So they began to pray specifically about it: Dad for guidance, wisdom, and clarity on the direction God wanted them to go on this subject, and Mom that God would take the idea out of Dad's mind if it really wasn't the right decision for them as a family.

Ultimately, they both felt led to teach their children at home, which at first proved to be a struggle for Mom. Not only was the bulk of the responsibilities for homeschooling assumed by her, but at that time there weren't the support structures and resources for homeschooling that are available today. In fact, in researching the materials to use that would be appropriate, a number of times she would call publishers or educational-resource providers in the hope of getting the proper materials. When the companies realized that Mom was interested in using their materials to homeschool, they refused to sell them to her.

Anyhow, Mom was determined to do it right and in the best way possible for us, and she stuck with it, tracking down materials or creating them herself. Her persistence turned out to be a wonderful blessing for all of us, not just because of the quality education we received, but also because of the flexibility that it afforded us.

Even though I was young, I understood and appreciated the flexibility that homeschooling provided. My parents were able to design the structure, schedule, and content however they wanted. During the sports seasons, they could shift the bulk of the workload to earlier parts of the day so that we didn't have a conflict with any afternoon or evening practices, games, or other activities. If they had to, they could also move studies to a different day altogether.

The flexibility with travel and sports was convenient, but the real success of homeschooling came from the fact that we were actually learning. Mom set the curriculum, and she could tailor her teaching to the needs of each of us. She used games or whatever methods were necessary to reach us and get the lessons across—a freedom she took full advantage of. In our house, school could be happening at any moment—even at meals—so you always had to be prepared. She'd put different placemats at various times at our places around the table—United States presidents, the periodic-elements table, state and world capitals—and we would be challenged to learn everything on our placemat before the others could. Everything with us always had to be a race or a competition; Mom knew that and used it to enhance our learning process. We even had manners contests.

Of course, as my parents would eventually find out, those placemats gave a decided advantage to Peter and to my sisters, Christy and Katie. My dad had long known that he was dyslexic, but it still took a while before my parents recognized that Robby, too, had dyslexia. By the time I came along, it didn't take them long to spot it in me as well. The fact that I was still struggling with reading when I turned seven was probably a pretty good clue that something in my head was working differently and that I had dyslexia.

Simply put, my brain processes things differently than most people. It's the same for my dad and Robby. All three of us are kinesthetic (or tactile) learners, meaning that we learn best by doing. My most effective learning style is not particularly visual, so I don't ordinarily retain as much simply from reading about something. I've heard others describe the feeling as reading when they're tired and looking back at a page, knowing all the individual words and yet not being sure what the page was about. That often happens to me in the normal course of reading anything, whether I'm tired or not. Therefore, I learned to use other ways to supplement my reading to make sure I learned all that I should.

Mom was always great with it. She had seen how things like this could stigmatize children and adults—into feeling that somehow they were less than, or not as smart or capable as, others. She had seen it in society, in schools, and in other settings, and she was determined that this would not be the case for her children. She explained to Robby and me that our dad has great intelligence as measured through his IQ score which is off the charts, but he just has to learn in a different manner. Through Mom, we learned and believed that it had nothing to do with intelligence, but was just the way our minds processed the information before us.

She helped me realize that dyslexia wasn't a disability, just a difference. My learning skills and information-processing abilities mean that I'm predisposed to learning much more quickly from "walk throughs," which football coaches love to have anyway, where the players literally walk through the plays they will want to execute during the game, and walk through them at a slower speed than actual live-game or practice situations.

Dealing with our dyslexia with wisdom, Mom not only affirmed that we were wonderful creations of God, with our God-given intelligence and abilities, but she gave us the confidence to learn as well. When subjects came more quickly to me, we could breeze through them, but if they were more of a struggle, we would slow down to focus on them. It was the same with each of my siblings—we were each able to discover alternate and better ways to learn, ways that were unique to us as students.

My mom would read articles to us from the newspaper, or have us read them ourselves as we got older, and then we would identify and discuss the character issues in them. We could always find something to talk about in most every article. As we ate breakfast together as a family, we would read through Psalms and Proverbs. Both of my parents were not just casually interested in our memorizing a large number of Bible verses; they required it. To help us, Mom would put the verses to music in songs that she had made up. Memorizing our verses paid off in a number of ways. One which was very important to us was that we knew we couldn't play sports or watch our favorite Saturday-night program, *MacGyver*—we all loved *MacGyver*, because it was the only Saturday-night program in English that we got in the Philippines—until we had successfully recited our five verses for the week. And it never seemed to fail that there was usually some frantic Saturday-afternoon studying going on in our house as the time for *MacGyver* crept closer.

Another thing that I think homeschooling helped me with was that we all learned how to talk to adults at a much earlier age than some of our friends. Or at least it seemed that way to me. Regardless, the ability we acquired in being able to talk with and be around adults has benefitted me greatly. Somewhere in that homeschooling process and travels I developed a comfort level in being able to talk to adults, to properly and politely address them, and to interact with them in so many different settings. I think that's because my parents made sure we were always included in most things they were involved in and around older adults. We weren't just surrounded by kids like ourselves all day who were just speaking at our own level of maturity and content. We were challenged to grow in being able to build and have relationships with others—of all ages.

Don't get me wrong. It was still school, albeit with really small classes: one teacher, one student. My mom gave us grades for every class. She was tough with the amount of work she gave us, but at the end of the day, she was a pretty easy grader, because she was always trying to encourage us. She did insist that we always take year-end tests, however, because she wanted an outside assessment of how we were doing. Also, she and my dad began to suspect I might have a chance at a college scholarship, so they wanted to make sure we all were exposed to testing.

People say you'll miss out on things by being homeschooled, like the prom and other traditional activities that you experience in an institutional school setting. The truth was that we were always so active in sports at various schools that we usually got invited to other activities like proms or other dances and really didn't miss out on the opportunity to participate in any of that if we chose to. Of course, there were things that, due to homeschooling, I probably missed out on. At times I wondered if there were friendships with other kids my age that I wasn't experiencing. Ultimately, though, being very active in sports and church helped a lot with that, since we made many friends through those outlets.

In addition to the friends I made through church and sports, I made other friends through an organization Mom started, which she called First At Home, about twenty years ago. It started small—there weren't many homeschool families at the time—but we had so many families that got involved in the years afterward that it became an integral part of the homeschooling culture. It involved participating together on a regular basis in various learning and recreational experiences. For example, we'd go on field trips as a homeschool group. So then we had all those new friends from other homeschooling homes that we got to know better and looked forward to being with, around Thanksgiving celebrations, and at numerous other activities.

For me, homeschooling helped keep my priorities in order and allowed me to work on the things that I wanted to accomplish at my own pace and on my own schedule. Later, in high school, if I had an opportunity to go on a recruiting visit to a college, I could take off on Friday and make up for it by doing more of the required work either ahead of time on Thursday or on Monday after I returned from the trip; and I never had to worry about missing a test. I would also schedule my workouts around my class schedule. I always could do everything I wanted to do athletically and academically because I was able to schedule things in accordance with the priorities that were built into me when I was growing up. And the neat thing was that I was able to do most everything I needed and wanted to do along the way, and that really helped me develop a sense of accomplishment.

It was during those growing-up days, when we were engaged in our games and chores around the farm, that I also had my first experience with the death of someone who was close to me.

Uncle Dick went to be with Jesus. He had health problems from emphysema and a childhood bout with polio, but I had never anticipated him actually dying. It was a sad occasion. We all loved him, and while we knew that he was now enjoying the rewards of heaven, we missed him and still do.

As sad as we were, we soon learned that Uncle Dick would continue to live on in a way that paid tribute to the great man that he was. Several years before Uncle Dick died, Dad was on a trip to the Philippines when he learned that an unwanted baby, whose mom died in childbirth, would be thrown in the river if someone did not take her. My dad's staff members Bert and Ray Gauran took her and named her Queen.

Dad has always been very sensitive toward widows and orphans, who the Bible says repeatedly we are to care for. So, when Dad heard Queen's story and realized how many children there were in the Philippines with similar stories, he went to the board of his organization, BTEA, with an idea to address the need of these orphans. He wanted to start an orphanage that would raise them. The board immediately embraced the idea, understanding the biblical mandate to help widows and orphans:

> *Pure and undefiled religion in the sight of our God and Father is this: to visit orphans and widows in their distress, and to keep oneself unstained by the world.*
>
> JAMES 1:27

In 1992, BTEA founded the orphanage in the southernmost part of Mindanao, Philippines. It's a relatively small orphanage, with just under fifty children, but it is making a large impact in those children's lives, caring for them and teaching them about Jesus's love for them. By God's grace we have had seventeen of our orphans graduate from college.

Much like my father, Uncle Dick understood the importance of helping those who are less fortunate, and when he died, he left a large portion of his estate to support the orphanage in the Philippines, which my parents then renamed "Uncle Dick's Home." It is a home of joy, providing unconditional and never-ending love to so many who need it. Renaming it in honor of the man who showed that kind of love to us and to so many others seemed to be the perfect tribute. I thought they'd have those little bottles of Coke and assorted flavors of popsicles for the kids who were living there, but Mom and Dad said they were going to take a different route on the meals and snacks for the children in Uncle Dick's Home.

I loved the idea, but I was still sad that he had died. There was certainly a hole left in our family with Uncle Dick's passing, a hole that was even more pronounced when Thanksgiving and Christmas came around. That hole would never go away, but it didn't take long for the newly renamed orphanage to become a vital part of our family. Through the wisdom of estate planning, Uncle Dick has had a great legacy of impacting many needy children.

For much of my youth, I played Pop Warner football at Lakeshore Athletic Association near where we lived on the west side of Jacksonville.

Lakeshore is a stone's throw from the St. Johns River but not near any lakes, as far as I could tell. It was a very strong and well-attended sports program that attracted a lot of top-flight competition and made me a better player. Initially I only played baseball at Normandy Little League and basketball in church leagues, but finally I wore my parents down with my begging and whining, and a few weeks before I turned eight, they finally let me play Pop Warner football.

The first week of football didn't go all that well. I got sick every day at practice with headaches, dizziness, and nausea. I asked my mom if there was something that we could do or something that I could take, and while she allowed me to take something to calm my stomach and head after practice, she was clearly hesitant about making a habit of it.

At the end of that first week my parents sat me down. It was clear to them that if these symptoms didn't stop soon, I would have to give up football. It was only a game, and they were not going to medicate me to play a game. My mom was particularly concerned, because she has dealt with Ménière's disease all her life. It's a condition of the inner ear that, for her, affects her balance. She wondered if I might have the same thing, especially since roller coasters, merry-go-rounds, and similar things have always made me ill.

Still, I didn't want to give up football, but I'd learned that the scriptures make it clear we are to honor our mothers and fathers. My siblings and I were fortunate to have parents who made that easy to fulfill—at least we could see they deserved to be honored by us whether we always demonstrated it or not. But it wasn't until later—when I wasn't with them all the time—that I began to realize all the reasons, in addition to the instruction in God's Word, that they deserved not only our respect and praise, but to be honored and loved. They cared for us, protected us, and nurtured us so that we could grow into the people God wants us to be. They guided us along the path on which they believe He had created us to walk. They did whatever it took to make sure following God's wisdom and direction was the path we took.

Well, my mom prayed with me that evening. She and I knelt beside my bunk bed and prayed that God might take away whatever it was and heal me so I might be able to play football. If it was God's will. That was always the standard for them, in anything they prayed for: if it was God's will . . . they asked for it to be done. And for whatever reason you might wish to assign, after that night, I've never had another issue with my head while playing football.

Well, there was one issue. But that was much later.

Once I got over my initial sickness, the Lakeshore Athletic Association football program was a great place to grow up and compete. Not only did it give me my first experience at playing quarterback—the only position I've ever wanted to play—it also produced a lot of talent that flowed into the high schools all over the Jacksonville area and beyond. From my Pee Wee football team alone, we produced a number of Division I athletes, including guys who played for South Carolina, Louisville, Houston, West Virginia, and Florida. And there were others who might have made it that far except for falling by the wayside through low grades, drug use, or other problems that cut their athletic pursuits short.

After playing baseball for years at Normandy, at age eleven I was invited to play on a traveling baseball team, the Tidal Wave. Because they wanted us to sample and enjoy different sports and activities, my parents had always discouraged us from playing only one sport for the entire year; however, they did allow me to play on this traveling team. I played three or four seasons with them, and during that span we won hundreds of games, playing all over Florida and around the country. During the summers, we'd play maybe ten or eleven games a week—with two each Friday, Saturday, and Sunday. I remember many Sundays where we'd leave church and I would change into my uniform in the car as we drove to a game.

At various times during those years on the traveling team, I was invited to play for teams in other states as well. I remember a couple in particular: one in Georgia and one in Texas. Here we were, just kids playing baseball, and for the sake of winning games, these people were willing to fly me to different parts of the country to play for them. My dad squashed that idea before it ever had a chance to take off. He was concerned with the time it would take away from the family and school studies, and he also worried that my arm would get overworked if he wasn't there to monitor my pitch count. He was a stickler for protecting our arms.

And, yes, he really did monitor my pitch count. After a great deal of talking with major league pitchers, Dad determined how much, in a game and in a week, I could throw without risking injury to my arm. One time in particular, Dad told our Tidal Wave coach, Matt Redding, that I had hit my pitch count. Before I'd joined the team, Dad and Coach Redding had already been good friends, which was probably why I was allowed to play on a traveling team in the first place, but this day, Dad was getting a bit upset with his friend, the Coach.

Dad walked over to him at one point and said, "Matt. He's thrown enough." He didn't have to remind Coach about the terms for our participation on the team: only one pitching appearance per week, with a maximum of eighty-five pitches. Surprisingly, Coach didn't immediately respond, and Dad continued.

"Matt, either go out there and take him out, now, or I will. And if I have to do it, then it's the last time he'll ever play for this team."

No one would ever claim that God gave Dad the gift of subtlety or diplomacy, at least not when he feels strongly about something, and especially when he feels strongly about something that involves one of his children.

Coach took me out. That may be the only time that they disagreed on anything, which makes it so memorable; Coach was really good, and Dad trusted him with me.

My dad never coached us formally in a team setting because of international trips and his irregular schedule. What he did was spend lots of time with us, teaching us not only to hit, but also to throw. Apparently, some people have even commented of late on that throwing motion.

Dad's fault.

He was not only focused on our arms, but also on our overall well-being. Eventually I felt that I'd taken working out with surgical tubing attached to doors as far as I wanted or could and had done push-ups and sit-ups, for hours, and I wanted to start on weights. My dad kept reminding me that Herschel Walker had turned out to be a pretty fair player with only push-ups and sit-ups, but it did little to dissuade me—I really wanted to start on weights.

"Not until you get your first pimple," he would tell me. He was a health and human-performance major at Florida, and people in the athletic world had convinced my dad that there was no point in training with weights before puberty, when the body starts manufacturing enough testosterone to be able to effectively begin to build muscle through weight training. I had no reason to doubt him, but that didn't stop me from asking. Over and over.

Finally, he gave in. He says it was because I had hit puberty, while my recollection is that it was just a bit earlier than that. Either way, I finally got a weight set that we kept in the barn. I think Mom felt like the barn would give the furniture and other items in the house a level of protection. That was all I had asked for as a Christmas present, and it was a gift that allowed me to change and improve my training regimen.

I kept push-ups and sit-ups in my routine, doing four hundred of each, every day. I also began to add weights and certain exercises with them, but Dad wouldn't let me use any weight heavier than one with which I could do at least fifteen repetitions. He was still being cautious, not wanting me to be injured or somehow stunt my growth or otherwise negatively impact the proper development of bones, tendons, and the like. In the process, I think I built up as much in endurance as I did in strength. As I began adding strength later, I think that foundation of stamina served me well, which was an expected plus.

At some point, still in Little League, I believed and imagined that everyone around me was also trying to improve. In retrospect, I'm not really sure how much most kids were training at that age, but at the time, I was convinced everyone was working hard to get better.

And that's when I adopted one of my mantras for getting stronger and better and for all my workouts:

Hard work beats talent when talent doesn't work hard.

Because I assumed that everyone was trying to get better, I began looking for ways that I could get an edge, an advantage that would serve me in competition. I would end up doing things above and beyond whatever was expected to get an edge. I also began working out at odd times of the day and night, thinking, *I'll bet there are no other kids in Jacksonville working out right now.* Whether that was actually true didn't really matter—what mattered to me was that I *thought* it was true. It was just another thing that motivated me to work longer and harder.

I'm sure that God made me in such a way that I was willing to work hard, but there was certainly a lot of parental encouragement and nurturing as well. From the earliest days I can remember, my parents always told me they believed God had big plans for me, even though they didn't know exactly what they were. Mom used to quote her paraphrase of Isaiah 64:4 over and over to me,

> *We haven't even seen a God like ours who acts on behalf of the one who waits for Him.*

My dad would also reinforce that promise of God. For my whole life, he has told me that he and Mom have always prayed for me, and knew that God had a special plan for me. They told all their children the same thing. That's true, of course, for me, for my brothers and sisters and for all of us, because God clearly has a plan for all of us. But my dad felt that somehow the plan God had laid out for me was going to involve a lot of visibility. He didn't say it exactly like that but, rather, more like this:

"Maybe it's through baseball or football, but somehow, some way, what we do in the Philippines to share Jesus with people, you'll be able to do and share right here in America, in ways that we'd never be able to. I can't walk into any high school to share the gospel, but you'll be able to. I believe that God is preparing the way for that to happen."

That's a great blessing to give a child. To remind them, pray for them, and assure them that God has a great plan—in His terms and for His purposes—for their lives.

I tried to work as hard as possible in every area in order to live up to it. Waiting on the Lord, as referenced in the passage from Isaiah that my mom always quoted, doesn't mean being complacent. It means understanding that He has a time and a plan, and that we're not the ones in control. In the meantime, however, we need to strive to use our gifts and abilities fully and to the best of our ability for whatever He does have in store for us, whenever the time comes. I was beginning to see more clearly that God always has His hand on us—preparing us for His purposes.

And I began to see that as not only a great blessing and promise, but a great responsibility.

Chapter Five

A FAIR FAREWELL

I can do all things through Christ who strengthens me.
—PHILIPPIANS 4:13, NKJV

After I'd been playing at Normandy and Lakeshore for a while, it came time for me to start playing for a school. There was only one that interested me: Jacksonville Trinity Christian Academy.

I was the third in our family to play sports at Trinity Christian. Since we were all homeschooled, we needed a way and place to participate in sports, and Trinity had provided that and had been a good home for us for years. As if the three of us playing wasn't enough, for years my dad had been videotaping every one of Trinity's games for the coaches' use, so it really was a family legacy that we were building at Trinity. And we continued to build it when I, as the third Tebow boy, began playing quarterback on Trinity's JV football team in the eighth grade.

We were undefeated during my eighth-grade year, and I was called up to the varsity team at the end of that season. (The varsity season lasts longer.) I didn't play at all that year on the varsity, however, but was biding my time for ninth grade.

After the season ended, I continued to train and lift as much as I could, but it wasn't until I was preparing for my freshman-year season at Trinity that I realized how much progress I'd been making. Before going into ninth grade, I went to a youth camp that featured, among other events, an arm-wrestling competition. Robby was back from college and had gone along to serve as a counselor for the camp, while Peter and I were there as campers.

That competition was one of the moments when I realized that all my extra hard work was beginning to pay off, providing me with an advantage I hadn't planned for. It was no surprise that Robby, as a college football player, made the finals at a high school camp, but as someone about to be a freshman, I certainly didn't expect to make it. Sure enough, though, I found myself in the finals against my brother. Of all people, my big brother.

The finals of the arm-wrestling competition? Me, about to be a freshman in high school, against my brother Robby, a college football player, and six years older than me.

Funny, I just can't remember who won.

It was apparent, though, that all the additional training I'd been doing was having a real and noticeable impact on my strength. Seeing that progress and the results of it in different settings made me even more motivated to work hard.

Heading into that first year of high school football, we went on a church-planned weekend called the "Burly Man Retreat," in Hilliard, Florida, located about thirty minutes north of Jacksonville and just inside the Florida–Georgia border. The events of that weekend have become the stuff of family legend and probably illustrate as well as anything just how competitive I am.

But there also can be a downside to that competitiveness.

This retreat included adult men as well as students and offered a tug-of-war, wood chopping, and a number of other events. I'm guessing the church didn't even bother to try and get insurance to cover anybody or the church for that weekend—what insurance company would want to underwrite such events? Anyway, at the end of the night on Saturday, they had scheduled an arm-curl competition. As I recall, it was a fifteen-pound curl bar with two ten-pound weights on each end, weighing in at fifty-five pounds. I kept sliding back in the line as guys were taking their turns, because I was hoping to be the last one to go, in order to know the number to beat.

The number of repetitions that guys were doing kept climbing with each new guy. Thirty-five, forty, fifty. I think it was around fifty-five repetitions by the time it reached the guy who was next to last . . . me. Unfortunately, I wasn't able to slide all the way to the end of the line, so I was going to have to put up a number that the guy behind me—the last guy in the competition—couldn't beat. Better yet, I figured that I'd put up a number that he wouldn't *want* to beat—and that way beat him before he even got started.

And so I began curling the bar as fast as I could. Thankfully, form didn't matter, just raising the bar to your chest by whatever means necessary. Arching my back, jumping . . . whatever it took. Forty, fifty, sixty, and now I was the leader. I kept going, straight through one hundred, which seemed like a lot, but I wasn't sure. He was really big—the guy behind me, that is.

At 175, my arms were really hurting, but by 225 reps, the pain was pretty much gone and numbness had set in. *May as well keep going,* I remember thinking. I couldn't feel anything anyway and still seemed to have the stamina and energy to go on.

I put down the bar after 315 curls.

I won.

If "winning" had included being able to straighten my arms out afterward, I would've been disqualified. I had to pack that night to leave camp the next day with both arms bent stiff at right angles, and when we arrived at church the next morning, I still couldn't straighten them. My biceps were still almost fully contracted from what I had subjected them to in that contest. By the third day the lactic acid and muscle shock had finally worn off, and I could use my arms again.

By the time I was preparing for my freshman football season at Trinity, my strength began to show itself more clearly on the field as well. When I attended the BMW Camp in Ocala (BMW stands for the last names of former Gator quarterbacks, Kerwin Bell, Shane Matthews, and Danny Wuerffel, who ran the camp), I was named the top quarterback at the camp, even though I was still only an eighth grader competing with high schoolers.

I also had a chance to work out with Gannon Shepherd, my future brother-in-law. At the time, Gannon played for the Jacksonville Jaguars. Katie, an intern for the Jaguars, chose to quit her job and date Gannon, rather than conform to their no-fraternization clause. The first time she brought him home, I was amazed at his size. He was a defensive end at Duke and became an offensive tackle in the pros, backing up the great Tony Boselli. At 6'8" tall and 320 pounds, he was huge. While my parents and the other kids were inside with Katie, I was outside with Gannon, working on pass rush moves.

Between my success at BMW, my strength victories, and the year as the Trinity JV quarterback that I had under my belt, I went into my freshman year with a lot of confidence. Peter was entering his senior year, and I felt comfortable on the team, with the program, and with our family's history at the school. But then all that changed.

As the season got under way, Coach Verlon Dorminey insisted on moving me from quarterback to linebacker, despite the success I'd had at quarterback in eighth grade. Now to be clear, this was not the first time I'd had to face this concept. I get it. I always did. I understood where they were coming from. I was a big, strong, athletic kid, and I had an advantage over many of the other kids my age because of it. Coaches would therefore always project me to play somewhere else besides quarterback. They all seemed to have a particular body type and lack of athleticism in mind that they associated with that of a quarterback and therefore always looked for another position that better fit their stereotype of my body type.

Just because I understood this, however, didn't mean I liked it. I always wanted the ball in my hands. I still do. My very first experience with the "playing position by body stereotype" philosophy and approach to the game was in my first year of playing Pee Wee football at Lakeshore. They asked where we'd all like to play, and I, of course, answered, "Quarterback," so they put me at running back.

I didn't get it. And I didn't like it.

And so they played someone else at quarterback and me at running back for one game and then decided to give me a shot and switched us. I was excited for the opportunity and was determined to do everything within my power to demonstrate that they made the right decision. I played there for the rest of the year, and then the following year they moved me back to running back—for the next two years. I hadn't done anything wrong, I was told, but the second year, the coach's son played quarterback.

I lived with that decision for those years in Pee Wee football, but it wasn't very much fun. My family, though disappointed, supported me and the coaches' decision, something that helped especially during those times where I really wanted to get in there and start taking snaps again. I hung with it to be a team player, but I was chomping at the bit to play quarterback. Football was my favorite sport, but what made it fun for me was playing quarterback.

Finally, I got to play quarterback again in my fourth year of Pop Warner, and we made it to the championship. The next year before the start of the Pee Wee League at Lakeshore, my coach came over to the house to talk with my dad. He had some thoughts about where I should be playing.

"I'm thinking of playing Timmy at fullback," Coach said.

"Oh, okay." Dad replied. "I'm thinking about having Timmy play for another team." He was clear and firm. Apparently Coach agreed with Dad that I was the best quarterback on the team, but he, like the others, was always looking for a position that better matched his idea for my body type and athleticism. When Dad told him that I really wasn't interested in playing football at another position, Coach agreed and moved me back to quarterback.

So, here we were again, only this time it wasn't Pee Wee football; it was Coach Dorminey at Trinity, and he didn't want me at fullback; he wanted me at linebacker like my two older brothers. It was merely the latest edition in this long-running soap opera that always had the same dialogue:

"Tim wants to play quarterback."

"He's too athletic to be a quarterback."

Position by body stereotype. For that ninth-grade year, though, I stuck with it so I could play with Peter during his final season. It was Peter's time to shine. But it wasn't much fun. Some guys just have a nose for the ball on defense.

Not me. On defense, I just wanted to hit somebody.

But in all things we can find some good. Even though it was frustrating, I did, even in that latest move.

As I was struggling with the move to defense, I was continuing to work out and get stronger. By that time, too, Robby was in his junior year of football in college, and he started sending me his Carson-Newman College workout books and regimen that the team used. Of course, I always felt that I had to do more repetitions than each exercise called for, and I often added to the suggested workouts with additional running or extra exercises or more sets of those recommended exercises. Taken just as it was from Robby's college, it was a solid workout schedule. For me, it was a great starting point.

In addition to Robby's workout, I learned an exercise series called 10-10-E, which I used thereafter until I got to college. For your final set, you'd put about two-thirds of your maximum weight total on the bar and then do ten reps. After a short break of about a minute, you'd do ten more. Another short break, and then do as many repetitions until complete exhaustion; that is, you can't move it anymore. That number should be between five and eight. If you could do more reps than that, you were supposed to increase the weight for the next time around.

I didn't realize or ever give much thought to the fact that the body needs a rest period to effectively increase muscle, so for those first few years I made sure I worked out every day. My dad tried to tell me to alternate upper-body and lower-body exercises to give my body a rest, but I'm not sure I always heard him. After all, if four workouts a week were good and the number usually recommended, then seven a week would be much better, right? Eventually, I learned a better approach that would help me to get even stronger and more physically fit.

I also studied a number of different books to help with my exercise routines. My best friend since I was little has been Kevin Albers. From the time we moved to Jacksonville from the Philippines I was always hanging out with Kevin, playing with him at Lakeshore and being with him in Sunday school. In fact, the Albers's house was one of the few that I was allowed to go to without my parents. His dad, Gary, who trained to be a Navy SEAL, gave me my first book on weight lifting, and I immediately started putting the exercises and principles in that book to use on a daily basis. A number of times when I would go over to hang out with Kevin, Mr. Albers would suggest some new exercise, or some variation on one I was already doing, for me to try. And then there were always the Navy SEAL moments that Kevin and I had with him, which made my time there working out and learning even more fun. He would often say something like, "Grab my shoulder," and the next thing I knew, he'd have thrown me to the floor. He was always teaching Kevin and me various hand-to-hand combat maneuvers that he had learned and polished during his time in the SEAL training.

Along the way I also tried other exercise regimens too. I would add various items from each of these books or from research I was doing on a regular basis on the Internet, but the core exercise protocol remained the one that Robby provided early on, one that he also used, from Carson-Newman College and Mr. Albers's physical-training manual and additional Navy SEAL techniques. I also added exercises from *Rocky IV*.

In addition to all the training, I'd also been drinking protein shakes in conjunction with my workouts, something that had begun when I was in eighth grade, thanks to homeschool. The reason I had homeschool to thank was that for months I'd been trying desperately to convince my parents to allow me to use the protein shakes, and for months they'd been resisting. That is until my mom suggested that I do a homeschool project to prove to them that the protein mixtures were safe.

My parents' hesitation came from the fact that they didn't want us taking anything that wasn't simply from a natural food supply or some kind of appropriate and generally recognized vitamin. I persisted because I kept hearing about guys mixing protein powder with milk or water and drinking it before or after their workouts. The protein in muscles needs amino acids to regenerate, so I was interested in drinking these shakes high in protein to supplement the protein in my diet that my muscles needed to heal and grow. My goal was to let the science out there persuade my parents that additional supplements of protein in my workouts—protein shakes in particular—were safe for me to use.

All this created a perfect atmosphere for learning—for all of us. Because of my homeschooling, my mom gave all of us the latitude to study the things that interested us beyond the required course load we had each year. At this time, I was particularly fascinated by whatever might help me improve athletically, and so we turned the building of muscle and protein's role in that into a science project, with an emphasis on any dangers or side effects from supplements and activities that would stimulate or affect the building of muscle. For weeks I did a lot of research in books, magazines, on the Internet, and at the nearby GNC store, putting together what I believed was a well-thought-out and articulated presentation.

After all, my athletic preparation was riding on it. In addition, I figured, why not go ahead and try to win the local middle-school science fair while I was at it? I tested my output of energy through a given workout and how much protein it would take to generate that energy. I even calculated how much protein I could take in through diet alone, and I was able to show that supplementation was necessary to get enough protein.

When I was done with my project, I presented it to my parents. Any grade I might receive was secondary to what I really hoped to achieve with this project and all the research that went into it. It worked. It really was a killer presentation, showing them that the protein shakes from GNC and similar places were completely safe, and I had the science to prove it. From that point forward, I was able to use protein along with my working out.

And yes, I won first place in the science fair.

The protein shakes, though, were just the start. I paid a lot of attention to what went into my body, and around this time I also decided to give up soft drinks for a year. My parents had witnessed over and over how committed I was to taking care of and improving my health, and so on this subject they had decided to challenge me, talking with me about, and demonstrating to me through their own research, concerns about the detrimental effects of ingesting too many carbonated drinks. As an enticement to quit, they offered me one hundred dollars if I went without having one soft drink for a full year. I did it.

I should have held out for more money, but in the end, it was worth it. To this day, I still don't drink soft drinks.

While watching my diet and working out in the right way helped me train, much of my early strength came from working on the farm. Some days it was just for an hour before we'd begin schooling; other days it might be all day, especially if there was a particular project on the farm that needed our immediate attention. We put up fences, chased and herded cows back to where they should be, planted gardens, felled and cleared trees that were dead—or to create some clearings we needed for other things—chopped firewood, and did whatever other work that needed doing on the farm. We joked that we were getting ready to dial Child Services when the work got too tough.

And as if there wasn't enough for us to do on our farm, about six times a year or so, Dad would loan us out to a neighbor friend, Mr. Bell, to help with whatever needed doing in raising and caring for his chickens. If you thought that I was complaining about working on *our* farm, trust me . . . I wasn't.

Chicken farming was brutal. Mr. Bell had a hundred thousand chickens. Upon arrival each time Dad sent us over, we'd immediately begin putting the new biddies (young hens) into his chicken houses, while also removing any dead biddies and chickens that happened to be in those houses. He had four chicken houses, and it was common for us to easily fill up three good-size buckets with dead chickens from just a single house.

But the fun was just getting started. We would then take the dead biddies to Mr. Bell's composter, where we alternated layers of chicken manure, which we had shoveled up from the chicken houses, and the dead chickens we had also just gathered up from the henhouses. The job—the smell, as the chickens cooked after being mixed in with the fresh chicken manure—would be a shoe-in for that *Dirty Jobs* television show. It was horrible.

Farmer strong. On so many levels.

On occasion we'd need to empty the composter when it got ripe and ready, which, as you can imagine, could get full fairly quickly on a chicken farm with a hundred thousand chickens. This process happened shovelful by shovelful through a door down at the bottom of the composter, loading the end product of fertilizer into a trailer. We would then drive the trailer to our property and begin scooping it out, throwing and spreading it evenly onto the garden or pasture as someone slowly drove the trailer along.

How many times was the wind blowing—in the wrong direction—as we threw this concoction onto the garden plots? *Every* time. It never failed that it ended up all over us—in our mouths, on our clothes, and in our eyes, hair, and ears. It probably doesn't have to be said that Mom would never let us in the house when we returned but instead forced us to strip and shower outside.

Looking back, I don't know if it's funnier that we only got five dollars for working all day or that I thought it was worth so much more when I was young.

Funnier still may have been the days when Mr. Bell would drive us to Burger King as an additional treat afterward, and before we'd had our outdoor shower. It must have been painful for other patrons and the Burger King manager and employees—not a treat for them, to be sure.

In the end though, being farmer strong, being trained, taking care of my body—it all felt like it would be futile if I couldn't play quarterback. Despite the fact that I kept improving and had good practices when I was allowed to play at quarterback, the coaches still used a different starting quarterback. That was how my freshman fall at Trinity went, and as the season came to a close, my future as a Trinity quarterback didn't look very bright. I continued to play hard and did what I was told at linebacker and tight end, while my dad kept filming each game every Friday night, dutifully making copies and delivering them to Coach Dorminey. But even with that loyalty, we were all beginning to see that something needed to change.

• • •

Between football, homeschooling, and farm labor, that freshman year I kept pretty busy. And when I wasn't doing any of those things, I was busy at our church. My family attends First Baptist Church of Jacksonville, and I was involved in their plays and youth meetings and activities whenever and as much as possible. Every Sunday morning we were all there, and the other times were a bit more sporadic, weaving things in with the pretty regular schedule of sports, which was often easier said than done.

First Baptist always had great kids' musicals, directed by Miss Nancy, who has supported me through my acting and football careers. I would never try out for special parts in the Christmas musicals because of football, but I had some memorable roles in the summer ones. My first role, however, did not exactly portend greatness on stage. I was in second grade and was cast as the back end of the camel. Please, no comments. The next few years, I played some "front end" roles, but I only had action parts, never ones that required speaking. That would come later. In third grade, I was a sailor, a supreme court justice in fourth grade, and in fifth grade, I was chosen to play Superman. It was a fun action part with a great costume, but I had such a dilemma when I realized that the required dress rehearsal was the same time as the semifinals for the city baseball championship. My mom and I prayed (Dad was in the Philippines), and my team won without me. That meant, however, that the championship game was the same time as my musical. We prayed again. To their credit, my coaches made an appeal to the city, and the final game was changed to Monday. I learned a lesson about giving the Lord my burdens, and this was a huge burden to me at the time. With no game on Sunday, some of my teammates came to the musical. And we won the city championship on Monday. My final action part in a children's musical was the first summer after I started college. I returned home to play Goliath and had a ball with all the kids.

With football season behind me, I moved on to the other sports I played for Trinity—basketball and baseball—both of which had rigorous schedules. In basketball, it seemed that my strength helped me to level the playing field a bit, balancing my basketball abilities and performance against my young age. When we played against Hawthorne High, just outside of Gainesville, I faced Cornelius Ingram, even at that time a great football and basketball player who was taller than I was and two years older. He went on to play both sports at the University of Florida. When we played Jacksonville Country Day, their lineup included a seven footer. It was obvious each time out that I needed to find something else that would give me a bit of an advantage—a balance against taller as well as older and more experienced players.

On both of those occasions, I was the one assigned to guard the tall guys. I was able to more or less hold my own due to my strength and by playing physically. It wasn't pretty, however.

Baseball was still in the sports mix as well. In fact, it was probably my best sport and the one that seemed to come to me most naturally—I had played varsity since the seventh grade. We even played some golf on occasion. But we did it on the cheap—it was not one of those sports that at the time fit into a missionary's salary. So Dad let us take the weed whacker out into the pasture and create our own putting greens, and then we used the posthole digger to create the cups. We were able to create four holes on our own farm this way—one of them was even a water hole over the pond—and messed around with playing a few holes whenever we could.

As much as I enjoyed playing sports for Trinity, though, my parents and I were still troubled with the quarterback situation at the school. And so we came to the conclusion that the time had come for us to look for other schools where I could play football. It was disappointing for all of us in the Tebow family. Trinity had always had great talent. More important, I had played with Peter, and our football team was on a run that culminated with our being crowned as state champions—the first time in school history. Peter had a great year and a great experience at Trinity and was named best defensive player for the year, but as a family, we came to a place where we knew we had to figure out a different plan for my future. We weren't going to say a word about our leaving during the season, but once the decision was made, our search began in all seriousness to find the best environment for me to fully develop my passion, and what seemed then to be talent, for playing quarterback.

No one in the Tebow family was pleased about reaching the end of the trail they had been running, walking, and filming at Jacksonville Trinity Christian Academy.

It was a disappointment to us all, but somehow we all knew it was the right thing to do.

Chapter Six

OVERCOMING

*Be anxious for nothing, but in everything by prayer and supplication
with thanksgiving let your requests be made known to God.
And the peace of God, which surpasses all comprehension, will
guard your hearts and your minds in Christ Jesus.*
—PHILIPPIANS 4:6–7

Homeschooling allowed us to pick my next school much in the same way we'd picked Trinity all those years before, and it didn't take long for my family to start looking around for another school where I could play quarterback.

Dad visited several select schools and spoke with their coaches. Some coaches weren't interested in taking a homeschool player, and some coaches and schools didn't seem as though they would be a good fit. Dad was talking to people about the types of offense that schools were running, the character of their coaches, and other pertinent matters. To him, the goal was trying to match my passion for playing football with a situation that would more fully develop my abilities. He likened it to when my sister Christy showed a passion and aptitude for playing the piano. For quite some time, they saved money and eventually bought a piano for her, so she could practice, learn, and more fully develop her God-given abilities. The way my dad and mom looked at it, finding the right situation at the right school was a matter of being a good steward of my talents. They felt like it was always our responsibility to identify and fully develop the abilities, talents, and gifts God created within us.

That and the fact that I couldn't stand playing linebacker anymore.

Dad looked at schools in Jacksonville and even considered schools in south Georgia and Ocala, Florida, trying to find the right setting for me to play.

Dad called Kerwin Bell, the former University of Florida quarterback and current head coach at Jacksonville University, who ran the BMW Camp that I had attended and who at the time was a very successful head football coach at Trinity Catholic High School in Ocala. Coach Bell told us that he was very interested in having me come to play for him at Trinity Catholic. My parents were considering and exploring the significant challenges involved in my playing at a school that was a couple of hours from our home, when Dad also asked another good friend who he would recommend I play for.

He was clear and direct in his response. "Craig Howard," he said, "who has just been hired for the Nease High School head football coaching position, runs a wide-open, creative offense." When we met with Coach Howard, we knew in three minutes that he was the right coach.

Because Nease was a public school, Dad started checking into the Florida statutes, as well as the Florida High School Athletic Association (FHSAA) rules and the rules of participation governing play in St. Johns County. Under Florida's homeschooling law, homeschoolers can play at the public school within their district. However, as it turned out at that time, if you lived in St. Johns County, you could participate in sports at any one of the four high schools in the county, regardless of the particular district the school was located within.

It also happened that my dad's sister Sharon was just finishing some work on an apartment in St. Johns County that was meant to be for their parents' use in the future. Apparently the future was now, and she made it available for us to use so that we lived in the same county in which Nease was located, even though we weren't in its district.

My mom spoke to her good friend, Brenda Dickinson, whose deceased husband had authored Florida's homeschool law in 1985. In 1996, Mrs. Dickinson, now a Florida homeschool lobbyist, wrote the legislation that allows homeschoolers to participate in extracurricular acitvities. She carefully went over every necessary requirement with my mom.

Dad spoke to the head of the FHSAA and four different lawyers to make sure that our understanding of the law and governing rules was correct and that we were doing everything in an above-board, upstanding, and legal manner.* We were assured that we were. Dad knew that if I enjoyed any success, some might move to challenge my eligibility. Sure enough, challenges came from two quarters: one expected and one that was not. The one we expected might be forthcoming was from one of the other three high schools located within St. Johns County. The other one that had some people making some noise (though it never grew to a formal challenge of my eligibility) came from Jacksonville Trinity Christian Academy, the school we had just left. That was hurtful—we had wanted to stay.

We helped my dad's sister complete the work on the apartment, and then Mom and I moved there to live in order to make me eligible to play. By then all my siblings were off at college or married, and Dad was traveling a good deal, so this worked out well for Mom and me to live in St. Johns County. On the weekends we headed back to Jacksonville to visit with Dad, but during the week we did all our homeschooling in the apartment in St. Johns County.

Convenient as it was, it was still quite a change and transition for us. I missed life on the farm and regularly being around our dog, Otis. Dad was traveling both to the Philippines and within the States a great deal, so while we missed him, that wouldn't have changed even if we were home. Plus, I was staying so busy each day—schoolwork,

---

* St. Johns County later changed the districting rule to read that homeschoolers must attend the school in their district, but I was grandfathered in and could remain at Nease High School.

workout, practice, workout, schoolwork, bed—that it was probably tougher on Mom than on me. Once I started taking recruiting trips, however, even many of those weekend trips home ended.

In this transition, I could see both my parents playing different yet vital roles for me, roles that have always been crucial to my success—whether in school or on the field. My father is fiercely loyal and helped us to pursue our passions. My mom, meanwhile, is more nurturing, and a peacemaker. She always told us to never let the sun go down on our anger, but rather that we should address our issues before bed, if not earlier.

And then there was the team itself. I started at quarterback my sophomore year, and I was surprised by how much strength training and overall improvement we needed to make as a team. That first year, we played in six homecoming games—every one of our away games was for some other school's homecoming. One of the games was for ours, but we were everyone else's homecoming opponent—not ordinarily a sign of respect for a school's football prowess. It didn't seem to bother my teammates as much as I thought it should have. After all, they had only won two games the year before, and they seemed a little too willing to accept this as normal.

We quickly improved, however, at least on offense. We had one of the best offenses in the state, but we had an undersized defense. We lost a number of high-scoring games, scoring 45 points in a loss to St. Augustine, and losing in triple overtime to Palatka, the number one team in the state. That Palatka game, a much bigger and faster opponent, and that year as a whole, were both important from the standpoint of building confidence. We realized we could play with anyone.

They had no idea what they were in store for—after all, I was the nutty kid who would watch football whenever I could. I certainly didn't intend to be a part of a team where being every other school's homecoming opponent was accepted.

I worked as hard as I ever did and did my best, through my words and my example, to challenge my teammates to reach for something much more for themselves and the team. I even pushed one of my receivers when he mocked my use of the word *lackadaisical* (directed at the receivers, I might add) as "a pretty big word for a homeschooler." I didn't mind jokes about going to school in my pajamas, but I didn't want anyone to say I was soft. I probably shouldn't have pushed him, but I could see a change that day in how he viewed me. He wanted to pigeonhole me as this soft homebody. He realized soon enough that I wasn't. Before long, though, we were all on the same page.

Chapter Seven

PHILIPPINES, FOOTBALL, FAITH, AND OTIS

Trust in the LORD with all your heart and do not lean on your own understanding. In all your ways acknowledge Him, and He will make your paths straight.

—PROVERBS 3:5–6

When you're younger, every birthday feels like a milestone, and the summer of my fifteenth was no different. For many reasons, I was excited to turn fifteen, but perhaps the most important was that turning fifteen meant I was old enough to go on my first Mission Trip to the Philippines the following summer. For years, my dad had been leading a mission trip to the Philippines in July, and finally I'd be able to go too.

That's how we were raised, with a joy in getting to tell people about Jesus. For as long as I can remember, this was instilled in me: to have fun, love Jesus and others, and tell them about Him.

Go therefore and make disciples of all the nations, baptizing them in the name of the Father and the Son and the Holy Spirit, teaching them to observe all that I commanded you; and lo, I am with you always, even to the end of the age.

MATTHEW 28:19–20

It was a real and integral verse within the life of our family. Even more than that, it was a way of life for our family.

Though I'd grown up with Dad's frequent trips back to the Philippines and with hearing news about Uncle Dick's orphanage, I hadn't been back to the Philippines myself since we'd moved to Florida when I was three. But when I was fifteen, I was old enough to go to the Philippines, and so I took my first trip back to help spread God's Word.

This was not the first time I'd done mission work, however. Just as I was entering high school, I'd gone on a mission trip to South Florida. A small church down there had invited, and made the arrangements for, some of us from Jacksonville to come. They were looking to reach the surrounding neighborhoods in the area where the church was located. Kevin Albers and I, along with our friend, college student Joey Hamrick, all roomed together with an elderly couple from the host church that was kind enough to open their home to us for the week.

Every morning, after we ate the biscuits and gravy the couple made for us, we'd head out for the day. As Kevin, Joey, and I went door to door in trailer parks and other neighborhoods, we watched God use our inadequate but sincere intrusion into the area as almost thirty people committed their lives to the Lord. It was awesome yet humbling to see God work in that way—through our simply taking part in this church's outreach into its community.

The church simply turned us loose in our small groups. These days they wouldn't do it that way; instead, they would probably send adults along with us. We needed to be back at the church each day at a certain time, but we missed it every time, so caught up in the passion of our visits in the neighborhoods and trying to speak to as many people as we could. Much like my approach to working out— if something's important and a little is good, a lot is better, so why stop at a little?

In the process of doing that each day, I had a chance to give an impromptu talk to a randomly gathered group of people for the first time. We were walking past an arcade, filled with kids playing all sorts of games, when Joey, who had been trained by my dad on a trip to the Philippines, told us to gather all the kids together. So we asked—actually I believe it might have been more appropriately characterized as shouted—the kids if we could have their attention for a moment. We waited while they all finished up whatever games they were playing or whatever else they were doing. I guess they were curious, and we must have looked harmless, because nobody really resisted, and moments later they all formed a group.

That's when Joey turned things over to me. Looking back, since he was the one with the training, I'm not sure why I was the one speaking, but I remember being pretty intimidated, seeing those kids looking at me as I stood there totally mute for what felt like a very long moment. Then I began to speak, first sharing something from my heart. It must have gone okay and it must have been sufficient for God to use, because I spoke for a few minutes about the good news of the gospel of Christ, and we ended up praying with seven or eight kids to accept Christ right then and there.

That experience was amazing, a crucial step helping prepare me for the difficult task of talking about God with people I meet—something I would do a lot later in life.

For this reason, I knew that going to the Philippines would be a challenge, but what I did not expect was that it would change my life. My dad's Filipino and American staff works hard for months to put together a solid schedule for the Americans on the summer trip. America and the Philippines have had a long friendship; in fact there is a Fil-Am day every year, celebrating the relationship. Because of our friendship, Americans are very welcome in the communities and schools, and received with a great welcome.

With the permission of regional and district superintendents, and principals of schools, we tie into the moral and spiritual values program already in place in the schools. It is a non-sectarian program emphasizing the love of God and a personal relationship with Jesus Christ, and drug abstinence.

When possible we have an assembly with the whole student body, such as at their morning flag ceremony. At an assembly we have a short 10 to 12 minute message of the love of God in Christ. If we are unable to have an assembly, we share the same message classroom by classroom, which is much more speaking but more intimate. We almost always have a minute to shake hands and high-five students, which is a special time. (Perhaps this is where my tradition of high-fiving Florida fans after each game began.)

My dad gets us up early each school day, around 4:30 A.M., to get ready and fix breakfast; and then we get on the road often covering a good distance to get to the first school. We usually have two or three Americans on a team with two Filipino staff. The staff drives, does most of the talking to the principals and then translates the message to make sure everyone understands all parts of the message. We work hard all day until school is out. It is fun but exhausting. In a typical day a team will speak in six to ten schools, depending on distance and other factors. Sometimes less and sometimes a few more. When I am speaking I usually open with comments about being born in the Philippines. That creates a great connection with students.

Then I talk about the gospel. The word "gospel" means "good news." So I'll ask, "Do you like good news? The good news is that God loves you! He loves you so much that He sent His son Jesus to die for you. He made you special and wants to have a personal relationship with you and give you eternal life. But our biggest problem is that we have sinned. Because God is a Holy God, He can never have fellowship with sin. Sin makes a wall between us and God. Because Jesus had no sin He could die for our sins on the cross. Because Jesus died on the cross for your sins and rose from the dead, He has the power to forgive your sins, make you His child, and give you a home in heaven. That is the best news you could ever hear. You can't earn the free gift of eternal life, you can't pay for the free gift of eternal life, you can only receive it as a free gift, by putting your faith and trust in Jesus Christ alone."

And then I always end with an invitation to pray with me if they want to trust Jesus, praying something like this: "Dear Jesus, I know

I am a sinner and need a Savior. Thank you for dying on the cross for me. I open the door of my heart and ask you to come in. Save me now, Jesus. Thank you for saving me. Thank you for coming into my heart. Thank you that God is my Father and I am His child. Thank you that I have a home in heaven, and I will come and live with you some day. In Jesus's name, Amen."

Finally, I ask them several questions. "Did you ask Jesus in your heart?" "Where is Jesus right now?" "Is He ever going to leave you?" "He promised to never leave you, to never forsake you, to be with you forever. If you have Jesus and you died today, where would you be?" "If God is your Father and God is my Father, what does that make us?"

Personally it is so exciting to have the privilege to share this good news with other people. I know that God is the one who changes hearts, but I am always eager to try and plant a seed. There was one special day that a friend of ours, Jenessa Spaulding, and I spoke in nine schools to 29,000 people. The first school that day was over 11,000 students. Needless to say, it was a wonderful and fruitful day in the schools.

Many nights I got back to the hotel we were staying in with a terrible sore throat. As I would fall asleep, I thought there was no way I'd be able to speak the next morning, but sure enough every time, I would wake up refreshed, throat fine and ready to go.

In addition to the life-changing aspect of preaching the gospel and leading people to place their trust in Christ, it was great preparation for the speaking I would end up doing as I got older. Speaking without notes, learning to reduce or extend my remarks depending on the time allotted, tailoring my remarks on the fly for an intimate setting or for a larger gathering—the opportunities I had speaking in the Philippines provided great training for it all. I now actually prefer speaking without notes, because it ensures that I won't come across as scripted, and it gives me a chance to engage my audience with my eyes and my gestures. And also, without notes I'm assured that my comments will be real, authentic, and come from the heart. I still get nervous when I speak, but even so I would rather not have notes and instead simply have prepared enough to know the material I want to share, I might have several words jotted down to remind me of points I want to make, and I've found that being slightly nervous actually helps me, in that it boosts my energy and passion.

Full days. Packed classrooms and auditoriums, and being worn out at the end of the day. That's what our trips back to the Philippines were like. But we loved it, and I came back from my first mission trip to the Philippines renewed to fulfill my purpose of living for the Lord, whether here or there and in whatever place, setting, or game I found myself in.

Life was good back in the States, too, when we returned from the Philippines. For the most part, life was quiet for us other than my schooling and studying with Mom, working, and sports.

One of the hardest parts about living at the apartment during the week was that it meant I was apart from Otis, our beloved dog given to us by Peter's friend Philip Hurst. We'd always had a number of dogs on the farm, but many of them didn't survive—or didn't choose to stay—on the farm. Otis set himself apart in many ways, including longevity. We got Otis when I was around five years old, so he and I had plenty of time to develop a trusted and close bond.

Otis was loyal and protective, traits you'd hope to find in a dog. If you came by, you would see blonde-haired Otis, who looked to be a mixture of half Lab and half golden retriever, walking down our long dirt driveway at the farm and toward the house, keeping my mom company . . . and safe. He would wander the property, looking for threats to the family, including snakes. When he found one, he would neutralize the threat and then, proudly, leave the dead snake, I suppose, for us to see that he was keeping us safe. He must have done this a hundred times.

Once at a birthday party, we were all swimming in the pool, when all of a sudden one of us spotted a small snake in the pool at about the same time that Otis did. He beat us to it, thank goodness, and leapt into the pool, grabbed the snake in his mouth, and made sure it would never again end up in any pool. Then he climbed out with the now lifeless snake draped out of his mouth, carried it off, and laid it to its final rest in our backyard.

Otis met every visitor who came onto our property, whether invited or not, and usually before anyone else in the family had the chance. Our guests or any delivery truck or our large-animal vet—anyone and everyone—were all escorted—chased, really—as they came up the drive toward the house. He was always keeping an eye out for us and *on* all others.

For my birthday weekend in August that year I went with my brother Robby and Kevin to Disney World. When we returned home after the weekend, I couldn't put my finger on it, but something seemed different as we drove onto the property. My mom met us as we pulled up in front of the house.

"I haven't seen Otis all weekend." She seemed pretty unsettled.

That's what it was. That's what seemed out of place. Otis (the "first greeter") always greeted everyone on their arrival, always excited to see friends and strangers—even though he was too trusting of strangers until they showed him they couldn't be trusted. That's what was different. He wasn't there when we pulled up. And now Mom was telling us he seemed to have been gone all weekend? It wasn't completely out of the ordinary for him to take off for several hours, but never several days. We were concerned, so we all headed out to find him.

Getting more upset by the minute, I took off on foot, running around the farm, then decided that the car would be faster. So I got in and started driving around the property, calling as loud as I could, over and over again, for Otis. We covered the length and breadth of the property as well as some property off the farm, even though Otis had never left the farm before. I went back and forth, over and over, hoping at any moment Otis would come bounding and barking from behind the corner of somewhere—maybe even with a snake that no longer could harm us hanging from his mouth. I smiled thinking for a moment about what a welcome sight that would be.

I made another pass down the driveway, driving slowly, keeping my eyes peeled toward the underbrush on either side of the drive. There it was—that golden head popping up in the brush. I slammed on the brakes, jumped out of the car, yelled for the others, and ran toward him, calling out to him as I ran.

He put his head back down. In the past, he would have always come running to greet me. I reached him, afraid that maybe he'd been bitten by a snake. He looked fine, and I slowly and gently lifted his head. I still didn't see anything wrong, until he opened his mouth.

It was a bloody mess. His bottom jaw appeared to have been split down its full length, the two pieces hanging loosely. He was missing teeth, too, I would later learn, but I couldn't tell at the time with all the damage and blood. I looked down at his legs and realized that instead of being tucked under him as they should be and usually were, they were awkwardly splayed around him. Otis had been hurt bad, but I couldn't figure out by what.

I gently but quickly scooped him up, put him on the seat of the car, and raced back to the house to tell the others, so we could all head to the vet. And all the way to the vet, I was getting more and more upset and more and more frustrated with the state Otis was in. Not merely upset, I was getting angry as well, because the more I thought about it, it was becoming clearer to me—he wasn't attacked by a *what* but by a *who*. It appeared to me that he'd been struck with something repeatedly.

The vet agreed with my guess, and after he'd given Otis a quick look he suggested that it could have been the work of a baseball bat. He didn't close the door on another object or possibly a car, but a bat or board was his guess.

"Tim, his injuries are too severe." The vet told me that Otis's back, legs, and hips were all severely damaged and his jaw was radically fractured. Surgery would have been extensive and expensive, and there was absolutely no guarantee that at his age he would survive either the surgery or recovery period. Plus, the extensive rehabilitation that would be required might prove to be more than he could take.

So we brought Otis home to die and laid him carefully on his bed.

Only we forgot to tell Otis that was the plan. We forgot to tell him that these were his last days.

So, every day, I carefully lifted Otis and carried him to the pool. He had grown up swimming in our pool and our pond, but this was a bit different, and he seemed to know it. He didn't fight it, but it didn't excite him, either, as it had in the past. I gently submerged him on my lap up to his shoulders, and for several days we stopped at that point of submersion. We just rested in the pool in that position together for a while, and then I would carefully take him back into the house. Neither one of us was prepared to give up.

When I'd been doing that for a couple of weeks, I began gently moving his back legs and watching his reaction. We took it slowly and increased his range of motion over time to help his muscles regain some tone and strength. He didn't seem to want to move them on his own, so I would—and he let me—move them for him. Over time, I started moving my hand out from under his back legs, which would force him to begin to paddle a bit to feel like he was staying afloat. I never took my hand off his chest and never made him paddle much. Just long enough so he could take a few strokes with his legs and regain some confidence and strength in them.

It was hard to look at him, though, without feeling how painful it all must have been for him and how he still must have hurt. Missing and broken teeth. A jaw that was split and badly misshapen. Every time I looked at him, I could sense and feel the pain he was in.

Thankfully, Otis continued to get better, and over the next few months, with the regular pool workouts and lots of milkshakes—he loved vanilla—he regained the ability to walk again, albeit with a noticeable limp. He never ran again, but after an initial period where he seemed ashamed or worried that he'd done something wrong— which made me as upset at the physical injuries he'd suffered—he settled back into being himself, even though as a bit more frail version of the original Otis. But he was our Otis, no less, and the one we always knew and loved.

A couple of weeks later, football season began. It was my second football season at Nease, and we continued to make great strides to improve during my junior year. Throughout the off-season, the guys had spent much more time on their own—weight lifting, working out, working together on drills—looking to get better, to develop that edge we needed, and in the process to help make us a better team. And it worked.

Though we'd been a .500 team the year before, our performance had been unexpected, but this year expectations were higher for all of us—including me. My playing the previous year had attracted some quiet attention from college scouts, and while I had no idea where that would take me, I did know I was looking to make that quiet attention get a bit louder.

But more important than wanting interest from college coaches, I felt a lot of responsibility for helping to make our team better and for pushing all of us to fulfill our potential. This year a 5–5 season would not be enough for any of us—especially Coach Howard. It was Coach Howard's second year as head coach at Nease High School, and he'd had a full year to encourage us, set the bar higher for us, persuade us that his way would lead to success, and build his values and lessons into us, including one that he taught and reminded us about often: "Our job as coaches is to love you guys; it's your job to love each other."

And as time passed, they did just that with all the players, and we did with each other. It all began to make a difference—both on and off the field. We could tell that we'd improved in the off-season through 7-on-7 touch football tournaments that we played in. From Jacksonville to South Georgia to North Carolina, we won every tournament, and as an added benefit, improved our passing game timing. In the process, games got to be more fun. We had enthusiastic, energetic fans. Students started coming more regularly and ended up creating what I still think is one of the coolest cheers around. When we had scored and were getting ready to kick off, they would begin chanting, "Mo . . . Mo . . . Mo . . . Mo, Mo, Mo, Mo," getting faster and faster until the ball was kicked. The idea was that momentum ("Mo") was now on our side. They then began raising one hand, spreading all five fingers toward the sky, acknowledging Coach Howard's goal that we get the ball back—and score—within five minutes of kicking off.

We were scoring quite a bit, really rolling and undefeated headed into our midseason game against St. Augustine. We had improved and knew we had a good chance to beat them. In fact, we led until the very end. They scored a touchdown with about twenty seconds left in the game to take a 33–30 lead, after which we ran the kick-off back to around our own thirty-five yard line. With only a few seconds remaining, Coach Howard called for a Hail Mary pass, but my attempt landed harmlessly at the goal line as, once again, St. Augustine won. However, the combination of our effort during that game and the continuously improving football culture at Nease High School helped me gain even more interest from colleges, which began to take note of me in larger numbers. It didn't hurt the interest that the ball had traveled seventy yards in the air on that final throw against St. Augustine.

Throws like that may have put me solidly on the radar screens of many college recruiters that season, but as a team, we played football that was worth remembering.

In the first round of the playoffs, we played Citrus High School, from Inverness, Florida. Coach Howard had asked my dad to do the chapel service for the team. Dad mixed together Bible verses with clips from *Saving Private Ryan*, a combination that apparently worked. One of Robby's college teammates, Angel, drove up from his home in Miami for the game, but unfortunately for him, he arrived a few minutes late, and by then it was all but over. I threw for three touchdowns in the first five minutes and seven in the first half, resulting in a 55–0 score at halftime. Setting numerous records in that game, we coasted, resting and playing all the members of the team, to a 76–6 final score.

In the next round of the playoffs we faced our nemesis, St. Augustine, again. We were so jacked up and believed we were ready for this game. It was going to be the perfect setting for finally breaking through to beat them—we had lost twelve straight games to them. Looking back on that night, I think Dad should have gone with *Saving Private Ryan* again. It was back and forth early, then our turnovers contributed to their taking a big lead. We were so far behind by halftime that it seemed like we had no shot at getting back into the game. To our credit, though, nobody in our locker room lost heart or turned it in, and we continued to scrap and battle, slowly chipping away at their lead.

Finally, we had driven close to their end zone and trailed 35–28 with just seconds left on the clock. The danger in calling a running play in that situation, of course, is that the clock would continue to run unless we got the ball out-of-bounds. We had enough time remaining, however, that we knew that even if we didn't score, we could still line up quickly and spike the ball to kill the clock and be able to run another play, or simply quickly line up and run one more play without having to stop the clock.

I kept the ball on a power-keeper play and lunged halfway across the goal line in the middle of a pile of bodies. The referees never made a call one way or another, continuing to unpile players, and while they were unstacking players, they never stopped the clock. When they finally got to the bottom of the pile, they should have found me with my entire upper body and the ball across the goal line, but somehow they didn't see it that way, ruling that the ball never got across the goal line.

No touchdown.

No time left.

Game over; 11–2 for the season, with both losses to St. Augustine.

St. Augustine raced off the field jumping up and down, cheering and hollering in celebration, while we stood there, in stunned silence, our season over.

Through the off-season and the summer, we kept growing together as a team, and by my senior year, in 2005, we were an incredibly tight-knit group—brothers-in-arms ready to go out together to face whatever was before us. We had all gone to camp together that summer to work on our football, a commitment that some had avoided in the past. We began meeting every Wednesday night and talking about important things, something pretty rare among high school students, even rarer especially since we were guys. We were truly trying to live out Coach Howard's mantra:

CHARACTER
STRENGTH
HONOR

Coach posted those words on the locker-room wall. Every day they were right there, in our faces. After that 11–2 record of improvement capping my junior year, we now had even higher expectations for my senior year.

At the same time, there was a lot of attention on me and whether I would perform at the level everyone expected. In the lead-up to the season, I'd learned that Ken Murrah of Ponte Vedra Beach wanted to film a documentary about me, which was scheduled for broadcast on ESPN. It certainly fit within the framework of the admonition of Proverbs 27:2 to "Let another praise you, and not your own mouth; a stranger, and not your own lips." It was very flattering that they would want to do that, and even though it was very well done, I couldn't help but be pretty embarrassed by its filming. And the title was the worst part of the embarrassment.

The Chosen One.

They interviewed coaches, teammates, and other key people from my life. And while I didn't really want the extra attention, it turned out to be really fun and led to other guys getting scholarships because of all the attention focused on our program. It was also a great Christian witness, because the final documentary showed my dad reading Bible verses.

But I'd have at least changed the title.

Luckily, though, the attention from the documentary didn't get in the way of our team's ability to focus. This was critical as we were immediately put to the test, opening with the first nationally televised game on ESPN at Hoover, Alabama, against the Hoover High School Buccaneers, who at the time were nationally ranked. We stayed close for most of the game, but after tying the score, we gave up twenty-one unanswered points and eventually lost, 50–29.

We breezed through the rest of the regular season, with scores like 70–21, 49–13, and 53–0.

St. Augustine was a different story. We spotted them twenty points to open our game, and in a steady rain, our rally fell short, 20–14. We had battled back and forced a punt late in the game to give us a chance, but we were penalized for roughing the punter and never got the ball back. We simply dug too big of a hole for ourselves early in the game. The then head football coach at Alabama, Mike Shula, watched it all from the sidelines, as some of the Florida coaches sat in the stands.

Same outcome as always when it came to St. Augustine. I joked that I didn't want to have something like that in common with Peyton Manning, who had a great college career but whose Tennessee Volunteers could never beat the Florida Gators in their four tries. I was wrong, as I lost four times to St. Augustine.

Hopefully I can find other ways to mirror Peyton's career.

It wasn't funny at the time, however. Losses crush me. I work so hard off the field and am so physically exhausted after games that I've been known to cry at times after losses, and occasionally even at wins. That night one of my coaches at Nease, Wesley Haynes, noted that crying wasn't at all unusual for me after a St. Augustine game. I just get so exhausted after games—not to mention that I'm pretty sensitive and seem to wear my emotions on my sleeve—that all the emotions just flood out of me, much to the delight of opposing fans, it seems. After that St. Augustine game, my brothers were trying to surround me to stop St. Augustine fans from taking pictures of me crying. It just happens. It's the way God made me.

Of course, plenty of people have seen the other side of me as well, the way that I get so intense and fired up during a game. That's a challenge for me, becoming so intense and yet still staying in control enough to show good sportsmanship. That's something my parents have worked on with me for years.

Two weeks later, while we were playing Columbia High, I heard a pop in my lower leg, but I didn't want to come out of the game. Coach Howard asked if it was broken, but I didn't think it was, mostly because I had already been down this path two years earlier.

My sophomore year, in 2003, we'd been playing Menendez High, and I'd thrown an interception right at the end of the first quarter. As

I was releasing the ball, a defensive lineman hit my right leg, which was planted, and I heard a snap. I hobbled off the field as our defense headed out.

Coach Howard asked if I could go back out. "Asked," may be the wrong word, as he told me that this was what legends were made of, that it was probably just a charley horse, and that I should gut it out. We were trailing 17–0 at the time, and I went back in. At halftime, with my leg still hurting pretty badly, I tested it out for our trainer, who thought I should come out of the game. My dad had even come down from the stands to the locker room to ask how it was. I told him it really hurt and I could feel it click on every stride, but I was okay.

I stayed in, and late in the game I scored on a long run to tie the game. My mom said people in the stands were wondering why I wasn't running any faster! In fact, when I scored on that run to tie the score at 24 with ten seconds left, I collided with their safety in the end zone, snapping his leg. Unfortunately, Menendez returned the kickoff to our thirty yard line and kicked a field goal to win the game. It's probably a good thing that we avoided overtime, as I headed straight to the hospital where x-rays revealed I'd been playing with a complete break to my fibula.

So at that moment in my senior year against Columbia, I probably would have given Coach Howard whatever answer kept me in the game. I told him I didn't know if it was broken, which was accurate. I didn't. It hurt, but not as bad as when I'd hurt my leg during my sophomore year. It was a whole lot less painful to put my weight on it when I walked or ran. And so I went back in.

As it turned out, it was only a high ankle sprain. To give it a better opportunity for healing but still allow me to play, we cut down on the amount I ran for the next few games leading up to the playoffs. It required a lot of restraint on my part, but by that point our offense had clicked enough that we knew how to win against opponents without my running game. In fact, I didn't even play in a couple of games at the end of the year.

All that ended when we got to the playoffs. We opened our run in the State 4A playoffs against Leesburg but I only played in five plays—four of them were passing touchdowns—before my day was over. We then had a battle with New Smyrna Beach High School, and, once again, we assumed that my ankle wasn't healthy enough for me to run. We were right. Not to mention, I had a hard cast over my ankle that Mike Ryan, the head trainer of the Jacksonville Jaguars, made for me.

Late in the game it was still close; they were dropping nine guys into pass coverage, rushing only two, because they knew I couldn't run.

Finally, I told Coach Howard to let me run, and he saved the moment for late in the fourth quarter, as we faced a fourth down with two yards to go. I ran. We scored. I ended up running one more time, and behind some great blocking, we scored then too. Most important, we survived to move on to the next round. That's what playoffs are all about—in any sport—surviving to play again. Sometimes it seems like our days are a lot like that too—just getting through the stuff and challenges of the day, knowing that God is still there and allowing Him to use it all to prepare us for another day and the things He has planned for us to do tomorrow.

For that next round of the playoffs we traveled to Gainesville, and with my leg feeling better, we beat the Eastside High School Rams by a score of 57–21. I rushed for sixty-two yards, and with that running threat something they now had to defend against, our offense was freed up, allowing me to throw for over four hundred yards. The following week, we played Pensacola Pace. It was an intense game with a record crowd. In the crowd were many of the Alabama coaches, while Coach Meyer paced the sidelines, making comments to my two brothers. Near the end of the game, we used a play that Coach Howard had gotten from the University of Florida—"Bullets." I threw a ninety-nine yard touchdown using their play. After winning that game, we found ourselves in the 4A State finals in the Miami Dolphins stadium, facing Armwood High School, a school located just east of Tampa.

Armwood had won the 4A State Championships the prior two years and were looking to make it three straight with a win against us. From the start, we played very well and jumped out to a big lead. At halftime Coach Howard congratulated us and said about our 34–15 lead, "They can't come back from nineteen points against you guys." He would have been right if we hadn't eased up, I'm sure, but instead they came storming back. We finally woke back up in the fourth quarter and scored a few more points while our defense stiffened and hung on for a 44–37 win.

Our offense was solid, and as a result, I had a good game, passing for over 200 yards and four touchdowns and rushing for 183 yards more and two touchdowns. With that effort on offense, those six touchdowns set a Florida championship-game record. It was a phenomenal feeling as we celebrated the achievement that our hard work had brought to us as coaches, staff, and players individually and as a team, and as an entire high school.

It was a wonderful moment.

In no small part because of Coach Howard and his staff, as well as the commitment that all of us as players made to one another and the success of our program, we won the state championship.

Along the way, I'd also managed to amass a high-school career I could be proud of. By the time I was done, I had been named to the First Team All-State team twice, was named 2005 Mr. Florida Football, and with the support of my teammates, set career marks in Florida for total offense, passing yards, touchdowns, and completed passes. I also now held the single-season records in Florida for total offense, passing yards, touchdown passes, and total touchdowns. I had worked hard, and my coaches and teammates had worked hard, but I had also been richly blessed by God and so many around me, who made me better as a person and student-athlete.

The day after we'd won it all, my mind had already moved elsewhere. It was now time for me to turn my attention to deciding what college I would attend. Earlier in the fall, I'd committed myself to making a decision by that next week, and I had no idea what I should do.

And Otis heard about it all.

Chapter Eight

WHERE TO GO, WHERE TO GO?

"I know the plans that I have for you," declares the Lord, *"plans for welfare and not for calamity to give you a future and a hope."*

—Jeremiah 29:11

One day during my sophomore year I came home and found two letters in our mailbox addressed to me: my first ever recruiting letters. One was from Ohio State, and the other one was from Louisville. I was so jacked, even though they were not personalized and were clearly generated by a computer. Still, they were from colleges, and they were to *me*.

They arrived on a Monday, and as I sat with my parents that night watching *Monday Night Football*, I couldn't help myself—I was still so excited about my first ever recruiting letters. And so when the players introduced themselves at the start of the game ("LaDainian Tomlinson, Texas Christian University"), I tried it out for myself from the security of my couch.

"Tim Tebow, University of Louisville."

"Tim Tebow, Louisville."

"Tim Tebow, THE Ohio State University."

It was a fantastic night, rereading those two letters, watching the game with my parents, and daydreaming about someday playing college football, and who knows what else after that. We were laughing, having fun dreaming about it throughout the game. I still think it's pretty fun to think about introducing myself for a *Monday Night Football* game.

As it turns out, the letters didn't stop with those first two.

Instead, they continued to roll in, creating quite an impressive stack of interest over time. Lots of schools, and lots of conferences. The University of Maryland, the University of North Carolina, North Carolina State, Florida State University, Miami, Michigan State, Notre Dame, Ole Miss, Iowa, Illinois, Ohio State, Oklahoma, Oklahoma State, Colorado, and others. By the time I had graduated, I had over eighty scholarship offers from schools across the country. When I started high school, I was simply hoping for one. It was a very humbling as well as heady experience.

One school seemed to have had an advantage initially for me, and it made for another great story line during our high school football seasons: Alabama, because of its fans.

Seriously. The University of Alabama fans. Honest to goodness, they used to come to our games en masse at Nease High School in their red and white Roll Tide gear, holding up home-made signs for me, encouraging me to head to 'Bama. I'd always liked the idea of a Southern school, not to mention one that was football crazy. It was very effective on this young and impressionable player.

And it needed to be effective, since I grew up in a room decorated in Florida Gator stuff. Orange and blue colors in all sorts of things and outfits had been decorating the walls, tables, and closets around our home for as long as I could remember. Of course, it was only natural that I would grow up with Gator stuff, since both my parents and my older sister Katie attended the University of Florida. And by my sophomore year of high school, Peter was already in Gainesville and enrolled in school there as a freshman. Three graduates of the University of Florida and another on his way, all in one family.

Given that background, you'd think that this would be the easiest decision in the world, but in truth I was pretty open-minded about schools, if only because I was such a big college-football fan in general. I'd grown up watching just about every game I could on Saturdays—that is, when Dad didn't make us work around the farm. So I was very receptive to considering other options besides Florida.

My sister Katie claims that she did more to overcome that openness of mine and recruit me to Florida than anyone else. At her wedding, when I was fifteen, she recalls that I was very impressed with how pretty and nice her bridesmaids were. Apparently I also took notice of the fact that they were all classmates of hers during her college career at Florida. In fact, I'd remembered some of those bridesmaids from a couple of years earlier when I'd had a baseball game in Gainesville. For some reason, my parents were busy, so my friend's dad drove me and him to Gainesville and dropped us off at ADPi, my sister's sorority. There we were, two twelve-year-old kids hanging out; then my sister and two of her friends, Brooke and Stephie, took us to our game. We struggled to pay attention to the game, especially my friend, who kept going over to talk with the girls, hoping that those college girls would fall for a twelve-year-old. No such luck.

Later, along the way, I at least tried to justify my decision as to which college I would ultimately attend with more principled reasons than simply recruiting letters, fan or family apparel, or gorgeous bridesmaids.

During my sophomore year, my parents and I had begun making unofficial visits to schools and continued those visits throughout the rest of my high school career. If we felt a particular visit would be helpful to my decision-making process, then we made the trip. Although you only get five "official" visits, where the school pays for your trip, you can take an unlimited number of unofficial visits on your own dime. Thankfully, my parents were willing to take the time and underwrite the expense to allow us to do that. On occasion, when for one reason or another my parents couldn't go, different people—usually my brothers or my friends—would accompany me on trips. It was great since it was a chance to see great college football and some great educational institutions up close.

One unlikely trip we made was to see the University of Virginia play at Florida State. I say unlikely since I had never been a particularly passionate supporter of FSU, to put it nicely. When I came of age as a Gator fan, FSU was the program that we seemed to be having the most trouble with, and being right there in the same state . . . It left me in the unusual position of liking and admiring Coach Bowden but not Florida State. That particular day, it was all about the football, though, as Dad, Peter, Kevin, and I caught the game between the Cavs and Noles at noon and then drove down to Gainesville to see Florida play Louisiana State University that night. One day, two unofficial visits.

Over those high school years, we also traveled to Alabama repeatedly, along with LSU, Florida State, Miami, Ohio State, Michigan, USC, and Florida, among others. Some of our experiences were unique, for reasons other than the game. I couldn't believe how cold South Bend, Indiana, was when we saw Notre Dame play Boston College; we scratched them off my list for just that reason. I couldn't imagine living there for four years. And at USC, I loved the energy of Pete Carroll and his assistant coaches, including Steve Sarkisian and Lane Kiffin, but it was so far from my home and support base.

Robby even came back from one of our trips to LSU with a girlfriend, which complicated matters. During our weekend trip that year to Louisiana State, we ended up driving all around Baton Rouge with my dad, Mr. Bell (our chicken-farming neighbor), and Robby's new girlfriend in the front seat, and, along with me, Kevin and Robby in the back seat. That crowd in the car made for a crazy trip.

And, of course, along the way Dad and I saw some great football, because Dad thought we should make the recruiting process a fun life experience: Florida–Tennessee, Florida–Florida State, Ohio State–Michigan, Florida–Alabama and then Miami–Virginia Tech for the ACC Championship.

We also visited Clemson University a couple of times, but I ended up not making an official visit there. That school could have been a good fit for me: it fits in nicely and similarly with the Floridas and

Alabamas of college football—a football-crazy, knowledgeable fan base, at a Southern school. The uniforms, the fans, the sweet tea, the passion, the traditions—including Howard's Rock that the team touches as it runs down the hill and onto the field before every game. Clemson was awesome. Plus, Charlie Whitehurst was just finishing, so I would have competed to be a four-year starter at quarterback, which would have been nice. I couldn't quite put my finger on the problem, but I wasn't sure we would be able to compete for championships, at least not compared to Florida and Alabama. But I was seventeen. It's hard to make that determination at any age, but especially when you're seventeen.

Once schools started getting more serious about recruiting me, it was important to discern whether they were being honest. That was the most difficult part—trying to figure who of all those I met was being truly honest and forthright in how they dealt with me. It wasn't always easy, but over time I felt like we were able to figure it out.

It was also interesting to see how well they'd done their homework on me and my family. Alabama may have been the best at this. Every single time we visited, we were surrounded by the most beautiful girls, who had Southern accents, were smart, and loved the Lord. And if that was all an act (which I seriously doubt), they certainly had all the vocabulary and talking points right! On the other hand, at some schools you'd be surrounded by girls who would be throwing themselves at you—I was surprised at how effective an approach that was with certain recruits, but I guess I shouldn't have been all that surprised.

Still the contrasts between all the schools kept bringing me back to Alabama. I kept telling my parents how much I liked the quality of the people there, and my dad kept reminding me to look beyond the Campus Crusade girls who were with the recruits all weekend. I did my best to heed his words and advice.

A few schools helped make the decision for me. Once Georgia had a commitment from Matthew Stafford, they quit recruiting me. I understood. They were, as you would hope, very gracious and up front about it with me. On the other hand, I visited Tennessee on an unofficial visit my junior year and was excited to be there. To me, it had a number of the same qualities as Alabama, Clemson, and Florida, so I was very intrigued. However, my unofficial visit didn't go very well for us, as Jimmy Ray Stephens (a former Florida player) was the only Tennessee coach to talk with me or my family all weekend. The other coaches were busy spending time and interacting with Jonathan Crompton, who was a high school senior at the time. It was easy to read their preference, or at least so it seemed, so I moved on.

In August of my senior year, coaches were allowed to call me after 12 midnight on a specific day. I received my first call at 12:01 from Louisville, and the calls continued from there. Recruiting was also a good time to listen and learn more football. There were some great offensive minds in the mix of colleges that recruited me. I would look forward to the calls from some of those guys, like Jimbo Fisher, then the offensive coordinator at LSU, Ralph Friedgen, the head coach of Maryland, Dabo Swinney, then the receivers coach at Clemson, and Marc Trestman, then the offensive coordinator at North Carolina State, just for the chance to learn more football.

Choosing between the many scholarship offers I was blessed to receive really boiled down to relationships. As with most areas of our life, whom we will work with and who will be our friends makes all the difference. I wanted to be in a place where I could improve my skills and win championships. The relationships I developed with certain coaches began to separate their schools from the pack. During the recruiting process, I became very close to Les Miles at Louisiana State, Mike Shula at Alabama, and Urban Meyer at Florida. These men were the main reason I chose these schools for three of my five official visits. In the end, the other two official visits I went on were to the University of Southern California and the University of Michigan. I grew up such a big college-football fan, and they are, after all, Southern Cal and Michigan.

My senior year we traveled to Baton Rouge to see LSU, ranked tenth in the nation at the time, play Florida, which was ranked eleventh. We had a lot of company, as it was the largest crowd to see an LSU game in the history of Tiger Stadium, and they've had some big games and big crowds through the years. What a great stadium that is, with its passion and the night games and a live Bengal tiger in a habitat—located far too close to the visitors' locker room, something I would learn more about a few years later. Florida led that game until the very end, at which time JaMarcus Russell and Joseph Addai carried LSU to an impressive and exciting come-from-behind win. It was a great game and a great trip, but it also underscored just how difficult the recruiting process was for me.

Sometime a few hours before that LSU–Florida game in Baton Rouge I was talking with LSU's Coach Miles, and as we were speaking in the middle of that madhouse with both teams on the field in warm-ups, I spotted Florida's Coach Meyer looking my way from across the field. We locked eyes, and I smiled at him. His expression never changed but remained as serious as ever as he slowly shook his head and turned away.

I liked LSU, but I was having trouble moving them into my top two. In fact, as great as Coach Miles and Coach Fisher and the others there were, for a lot of reasons related to Alabama and Florida, I never could get them above third place.

My official visit to Alabama seemed just as crazy as the one to LSU—it was my fourth trip there, after three earlier unofficial visits. I was with my brother Peter and my parents, and as we came out of the tunnel onto the field before the game, we were greeted with chants of "We want Te-bow" and saw signs and banners that read:

STABLER
NAMATH
TEBOW

That was really flattering to see.

We even got to meet the legendary Hall of Fame Coach Don Shula on the sideline right after we came out of the tunnel. That was so cool, just standing there on the sidelines with Coach Shula in Tuscaloosa, Alabama. I loved everything about Alabama, including the Shula family. Maybe even, especially the Shula family.

In the meantime, Coach Meyer and I had also become very close. He said he'd first heard of me when he landed in Gainesville at the

University of Florida in December of 2004 as their new head coach, coming there from the University of Utah. Then, a few weeks later, he attended a coaches' convention in Louisville, Kentucky. He claims that my coaches from Nease High School were everywhere in their green and gold shirts, helping to keep me foremost on Coach Meyer's mind.

That following spring of 2005, my junior year in high school, he'd seen me for the first time in person during a Nease baseball game. We both remember that game, but for different reasons. It was the district championship game against St. Augustine, in which I homered in the last inning to win it (it was just football that I never could beat them in). Coach Meyer says that he remembers observing my leadership during the game and on the field, and that he'd never seen a right fielder impact his team the way I did. Whether I really did or not, I'm glad that *he* thought I did.

Simply put, Coach Meyer loves football and loves winning. That was a good place to start for me. In the beginning, we had a blast just sitting around and discussing the philosophy of the spread offense that Florida ran. And Coach Meyer continued to recruit me seriously, even when other coaches might have bailed. Jevan Snead was a quarterback out of Texas and was highly recruited. He committed to Florida, but Coach Meyer continued to recruit me anyway. That was fine by me—if Florida ended up being the best fit for me, I didn't mind the competition. Apparently Jevan felt otherwise about Florida's continuing to recruit me. We had met before at an Elite 11 quarterback camp in California. Sometime after Jevan Snead's verbal commitment to Florida, Coach Meyer called me one day and asked if I was still truly interested in Florida. I said I was, but that I hadn't made a decision yet. He told me that my answer was good enough for him.

I later heard, even though I didn't hear it from Jevan, that he had called Coach Meyer and told him that he would decommit from Florida if they continued to recruit me. I guess Coach Meyer had gauged my continuing interest with that phone call, and when I told him I was still interested, I understand he told Jevan that they were still interested in me as well. At the end of the day, Jevan decided to decommit and sign with the University of Texas instead.

That kind of character and commitment was typical of Coach Meyer, but he also had a work ethic and drive that were unparalleled. It is clear to anyone who watches him recruit or is around him for any period of time that his charisma around others is attractive, sincere, and compelling. No matter what was going on, he was always engaging and enjoyable to speak with, and yet somehow he was able to balance that by being totally focused on championships. He possessed an overwhelming drive and determination to win championships—so strong that I had no doubt he would succeed.

My official visit to Florida was impressive to all my family members who attended: Mom, Dad, Robby, Peter, my sister Katie, and her husband, Gannon. Four of the six were Gator grads and Florida beat FSU that day. We ate dinner with University of Florida president, Dr. Machen, Athletic Director, Jeremy Foley, and of course, Coach Meyer and his family. Very impressive.

In addition to my relationship with Coach Meyer, I also really enjoyed my time getting to know Greg Mattison, Florida's co-defensive coordinator at the time, who was my primary recruiter. My relationship with Coach Mullen, then Florida's offensive coordinator, developed more after I got to Florida. Coach Mullen told Peter during one of my visits that it would be fine if I came to Florida, but he so believed in the offensive system he ran that he felt he could play any number of quarterbacks in the system and it would work, so to him, I was just another guy. That was one thing that Coach Mullen and I had in common: we believed in Coach Meyer's offensive system. The difference was I thought I actually could make it even better.

On the other hand, Mike Shula never gave me the impression that I was "just a guy" to him. Rather, he was always very clear about how they viewed me and what they wanted me to do, which was to do some Michael Vick–type things on the field. He was also focused on championships at Alabama and returning them to their prior levels of success. More low-key than Coach Meyer, his faith and that of his staff was appealing. Many of the position coaches, for instance, prayed with their players. I enjoyed that—and in my experience it was unique.

It was sometimes hard during the lengthy and intense recruiting process to figure out others' agendas; they all had them, we all do, and so much of the typical recruiting process is insincere and depends on how good a salesman the recruiter is. Those coaches, as well as some of the others I've mentioned, however, stood out for their honesty and integrity, and as a result, I faced a difficult decision.

I told each of the coaches who were recruiting me that I would decide by the middle of December, shortly after we finished our season, for two reasons. First, because of homeschool, I had the flexibility to start college early. Wherever I ended up, I wanted to begin in January so I could participate in spring practice. Second, I wanted to help my college recruit if I could and if it would be helpful. Through my unofficial and official visits and playing in all-star games, I had gotten to know some of the players who were looking at similar schools. If I waited until signing day, which was the first Wednesday in February, to commit, then I would lose any ability to influence who could be some of my future teammates. By deciding early, I could try to help convince others to attend with me and in the process hopefully increase our chances of winning championships in the future.

Unfortunately, the decision to attend early meant I also faced a difficult decision with respect to being able to continue playing other sports. My senior year of baseball was approaching, as well as basketball, and my dad really wanted me to keep going with baseball. Baseball had continued to be the sport at which I felt I was most naturally gifted. I was named to the All State team my junior year, and we went to the State Championship. My head baseball coach at Nease, Boo Mullins, tried to talk me into staying for that year, telling me that I was a "five tool" player and that many major league general managers were contacting him to set up private preseason workouts in January. The term "five tool" is used to identify position players (as opposed to pitchers or designated hitters) who can: (1) hit for average, (2) hit for power, (3) have excellent base-running skills and speed, (4) have good throwing ability, and (5) are good defensive players. I was flattered. My coach and my dad would tell

The baby of the family: My mom and my brothers and sisters with me shortly after I was born.

I had football on my mind from a very early age.

With my mom.

When I was growing up, my brothers and I were inseparable. Once we moved to the farm, we'd play just about any sport we could together.

Playing football in the yard with Uncle Dick.

Uncle Dick's love and generosity provided a start for the orphanage in the Philippines that was eventually named after him.

Here I am with my favorite teacher, my mom.

No matter what sport I was playing, I only knew how to play one way: hard.

With our beloved family dog, Otis. Whenever we came home, he was there to greet us.

When I first played football, I played at the Lakeshore Athletic Association in Jacksonville.

With my brothers after a church play.

Life on the farm made our entire family "farmer strong."

My sister Katie and the infamous "bridesmaids."

When I was fifteen I went with my family on the first of many mission trips to the Philippines. It was my first time back since I was three years old.

With my dad *(left)* and Coach Howard *(right)*, my high school coach at Nease.

In my sophomore year of high school I began playing quarterback for Nease High School.

With Carl Johnson, Brandon Spikes, and Percy Harvin at the U.S Army All-American Bowl following my senior year of high school.

My senior year of high school, rushing for a touchdown in our state championship game, which we went on to win.

2006, Florida versus Southern Mississippi: My first touchdown as a Florida Gator.

2006, Florida versus LSU: The first jump-pass touchdown of my career. ("Jump Pass" © 2006 Daniel Stewart)

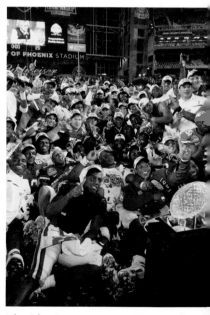

Florida Gators, 2006 National Champions.

Working hard with my teammates.

After being awarded the Heisman Trophy in 2007.

When that smile came across Coach Meyer's face toward the end of a game, we all knew we'd done a good job.

With Coach Meyer the night after winning the Heisman Trophy.

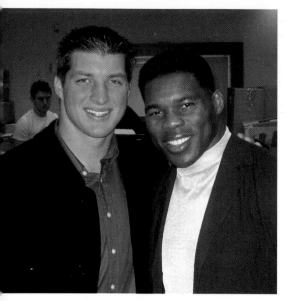

Hanging out with fellow SEC Heisman Trophy–winner Herschel Walker during the Heisman weekend festivities.

With our dear family friend and one of my favorite people in the world, Uncle Bill.

Throughout college I continued to take mission trips back to the Philippines. Being at Uncle Dick's Orphanage with all of the kids is always an amazing experience.

When I'm in the Philippines, speaking in front of large groups is a terrific way to spread God's message of hope and salvation to as many people as possible.

A promise was made . . .   . . . and now it was time to back it up.

There's nothing like Florida versus Georgia—especially since it's in my home town.

2008, Florida versus the team out West: This was my favorite game against them. . . .

The more it rained, the more we Gators felt like we were at . . .

. . . the Swamp.

Jump pass to seal the victory in the 2008 National Championship Game versus Oklahoma.

The only personal foul of my career—and it was worth it.

Giving thanks.

As a team,
we had
accomplished
our goal.

Florida Gators,
2008 National
Champions.

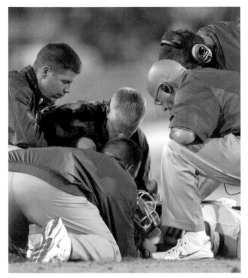

My 2009 concussion: I'll admit he got me good, but at least I still held on to the ball.

Senior Day: Running out of the tunnel for the last time at Ben Hill Griffin Stadium.

2006–2009: 4 wins, 0 losses versus the team out West.

My last victory lap at the Swamp.

With my parents at my graduation from the University of Florida.

2010 Sugar Bowl: Florida 51, Cincinnati 24. We finished strong. Thank you, Gator Nation.

My first day as a Denver Bronco. Excited to still be wearing orange and blue.

Draft night in Jacksonville, Florida, with my brothers and friends (*from left to right*: Peter, Bryan Craun, Robby, Kevin Albers, Angel Gonzalez).

December 19, 2010, Broncos versus Raiders: My first NFL start.

October 10, 2010, Broncos versus Jets: My first NFL touchdown.

December 26, 2010, Broncos versus Texans: My first home start . . .

. . . and it was a great comeback win for our team.

2010—the Tebows and the newest addition to our family, my dog Bronco.

scouts that my character made me a six-tool player. Of course, to my dad, that sixth tool was the only tool that mattered. Dad kept pushing baseball and had been making a compelling argument from when I was young: if you're good enough to have a professional career in baseball, it's usually longer than a football career, injuries are less frequent, and the pay is greater.

He was right, and I did love baseball. Turning and connecting on an inside fastball is a great feeling.

But football was my *passion*. More specifically, playing football as a throwing quarterback has always been my passion, and I was not going to let baseball get in the way of my making a timely decision.

My relationship with my top two head coaches was good. No, great. Both men were first-class football coaches as well as men of character, integrity, and caring. At Florida, I knew I probably wouldn't be able to beat out the senior, Chris Leak, at quarterback as a freshman and therefore didn't know if I'd play at all during that first year. At Alabama, I might have had the chance to compete with John Parker Wilson to start that first year, but I didn't know for sure. It didn't really matter—I wanted to play for either one of those coaches, whether I got on the field that first season or not. And for those who think that coaches should be able to leave a particular school without repercussions but the athletes should be bound to the school, all I can offer is my own personal experience in the whole recruiting process: the identity of the coach was critical in making my decision.

Decision Day rolled around, and I still didn't know what I was going to do. Earlier in the day, I had already called Coach Miles at LSU, Coach Carr at Michigan, and Coach Carroll at USC. I told them I appreciated their time and interest but that I wouldn't be coming to their school that next year. It was down to the final two. I had been praying about it regularly, and my family was praying as well. I had no doubt that the Lord was leading throughout this whole process, but what was unclear was determining *where* He was leading.

People often seem to think that when you're following the Lord and trying to do His will, your path will always be clear, the decisions smooth and easy, and life will be lived happily ever after and all that.

Sometimes that may be true, but I've found that more often, it's not. The muddled decisions still seem muddled, bad things still happen to believers, and great things can happen to nonbelievers. When it comes to making our decisions, the key that God is concerned with is that we are trusting and seeking Him. God's desire is for us to align our lives with His Word and His will.

But that's part of faith, what the writer of the book of Hebrews describes as a belief in things that we cannot see. Still, it would have helped if He had yelled down from the heavens the direction He wanted me to take or had just written the answer with His fingertip in the clouds—I certainly would have been listening and watching.

Unfortunately, I wasn't feeling any of that direction as the time approached. No guidance, even though I knew I was being guided, and no peace, even though I knew He was there, offering it to me. Postponing my decision wasn't going to help. I wasn't going to grow further apart from either Coach Meyer or Coach Shula in the next two months, but rather and most likely the opposite would occur. If anything, the decision would grow even harder.

Therefore, on Tuesday, December 13, 2005, just three days after we had beaten Armwood High School to win the state 4A title, I stood behind the stage with my parents and family. No one could help me decide—my family understood my dilemma. I am sensitive to the way others feel and didn't want to tell either of these two coaches no. More important, I actually wanted to play for both of them.

We had just filmed the presentation of the Florida Dairy Farmers High School Player of the Year in the school auditorium and took a break before they were to film my college decision. The crowd and cameras were ready. We were not.

Thirty minutes until show time. Still no idea. I was overcome with emotion and trying, unsuccessfully, not to cry behind the stage. It had been a long, arduous, and, at times, emotional journey. I wanted to make the right decision.

Twenty minutes. I owed them answers.

I gulped and picked one.

"I'm going to Florida," I told my dad. "I'm going to call Mike Shula first and let him know."

I called Coach Shula. As I told him I was going to Florida, my tears turned into sobs. I doubt he could make out anything I was trying to say, but he was getting the point. He cut me off.

"Tim," he began, "I love you as a person and a player. When I told you that you were going to have a great career and life of meaning, I meant that. I wanted it to be here, but it's still true. I still love you, and you're still going to do great things, even if it's not at Alabama."

I have no idea what I said to him after that, but we hung up and I turned to my family.

"That's the coach I want to play for—Coach Shula's so great. Maybe I should call him back and change my answer." First, though, we decided, I should speak to Coach Meyer and see how that left me feeling.

"Coach, it's Timmy. " He laughed nervously, as if he didn't know who was calling. He told me he'd been driving around much of the day to stay busy while waiting for my call. In fact, he had been trying to stay busy all day, but every turn brought him back to my decision, he said. He had gone for a jog that morning and passed several runners who called out, "Hope you get Tebow!" Then, at the office, Jeremy Foley, the athletic director at Florida, stuck his head in.

"Any word from Tim Tebow?"

Of course there was no news to speak of. He'd then headed out into the stands at Florida Field, where he sat on the forty-fifth row. Forty-five was his lucky number, and since he couldn't think of anything else to do . . .

Finally, as he was stuck in traffic, I called.

"Coach," I continued, "I've been thinking about it, and . . . Coach? Are you there? Coach?" He wasn't. Dead silence on the other end of the line. I later learned that his phone had died after he'd been driving around and using it all day and that he didn't have his car charger with him. As intense as he is, I knew he wasn't taking this development of a dropped call from me very well. He could tell that I had been crying and he wasn't sure how to interpret that.

Now I had no idea what to do. I was thinking, *Do I stick with Florida since that had been my final and maybe knee-jerk reaction, or do I switch to Alabama based on the always-classy Coach Shula? But if I do that, shouldn't I tell Coach Meyer first that I'm not going to come to Florida?* I couldn't get through on his phone and didn't know why.

I took the podium and quieted myself and focused. Earlier in the day, I had typed my prepared statement with a long list of thank yous. I concluded my statement with "Next year, I will be playing football at the University of _____." I had left it blank, trying to decide.

Ninety miles away from that podium over in Gainesville, Shelley Meyer called her husband in from outside. She had the television on. Coach Meyer had driven home and was playing catch with their son, Nate, nervously passing the few remaining minutes until the announcement.

ESPN had me miked up before we went on the air, and I could see the cameraman's look of amazement as I turned to my family members, trying to decide at the last minute where to go. Coach Meyer's passion flashed into my mind.

"I will be playing college football next year at the University of Florida." There, it was done, and the peace that I had been waiting for throughout this whole process was still nowhere to be found. But at least the decision had been made.

Unfortunately, it wouldn't turn out to be the last time I cried over a Florida–Alabama outcome.

Chapter Nine

RUNNING DOWN A DREAM

Whatever you do, do your work heartily, as for the Lord rather than for men, knowing that from the Lord you will receive the reward of the inheritance. It is the Lord Christ whom you serve.
—COLOSSIANS 3:23–24

And so it was over. But then, it continued. It really is true what is said about the recruiting process—it's never ending.

Florida's 2005 season had been good by most standards—9–3 overall, tied for second in the SEC Eastern Division—but not by Coach Meyer's standards. It was his first year at UF, and he made it clear that he wanted the incoming freshman class to help the program hit loftier heights. As such, one of my first moves was to begin calling many of the other guys I'd met as teammates at the CaliFlorida All-Star game and the U.S. Army All-American Bowl, guys like Percy Harvin, Brandon Spikes, Jarred Fayson, and Carl Johnson. I don't know if my calls made any difference at all, but we all ended up at the University of Florida together, in what was dubbed by all those who opine about such things "a talented group of freshmen."

I wanted to prepare for the 2006 season in any way I could, and in the weeks before I made my commitment to Florida, I'd spoken to Coach Meyer about foregoing my spring baseball season at Nease to enroll early at Florida, which my homeschooling made possible.

Then about two weeks before I committed, Coach Meyer had called and suggested that maybe I would want to play baseball with my high school teammates one last time instead of showing up early at Florida.

"What's going on, Coach?" I was puzzled, because Coach Meyer had been excited about my plan to enroll early. He came clean. In the recruiting process, no one had blinked about my homeschooling, but now the admissions office was raising some red flags. It wasn't a matter of my coursework or test scores, but they were simply hesitant. Coach Meyer and I discussed it a great deal, and he ultimately approached the university president, Dr. Machen, directly, personally guaranteeing my academic performance.

Two weeks after I'd committed, it was still unclear if I was going to start at Florida in the spring semester or if I'd have to begin in the fall with the other freshmen. Coach Meyer was also concerned that I might go pro in baseball if I didn't enroll. In early January, I played in the U.S. Army All-American Bowl in San Antonio, but as I returned home, I still didn't know whether I was going to begin my college career the next day as we'd originally planned. And then after landing, I got word from Coach Meyer that everything was arranged. As of the next day, I was going to Florida.

I arrived at the University of Florida that January like a typical freshman, without much fanfare. Actually, I may have arrived with even less fanfare than most; the night before my first class was to begin, I caught a ride to Gainesville with Peter in his pickup truck, carrying only a duffel bag's worth of possessions with me.

I slept on Peter's couch in his apartment for a few hours until I had to head over to our first workout in the wee hours of the morning. Football started right away—even before classes. We met that morning in the Team Meeting Room in Florida Field, a precursor to orientation to football and early workouts. Then I had to shift gears and head off to my first class.

My first class at Florida was in public speaking with Professor Stephanie Webster. I know I was at an advantage with regard to most of my classmates, because of all the times I'd already spoken in the Philippines and elsewhere. But it was still interesting, and never ceased to amaze me, how concerned people were about standing up and speaking before a group. This class itself was particularly easy, because our exercises were all simply short talks on any subject we chose that we knew something about, like, for example, where we bought our shoes. Nevertheless, I remember students saying that they couldn't wait until the final exam, knowing they would have gotten past the period of having to give two-minute talks in class.

My brother Peter, an engineering major, spent the better part of the spring semester appealing the school's denial of his high school language credit, an issue on which he found himself growing more irritated with the bureaucracy with the passing of each day. I didn't have the same problem when I was admitted to Florida—they looked at my two years of Latin and accepted it immediately to meet my language requirement. That was appropriate, I felt, since Mom had brought in a teacher with a degree in Latin, who knew the language very well, to help me: one of the benefits of homeschooling, again, in my opinion. As for Peter, in fairness, UF hadn't had to deal with that many homeschool students at the point of his enrollment, or at least that was our perception, which may have added to the problem.

Why was Peter so irritated?

Well it was because . . . we took the very same Latin class, sitting side by side for two years. Finally, Peter got his credit, but not until I had a chance to point out just how advanced my language skills in Latin, at least, were in the eyes of the university.

Two weeks later I presented myself in the old Florida Gym for the first of our off-season workouts. It was mid January, very early in the morning, and still dark out. I was totally fired up. By now that shouldn't surprise anyone.

I am too young to have ever seen Florida play basketball in the Florida Gymnasium, affectionately nicknamed Alligator Alley, which was home to the basketball games for the Gators from 1949 to 1980. It was an intimate setting—small and very cramped—and always good for at least a ten-point advantage to the beloved home team and the scene of many a miraculous upset within the stretch of a long and difficult Southeastern Conference season. Since those days, it has functioned in various capacities for classes and teams, as well as pickup basketball games for would-be Gator basketballers of any age. It also served as Mickey Marotti's personal torture chamber.

That first morning I was not concerned with its history. Like the rest of the newcomers, some of whom had just finished their freshman football season but hadn't yet gone through a stretch of offseason workouts, I was simply concerned with survival. Being able to walk out of the doors of Alligator Alley each week under my own power was an achievement.

I'd first met Coach Marotti during the recruiting process, and while I had heard the stories of his legendary workouts, I also knew that hiring him was one of Coach Meyer's first acts of business when he arrived at Florida. If Coach Meyer believed what Coach Mick did as head of the football team's strength-and-conditioning oversight was that important, then I was all for it.

And, like with most everything else I undertake, once it began, I no longer wanted to simply survive; I wanted to excel. Especially if it was going to make me a better player.

On that first day, I learned to love Coach Marotti's mat drills. Love. We had done a version of mat drills at Nease High School, but these in Alligator Alley were far more intense. To be more accurate, the mat drills were awful, and to say that you love them should put you first in line to see the psychologist at the campus infirmary. However, I loved them because they gave you the chance to compete in drills that were unique because they blended both the mental and physical aspects of becoming better—not just as a player, but in your approach to anything you might face. Anyone could be in great shape, but to compete against another person . . . I viewed it as a test of will.

They began with Coach putting us into two separate lines. The first player in line A took his position on the wrestling mat, lying facedown. Coach then grabbed the first player from line B and had him lie facedown also, but on top of the first player who was already facedown on the mat. On Coach's whistle, the player underneath had to use whatever means he could—run, walk, roll, or crawl—to reach a line ten feet away, while the second had to use *whatever* means he could (use your imagination) to keep him from reaching the line.

That first day, after spending forty-five minutes on conditioning and quickness drills, we did a variety of mat drills to finish the hour, pitting one against another, to the point of complete exhaustion. I was pleased, however. I hadn't lost one drill. It might have been all the farm work. It might have been the years in the barn, lifting. The protein shakes certainly helped. So far, so good.

On the whole, my classes went well that spring. To be honest, it just wasn't that hard. My mom's homeschool classes had prepared me incredibly well. I'd thought college was going to be much harder than it was. I learned it was important to attend all my classes, stay up on my reading, and do my assignments. I was living with Percy Harvin, and some of the football players and I spent our free time playing pool basketball at an apartment complex near campus. Between football, classes, and pool basketball and the occasional paintball games, we all stayed pretty busy.

Throughout the spring we continued to work on our conditioning with Coach Mick. Days were varied in the exercises he had us do. Some days we had mat drills; some days, running, like running all the stadium steps at Florida Field. I loved it. One morning during conditioning drills in our regular weight-room session in the stadium, I was paired with a defensive tackle in tug-of-war. Unlike times when I'd done a tug-of-war in the past, here there was no line to pull the other guy over that would have marked victory and ended the drill. Instead, this tug-of-war lasted until one of us conceded.

Again, a drill with a mental aspect.

We battled against each other and neither gave up until he eventually lost his balance. But he didn't quit. I dragged him hanging off the end of the rope, walking backward with him all across the room. He still didn't concede. I kept walking and dragging until I reached the wall. Still didn't concede. By that time he had scrambled back onto his feet, and as he did, I saw that I was next to the door to the men's room. I kicked the door open, positioned my body into the opening, and kept pulling and pulling, backing my way into the room. I did the same thing once I reached a stall door, kicking it open and continuing to pull, hand over hand, pulling on the rope with him hanging on and pulling as hard as he could against me from his end of the rope, pulling him into the bathroom and toward the stall. Finally, when I had pulled him into the stall with me, Coach Mick blew the whistle and brought an end to the drill.

About a month into off-season conditioning, I still hadn't lost at tug-of-war, and Coach Meyer decided to up the ante for everyone.

"Offense, defense, pick your best two!" Offense vs. defense, two-on-two tug-of-war, with the loser having to run suicides (repeated sprints) across the field. A lot of them. The defense selected Joe Cohen, a senior defensive tackle weighing over 310 pounds, and junior Brandon Siler, a 240-pound linebacker, while the offense selected a big offensive lineman, over 300 pounds . . . and me. Coach Meyer later told me that he was stunned that the players had chosen a freshman, someone who had only been on campus for a few weeks. Maybe it was because of my coming in and lifting 225 pounds twenty-five times on the bench press that caused them to put such confidence in me. Maybe it was my performance dragging the defensive tackle into the bathroom stall, or maybe it was my relentless determination to never lose any of the drills; but for whatever reason, the offense selected me—a freshman quarterback. I was so excited.

We killed them and watched as the defense had to run.

All those drills, in addition to physical conditioning, were also great psychological and confidence conditioners for us as a team, even for the guy who ended up in the bathroom stall. Because for the next four years, whenever we took the field, we knew that our opponent hadn't gone through anything at all similar to what we had. Coach Mick's mind-set dovetailed perfectly with my mantra: *Somewhere he is out there, training while I am not. One day, when we meet, he will win.*

We were the ones doing the extra work, and we knew it.

On top of all that conditioning, spring football practice in 2006 went well also. I knew that it was Chris Leak's team as the starting quarterback. He was a senior, he knew the system, and he had a lot of experience. I didn't know if I'd even be able to contribute that first year, but I certainly hoped to have the opportunity to do so and was prepared to compete for playing time. Coach Meyer always said that he felt blessed to have two leaders at the quarterback position that year.

I played pretty well in the Orange and Blue Game that spring and led my team to victory, but the thing I was most proud of? I never lost once in Coach Mick's mat drills, and after that first year of drills, he told me that I wasn't going to be doing them anymore. As a quarterback, they apparently didn't want to risk my getting hurt trying to open a bathroom stall door.

And, thankfully, throughout everything, Coach Meyer didn't pay attention to any of the media reports. Some sports writers took it upon themselves to write articles proclaiming that my style of play would never work in college football. In many ways I thought I'd silenced this debate from my freshman year of high school with how I'd played, and yet here I was again, four years later, hearing the same old "playing position by body stereotype" argument—only this time it was disguised as analysis:

My type of quarterback wouldn't work in college.

I didn't have the right body type to run the spread offense.

I wouldn't survive in the SEC with my style of play against the kind of defenses we would see.

I could help the team more at a different position.

I should be a tight end.

Or a fullback.

I read the articles, and they simply served as more fuel for all my workouts. I would show them, and I would stay a quarterback.

After all, I think I did okay in high school. My first summer at Florida, my mom and I went to pick up a trophy at an awards ceremony at the National Quarterback Club in Washington, DC. I won for high school, Vince Young for college, and Ben Roethlisberger for the pros. The trophy was enormous—it came up to my waist. Making matters worse, I couldn't check it for the flight, so I had to carry that huge trophy through the airport and onto the flight. Embarrassing.

Chapter Ten

GETTING MY FEET WET IN THE SWAMP

In everything give thanks; for this is God's
will for you in Christ Jesus.
—1 THESSALONIANS 5:18

By the time the regular season rolled around, I was feeling relatively comfortable in the offense. There was a lot to learn, but I was pleased that I had come in early and been there for spring practice. The offensive plan was getting more familiar, and I was getting more comfortable with my ability to execute it at some level if given the opportunity.

Before I knew it, our opening game had arrived—against Southern Mississippi—a home game at the Swamp. It really did seem like it was still part of an earlier childhood dream. I remember how excited I was to walk off the bus and through the Gator Walk, a gauntlet of exuberant fans, into the stadium. And to run out of the tunnel for the first time. To be a part of all the excitement. Putting on the uniform with my new number, 15 (when I arrived, Bubba Caldwell already had my high school number, 5), and heading out for my first pregame warm-ups as a Gator. As we gathered in the tunnel, seeing the footage of live alligators on the video board and hearing the voiceover: "The Swamp. Only Gators get out alive." The crowd working itself into a frenzy. It all still seemed like a dream, but it was one that my teammates and I were living.

I had grown up watching Florida quarterbacks from Danny Wuerffel to Doug Johnson and Rex Grossman, and I'd heard about so many others like Wayne Peace and Kerwin Bell. Robby, Peter, and I had played so many games together on the farm over the years, those three-man football games. I remember saying I was Danny Wuerffel or one of the others when I was the quarterback, or Ike Hilliard if I was the receiver, or Lito Sheppard when I was the defensive back. And now I was getting to be part of it all.

Finally, the voice of the Gators boomed "Heeeeeeeeere come the Gators!" as we rushed out of the tunnel. Coming out of the tunnel with "Tebow" on my back for the very first time was such a thrill for me and for my whole family. The goose bumps were everywhere. Something you think about your whole life, and then in a surreal rush it's actually happening. I felt blessed.

Throughout the game, I had a headset on listening to everything that was being said. It was great and I was so excited. It's a wonder I was even able to keep up with all that was going on during the game. We threw a pick to them early, which they converted into a score, keeping it close for a while. But our defense manhandled them throughout the game, and eventually we took charge.

We were just beginning the fourth quarter, after my first sideline experience of listening to a stadium full of fans swaying, singing "We Are the Boys of Old Florida," and I got the call to go in. I thought I'd have a shot to go in because we'd just gotten a turnover on about their six yard line, and sure enough the coaches threw me in. The first play of my career was supposed to be a handoff play out of a shotgun formation to Kestahn Moore. I was nervous even calling the cadence, but once the ball was snapped, all the nervousness went away and—this may seem odd to say—it was just like I was playing football again.

The ball was snapped way low and to the left, so I ran and picked it up. I didn't even think; I just reacted to the situation, which was fun. I picked the ball up, ran left, stiff-armed a guy, dove, and laid out toward the end zone, scoring a touchdown. I was so ecstatic at scoring my first touchdown that everybody watching must have seen it, like the guy who hits his first home run in baseball and fist-pumps and laughs all the way around the bases. After I scored, my excitement bubbled over as I just kept running around and giving everybody a hug. I was so pumped up.

In practice the next week, we prepared for Central Florida, and I had a little bit more in the way of snaps, plays, and involvement, since we anticipated and hoped that we'd be far enough ahead to get me into the game. I went into the game for a few series in the second quarter and had some success. I handed off to Kestahn Moore once we got down close to the end zone, and he scored—a good start for me. I felt like I had some nice passes and decent runs. So far, so good. I did, however, throw an interception too; and anytime you throw a pick in a game, it stays with you for a while. Some good moments, some not so good.

The game played out as we hoped and planned, and so I got to play a lot in the second half. I had a decent day of passing, and that gave the coaches a chance to see that I was more than just someone ("playing position by body stereotype") who could run around a little bit. It's one thing to be strong in the weight room or in Coach Mick's mat drills, or to do well in sprints and the physical competitions in practice or in the off-season, but it was important for them to see firsthand that I could actually break tackles and run. I think that's when it translated in their minds that I could play quarterback at the University of Florida, because I was never again allowed to be tackled in practice. Leading up to the Tennessee game, with the coaches now having a different perspective on my athletic talent, and in particular my ability to play quarterback, they put in a special package for me—all runs and all from shotgun. I was pretty excited to be able to have a specific and planned chance to contribute—against a team ranked number thirteen in the country.

On the first play they called for me, I had a running back with me, faking the option to him, but instead I just kept the ball and kept going. I broke through the first wave of defenders, the defensive line, running as fast as I could, and I got past the linebackers. At that point I could see that there was nothing between me and the rest of the field but Jonathan Hefney, a safety. I remember looking into his eyes and thinking, *he doesn't want any part of this*. He went for my ankles and made a good tackle, a solid tackle. It was then, though, right at that moment, that I knew I could play in the SEC. Hefney was one of the better safeties in the conference, and he chose to go low, at my ankles rather than try to take me on straight up.

With that positive play of ten or fifteen yards coming the first time they'd called my number that day, I figured they'd probably call my number again, which they did. Throughout the game, I was able to consistently get in there on different plays and help the team in a variety of ways. Finally, in the fourth quarter, we were on the short end of the score, losing 20–14, and we were faced with a third down and six yards to go for a first down; Chris Leak ran for it and was stopped just short of the first-down marker.

Now we were facing fourth and a long yard, almost two yards, for the first down. Coach Meyer called a timeout, and I'm standing there before him, staring at him, *willing* him to put me in. I saw him looking straight at me, no doubt thinking, *He's only a freshman*. This was the biggest situation in the season so far against one of our biggest rivals. It was probably our last drive of the game—Coach was faced with a big decision.

He didn't hesitate in sending me out there. I'd like to say that as I ran onto the field, I was thinking about proving him right or winning the game, but all I could think was, *Holy cow, this is the loudest place I have ever been in*. The crowd was going crazy, absolutely crazy on fourth and a very long one.

Seeing all the linebackers cheating in so close behind the defensive line brought me back to the moment. I had to get this first down. I just kept thinking, *I have to get this, I have to get this. I'm going to run as fast as I can, downhill*. I thought of Coach Mick and those mat drills. I was going to get this first down, *If they get in my way, they will pay the price; they're going to take some punishment.*

I clapped my hands—it was a silent cadence because of the crowd noise—took the snap, and hit the hole quickly, running as fast as I could. I knew we had gotten the first down as soon as I hit the hole because I could sense that my momentum carried me well beyond what I felt was sufficient; I was so jacked up that I popped off the ground as we unpiled. Two plays later Chris Leak hit Dallas Baker on a crossing route for a touchdown, and Reggie Nelson ended Tennessee's last drive to try and score with an interception. Not only had we beaten Tennessee, 21–20, but in my first Southeastern Conference game I had really helped the team. I felt like I had substantially contributed to the result and helped out all the guys who were the mainstays, the studs on the team, guys like Brandon Siler, Ray McDonald, Joe Cohen, and Dallas Baker, all those guys that I looked up to. It was an awesome feeling to have helped those guys and the rest of the team win a big game.

So far, so good. I had played in three games in a limited role, and it had gone pretty well. I understood that I was a very willing freshman among very talented and experienced upperclassmen, and rather than feeling impatient about my position on the team, I was pleased just to contribute. Chris threw a real pretty ball, and I knew it would be his team all year long. I was fine with that. I equated my situation to what Jesus said: if you're faithful in little things, I'm going to give you more.

That's how I approached the season. That's why my few plays in the Southern Miss and UCF games were so big to me and the Tennessee game plays were huge. Not just for my confidence, but for the coaches' confidence in me as well. Taking care of the little things, one play at a time.

For me, more important than winning the quarterback job was earning some playing time, being part of the team, building the trust of the coaches and my teammates, and being able to contribute. That's what I took so much pride in and what I wanted to accomplish. I hoped to carve out a role for myself that contributed to the good of the team in every game.

After we returned from Tennessee, I was asked to meet with Zack Higbee, a member of the University of Florida's Sports Information Department. Zack was our assistant to Steve McClain, our sports information director for football. I headed up to Zack's office, which was tucked inside the west stands of Florida Field, wondering what he needed from me.

As it turned out, I'd been receiving a number of requests for personal appearances in and around Gainesville—even though I hadn't been playing a lot. Florida was trying to come up with a plan that might accommodate some of those requests, while still giving me sufficient time for football and classes. Zack became the point man for UF and me in this effort with the community. Between the two of us, we devised a plan for dealing with requests, giving highest priority to the ones where people needed help the most and we might be able to make a difference.

He suggested we visit the hospital. I'd never done a hospital visitation in Gainesville before, but we headed to the oncology floor at Shands Hospital at the University of Florida to see a longtime Gator booster. He was there with his wife, and they were struggling with his recent cancer diagnosis.

I suppose I was there to encourage them, and maybe I did, but a good bit of the reverse happened. They did a lot to encourage me, and as I walked out of the room, I realized that I really enjoyed hospital visitation for the opportunity it gives everyone—patient and visitor—to be encouraged, lifted up, and joined together in fellowship.

Zack started making arrangements for us to go to the hospital on a weekly basis, especially to the pediatric wing. I loved seeing the kids. I hated that they were going through challenges at far too young an age, but I absolutely loved them and their spirit. I always came away encouraged and inspired by their courage. I could only pray that I left them lifted up a bit with a measure of encouragement for that day, the next, and every day beyond.

That next weekend Kentucky visited the Swamp, and we all knew that we couldn't have a letdown after such a big win against Tennessee the week before. On my first three plays I had long runs of twenty and thirty yards, taking us down to inside Kentucky's ten yard line. On one of the runs I broke to the right, running toward their sideline, and stiff-armed their safety who had come up to try and make the tackle. I actually stiff-armed him all the way out of bounds, and the officiating crew called it a personal foul on him. Not a bad break as it turned out.

We were inside the ten yard line after the half-the-distance penalty was assessed, and the coaches replaced me with Chris. I was fired up from the entire drive, but I noticed some booing from our home crowd as I left the field. Chris handed off, and we scored, but the booing really dampened my spirit. There was no need for it. I knew the boos weren't aimed at me, but it was embarrassing to be a Florida fan at that moment. Sure, Chris Leak and I were competing for playing time, but at the same time, we got along fine and the coaches were doing a great job in coordinating our playing time effectively for the good of the team. We were winning, we were undefeated, we had good plays in a row, and we scored. As a fan, what more could you want?

Being a competitor, I wanted to be out there helping and felt that I was ready to be involved whenever the coaches felt they needed me. The hardest part was not knowing—warming up to stay ready and then not knowing when your number will be called. It was a "wait, then hurry up, and then wait again" situation, like much of life. You never know when an opportunity to help, to do something good, to lift up someone, or some situation will come your way. Always be prepared so that you can do your best when it's time.

Later in the game we ran a fake option right, and then I spun around to the left and threw a comeback screen to Dallas Baker. We scored on it—my first touchdown pass in college—but they called holding on Phil Trautwein. As we came back into the huddle, Phil, who was a sophomore, apologized to me. He was a hard worker, team leader, and a true asset. Of course he hadn't meant to be penalized. I looked him in the eye and said, "No problem. That was only my first passing touchdown in college *ever*—don't worry about it." That became a running joke that I still remind him of.

The next week was Alabama, again at home. It was also the week-end of activities in support of the one hundredth anniversary of Florida Football Celebration Gala. We wore throwback uniforms and helmets. It was a big weekend, and I was heading into it still learning and accepting my role. Finally, I had gotten past the second-guessing about choosing Florida over Alabama, and even the lack of a clearly defined role didn't change that. As much as I loved it at Florida, it was hard not to think back to the difficulty I'd had choosing between the two schools. Though I was perfectly happy with the role I'd been playing for Florida, in all honesty there were times that first season when I wondered if I would have been playing more or even start-ing at 'Bama. Despite those normal "what if" thoughts that crept in from time to time, I had no regrets—none whatsoever—about my decision.

I did talk to Coach Mike Shula before and after the game. Of course, he was kind, as ever. He asked about my parents and the rest of the family and said again that he had a great time recruiting me and would always wish the very best for me. As always, he was great to be around.

It was a fun football game. The coaches had installed a play-action pass in the game plan for me that week, which I was looking forward to having a chance to run. Unfortunately, we started that game with Alabama's scoring a defensive touchdown on a botched snap, so I didn't go in as early as I might otherwise have, until we got a bit of rhythm going with Chris and the offense. But then I had a chance to go in a little while later. We had a fourth down and goal to go from the one yard line. They put me in, and although someone hit me at the line of scrimmage, I had such momentum that I carried him into the end zone with me. That was a sweet feeling, to do that at home against Alabama.

Later in the game we called that play-action pass they had specifi-cally installed for me; I threw it down the sideline and completed it deep into their territory. We continued down the field and scored on that drive. I didn't have many plays in that game, but the ones that I did have were pretty big. John Parker Wilson, Alabama's quar-terback, had a tough day, which helped us pull ahead. Once again,

Reggie Nelson sealed the win with an interception late in the game, adding an exclamation point to the win, since he ran that pick all the way back for a touchdown.

The following week, we faced our fourth straight SEC game, but thankfully it was our third in a row at home. We needed that—since we were facing LSU, who was ranked number nine in the country going into the game. We were ranked fifth, but we weren't really focused on that. We were simply trying to play well each week. In addition, Gainesville was hosting ESPN's GameDay coverage that week, which only added to the madness and led to a few interviews before the game about the two-quarterback situation Florida was using. Some people weren't sure our offense would hold up. Louisiana State had an unbelievable defense with Glenn Dorsey, Tyson Jackson, LaRon Landry, and Chevis Jackson, all of whom went on to become NFL players. In fact, the first three were all taken within the first six picks of the NFL draft in the years they were eligible to be selected.

That week in practice our coaches once again put in a few special plays for me and showed us a play from their days at the University of Utah. In that play they put their bigger fullback in at quarterback in the shotgun, and after he took the snap, he stepped forward like he was going to run. Instead, he stepped back and tossed the ball to the back of the end zone to a receiver who had made a fake block at the line and then released into the back of the end zone for the pass. When they showed us tape of the play from a game, it had resulted in a score against the U.S. Air Force Academy.

When we ran it on the practice field, I ran it wrong the first time out of the box—when I got the ball, I faked the run by running almost all the way to the line of scrimmage, but then I stopped, jumped, and threw the ball to the receiver who had worked his way into the back of the end zone. It worked, and the coaches liked the way it turned out and decided to keep it in the game plan as a jump pass.

We also had a play-action pass that I repped and repped and repped, both in practice and then even on my own afterward, in which I ran all the way to the line of scrimmage then dropped back to throw downfield, where we had one receiver on a post and another on a wheel route.

Early in the LSU game, they put me in, and on my first play they had me counter to the left; I then jabbed to the right and came back to the left, got about eight yards downfield, and then met their safety—right in the hole. I hit him square and head-on and just started driving him downfield for about ten more yards while others joined to push the pile—both on offense and defense—and we ended up gaining another fifteen yards in the scrum. I spun out of it, released, and almost scored a touchdown, except a guy tripped me at the last second. That was actually one of my favorite plays at Florida. The next play they kept me in for had me run a counter right and then a little draw play; then they put Chris in, and he threw a swing pass and had fourth and goal from the one. They put me back in, and I ran a goal-line dive play to the right and met Luke Sanders in the hole. Luke was a great linebacker for LSU and had actually been my host player when I took my official visit to the school. I got the better of the meeting on the field, though, and we scored.

Throughout the first half the momentum and advantage kept swinging back and forth—first to us, then to them, and back again to us. We got the ball with a minute or so to go in the half and drove down the field to inside the ten yard line. They put me in for a run, and we took it down to the one. We called a time out, and Coach Meyer pulled me over and asked if I thought we should run the jump pass or not.

"Tim, you cannot come down with the ball. The half will run out." His concern was that the clock would run out on us since we didn't have any time-outs left and we wouldn't be able to get the field-goal unit onto the field to set up to at least kick a field goal. "Got it?"

I nodded. I'm sure he could see my eyes blazing, ready to go in.

"All right, let's run it. One more time: either throw a touchdown pass or throw it out of bounds. *Don't get tackled, and don't come down with the ball.*"

So we set up, snapped the ball, and ran the jump-pass play, but Tate Casey, my go-to receiver on the play, was held coming off the line of scrimmage and prevented from releasing to the back of the end zone. He finally broke free, but by that time I was gulping hard and double and triple clutching the ball in the air, trying to stay up just long enough for him to break free. I finally let it go at the last second, even though he was barely coming out of his break. He was stumbling, so I just lobbed it in the air to the spot close to where I was calculating he'd end up. Tate, who was falling over but trying to hold himself up long enough to make the play, reached out as the ball floated toward the ground and caught it in his lap for a touchdown.

That's how the legend of the jump pass started.

Coming out of the locker room for the second half, we got the ball early in the third quarter in great field position, and when I was put in the game, we called the play-action pass, "Shift Swap Ace Right Run Pass 95 Zombie Stay Pistol H Cross." I'd practiced saying it all week for obvious reasons.

I took the snap in the shotgun, ran toward the line of scrimmage, and then dropped back into the backfield with what seemed like the whole LSU defense coming toward me. It must have been the whole defense, because no one covered Louis Murphy, who later told me he was so wide open it made him nervous. He caught my pass, took two steps, and just fell into the end zone. No one was anywhere around him, so we always kidded him from then on that he couldn't even run into the end zone, he could only fall in.

Late in the game they put me back in to try to run the clock out. We were running power right, power left. Counter right, counter left. We were successful in running, using up time on the clock and wearing down their defense and winning the game, 23–10.

There we stood after the first six games—undefeated. All the momentum was still behind us, and the potential out in front of us.

Chapter Eleven

ENDING UP IN THE DESERT

By grace you have been saved through faith; and that not of yourselves, it is the gift of God; not as a result of works, so that no one may boast. For we are His workmanship, created in Christ Jesus for good works, which God prepared beforehand so that we would walk in them.
—Ephesians 2:8–10

After the Louisiana State football game, we went to Outback Steakhouse for dinner, a whole crowd of us—my parents and brothers and sisters and a whole group of friends who had come in for the game from all directions. Since it had been a day in which I accounted for all three of our touchdowns—my passing stats for the game were two-for-two for thirty-six yards and two touchdowns—I found myself to be pretty popular, at least at our table.

What my parents remember most about that scene that day was the time I took with a really sweet but shy little boy in the middle of the throng of well-wishing Gator family and fans. My parents have learned not to be surprised when I do something like that; I've always got time for little kids, the kind of time I remember many others, like Uncle Dick, taking with me when I was growing up. Kids can be fragile and are so impressionable. They need lots of encouragement to help them see their potential; and, besides that, they're fun to be around. At times, I find I can be a lot more myself around them—a kid.

My dad reinforced that lesson that night, telling me, "You were on the GameDay set after the game, and they showed everyone in the country your jump pass, but your time with that little guy was the best play of the day."

I suppose it could have been the pressure of the Auburn week and preparing for our game with them at their place on the Plains, but if anything, we took Auburn too lightly: they weren't as good that year as their usual Auburn teams. The rest of the practice week was uneventful and pretty much the same as any week of preparation for an SEC game.

I was really looking forward to the game in Auburn. It was great being at Auburn. I loved their grass, their early-arriving fans, guys wearing ties to the games but still going crazy. I'm told the atmosphere was always electric for Florida games. That day was no exception.

My first play of the game I ran a counter-right and took it in for the score. I also learned a painful lesson on that play—as I scored, I eased up a bit even though I saw a guy coming at me from the side. I knew he wouldn't be able to keep me out. He hit my shoulder just as I crossed the goal line, and the hit sprained my shoulder. It was a relatively mild sprain, but it was irritating, because I had brought it on by easing up.

The game went back and forth between us, and I only played on about three snaps, one of which was in the backfield simply as a decoy with Chris as the quarterback. It was the fewest number of plays I played in a game all year, which was a little bit frustrating, watching from the sidelines and feeling that I could help the team more. What made it worse was that we did not play well, and as a result we ended up losing to a team that we shouldn't have, 27–17. And, to add insult to injury, on that one play, I'd hurt my right shoulder, which ended up nagging me throughout the rest of the year.

After the game, a reporter asked me how I would handle the loss. I gave them the verse that my parents had reminded us of ever since we were children, 1 Thessalonians 5:18:

"In everything give thanks; for this is God's will for you in Christ Jesus."

Six and one. Gimpy shoulder, and back searching as a team for that momentum again.

We had a bye that week, which gave us a chance to work on fundamentals. Also during the bye, I had a little more downtime than I'd had recently and had a chance to catch up with some friends.

Right before school started, I was the celebrity judge of a talent show along with Matt LaPorta, a UF baseball player; I think Coach Meyer's wife, Shelley, may have been one too. This one girl, in addition to being really attractive, was talented and bright. Everything she did was awesome, and she had a hysterical sense of humor, so at the end of the night, I gave her a perfect score. Apparently I wasn't the only one. Matt asked her out that night before I could even think about it, but she wasn't interested. I didn't give her another thought.

The following week, Butchie Rowley, a good friend and fellow teammate, invited me to go to a movie with him and a girl he knew from high school. He said he was hoping to ask her out on a date, following this movie, and that maybe I'd want to go in case she didn't seem interested; then the night wouldn't be so awkward for them. Butchie is a guy who shares my principles of how I think Christ wants us to relate to women—with respect, first and foremost—and he was trying to go about it the right way. Still I declined, thinking that the night sounded plenty awkward for me in case the two of them hit it off.

He insisted, and I found myself as the third wheel as we went to pick her up. It was, of course, the girl from the pageant, and by the end of the evening, it was clear that she and Butchie would remain friends, but she and I clicked.

We went out for a couple of weeks, but it never got serious. My family tells me that I'm the pickiest person they've ever met, and that may be true. Between my mom and my sisters, who have such amazing character qualities it's a tough standard for anyone else to meet. Plus, I've not yet been willing to devote time to make a relationship work.

Meanwhile the team tried to get refocused and headed to Jacksonville for our sixth SEC game in a row. I, of course, was looking forward to that week because it was the Florida–Georgia game. That was enough in and of itself, but Jacksonville was also my hometown and my parents' first date was to the Florida–Georgia game. I had grown up going to that game every year, so I was excited to finally play in it, but nowhere near as excited as my dad was. He grew up in an era in which Georgia was the big rival, and he spoke about this game much in the same way that I've heard Coach Steve Spurrier was always focused on beating Georgia when he was coaching the Gators. Quite honestly, we were beating Georgia pretty regularly when I was growing up, so they weren't nearly the archrival for my generation that Florida State became.

I remember going to Florida–Georgia games in the pouring rain and coming out of most of them pretty happy. Of course, there were a few of them that ended up very sad, like the year when Georgia quarterback Quincy Carter beat us. Several times we had a Pop Warner game beforehand, and we'd change in the car on the way to the Florida–Georgia game. As soon as the game was over, we'd head home, where my brothers and I would play in the backyard, mimicking the players we had just watched during the game.

My brother-in-law, Joey, went to Georgia. In fact, his entire family are Bulldogs, but—get this—most of the people at the church his dad pastors agreed to become Gator fans during the four years I played at Florida.

I was ready. I went into the game on the first drive and had a really good run on a 97 Q Power call, a quarterback run up the middle. I played on and off for the rest of the game, but the worst part of the game for me came in the second half when I was stood straight up on a tackle by a defender, and then got stripped of the ball by another player. My fumble was recovered by Georgia on our own ten yard line, and they scored a few plays later to cut our lead to 7. I was mad at myself, even though I'd been practicing good ball security—I just had several guys ripping on it while I was being stood up, and I didn't hang on. There was no excuse for it, whether I thought I was doing well on good ball security or not; it wasn't good enough. To me, and Coach Meyer, I'm sure, it was unacceptable. Very irritating. We hung on to win, 21–14 but didn't play very well offensively that day.

The whole next week I worked on ball-security drills by myself after practice, trying to make sure what happened in the Georgia game that Saturday didn't happen again, and I worked to hold on to the ball with as much force as I possibly could.

That next week I heard that the coaches debated playing me even more since we weren't playing our best on offense, but it was decided, instead, to stick with the approach we'd followed so far. Chris Leak still started in our game at Vanderbilt, of course, but I did play a little more, and it went well, including a thirty-yard run. Early on, things were clicking on offense, even to the point where, after one touchdown, Butchie Rowley, our holder on extra points and field goals, after fumbling the snap for the extra point after a touchdown, just picked it up, looked into the end zone, and completed a pass for a two-point conversion.

After a while, though, we stopped moving the ball effectively, and they mounted a comeback, scoring thirteen unanswered points in the fourth quarter. Chris struggled, throwing three interceptions on the day, totally out of character for him. Toward the end of the game, having just scored, Vandy lined up for an onside kick, still sitting on the short end of a 25–19 score.

I was out there on the hands team, too, to make sure we recovered the onside attempt, and I was able to cover the kick along with Dallas Baker. It was similar in some ways to the Georgia game of the week before, in that we found a way to get an ugly win over a team that was overmatched.

The day after the game, Robby called. It was a call I knew could come at any time, but I still wasn't ready for what he told me—it was so hard to hear that our beloved, faithful, and protective Otis had died. The limp had gotten better over time, but he had cancer and was thirteen years old. Because of football, I couldn't go home to help bury him. He was a great dog, and a great friend. Robby buried him down by the lake on the farm. Otis was an incredibly tough loss, and it was even more difficult because I was away from home.

In general it had been getting easier to be at school. Much like things on the field, school had also been going well. It was my first time away from home, but it had been a good experience. I was attending several churches and hadn't settled into any particular one. I was staying busy, which probably helped with the transition.

When I came to the University of Florida, I was tested for my dyslexia and because of it, I was allowed time and a half to take all my exams. I used that extra time my freshman year, and carried a 4.0. I'm not sure how necessary it was, however, as I was usually able to read and process most of the questions in the allotted time; and having 50 percent additional time didn't seem to make any answers that I didn't know come to mind. In fact, it invariably made me late to my next class, so by the end of my freshman year, I'd quit taking the extra time I was allowed.

Football-wise, we were in the middle of a tough streak. We were winning, but we weren't playing very well, and so we weren't really entertaining any serious thoughts that we were on our way to anything truly special that year. We were still focused on getting to the SEC Championship Game and winning that, but even in that commitment, I don't think we were very confident or excited about any other opportunities—like the National Championship—which we hoped might be in our future. There were a number of one-loss teams logjammed around the country, and they were all playing pretty well. We were just barely hanging on in games and then ending up on the good side of the score—except for Auburn, of course. It just seemed as though it was going to take something special to really fire us up and get the juices flowing again.

When South Carolina and the "Old Ball Coach"—Steve Spurrier—visited the Swamp, things didn't change much. As the game wore on, it became clear that the South Carolina game made it four in a row in which we still weren't playing very well. Other than a second quarter touchdown, our hopes of moving the ball regularly against South Carolina's man coverage just didn't pan out like we'd expected, although Chris Leak had one of his best games of the year. He passed for 258 yards that day, and in that performance he passed Danny Wuerffel to become the all-time passing leader in Gators history. Still tied at seven early in the fourth quarter, the coaches called a play for me on third and short yardage to try and get the first down; it was a fake run, roll out, in which I was to hit fullback Billy Latsko in the flat near the side of the field. I overthrew him by about a foot too high and, despite that, Billy made a great effort to make the catch, but I had overthrown him by too much. We had to punt, which was very frustrating and indicative of the way the game was going.

South Carolina took the lead, 16–10, with eight minutes to go—we blocked the extra point—and with four minutes left we started what seemed like it could turn out to be our final drive of the game. We faced a fourth and two from our own end of the field. They might have been able to run the clock out if we didn't get the first down to be able to keep the ball and keep the drive alive. We called 97 Q Power. For a brief moment I saw nothing but daylight on the play, but then a guy crashed into me from the side. Despite that, we gained enough for the first down and kept the ball. We kept moving down the field, and eventually we had the ball at South Carolina's twelve yard line.

We needed a touchdown. Coach Mullen called a run play for me, and after I hit the hole right up the middle that our line had opened, I jump-stepped over their safety at the five yard line, like a hurdler, dashing in for the score. The extra point was good, and we led 17–16. South Carolina still had time to move the ball and try and get into field-goal range. And move the ball they did. They eventually got down to our thirty-one yard line and, facing a fourth down with a few seconds left in the game, lined up for a forty-eight-yard attempt for the win.

By that point, I was praying full-time. We were holding hands on the sidelines, and when Ryan Succop went in to set up to try the kick, I just closed my eyes. I didn't want to watch; I was just praying and praying. I don't think my prayers were particularly rational and well thought out, but more like: *if You let us win this game, I will do as much as I can to honor You.* Truth be told, I should, and hope I would, do the same thing if Succop hit it sixty-five yards dead-center-perfect to beat us. To be honest, in that moment, I don't even know exactly what I was praying—I was just praying.

I know it sounds dumb to be praying over a football game, but if you've ever watched a close football game, then you've almost certainly seen one or two guys with their heads bowed during the closing seconds. I'm not sure God is into who wins or loses—He probably is more concerned with what you do in the process and what you will do with either result, to glorify Him and change the world by hopefully impacting one life. But since my parents raised me to pray about anything that's on my heart, I pray—even if some of those things are trivial in the overall scheme of things.

I had my eyes closed, we were holding hands, and praying when all of a sudden I heard the crowd erupt. I later learned that Jarvis Moss blocked his second kick of the day—preventing a crushing loss and securing a spot for us in the SEC Championship.

I opened my eyes to see Tony Joiner running to get the ball, and I realized from where he picked it up that it must have been blocked. The bench unloaded as we all just ran out onto the field. We celebrated for a long time on the field, a lot longer it seemed than ever before.

The next day in our meetings Coach Meyer had a video guy grab a clip off YouTube from one of the fans to show us how crazy the game was from the fans' perspective. The whole team was sitting there, stunned, thinking, *Wow, this is crazy. This is exciting.* For us to clinch the SEC Eastern Division and, with it, a trip to Atlanta to play in the SEC Championship Game against Arkansas was just another part of the dream of being there. There were some great memories for every one of us, and I was glad to be part of it: Chris's record-setting performance, Jarvis's two blocked kicks, and, personally, that fourth down, then later running through that huge hole opened by our guys so we could score the go-ahead touchdown. At that moment, we were only thinking about our goal of winning the SEC Championship. We were all pretty sure that Southern Cal and Ohio State would end up playing in the National Championship game.

Our 62–0 win over Western Carolina that next week wasn't the most exciting one for the fans that year, but I got to play the second half and really enjoyed it. Coach Meyer let me make checks at the line and call audibles and didn't really restrict me when we were winning; he just let me go ahead and play.

There would be no overlooking Florida State to focus on the SEC Championship Game for me, or for anyone else on the team. I grew up really not liking FSU. I had vivid memories of them beating us and ending Florida's undefeated season on Thanksgiving weekend of 1996 in Tallahassee. But then I remembered how nice it was when Florida returned the favor the next year in Gainesville. Oh, and who can ever forget that the Gators' only National Championship at that point came in a Sugar Bowl blowout over Florida State in January of 1997, just five weeks after that heartbreaking regular-season defeat?

It was close at the start of the game, and as is often the case with this rivalry, neither team was able to sustain any lasting momentum or advantage. We got the ball at our one yard line, and they put me in to try to punch the ball out to give us some breathing room so we'd at least have room to punt. We called a power play, and no one touched the nose guard. He came through scot-free and met me about two yards deep in the end zone.

My brain was screaming that I couldn't take a safety. I think the score was tied at the time 7–7. I was thinking, *I will not be the reason Florida ever loses to Florida State.* I hit him with all I had and began driving him forward, thinking, *no, no, I can't take a safety.* Later on, when we reviewed the film, it was pretty neat to watch my obvious determination. I'm driving him so hard that you can see his knees just snap back and he ends up flat on his back. I got the ball to the half yard line. Barely out of the end zone, but out. It wasn't the breathing room the coaches were hoping for with a loss of a half yard, but it was back out of the end zone. And it really wasn't a big play to the average fan, or most people watching, but it was something that the coaches took the time to praise me on and then played it again the next day when we watched the film as a full team.

Otherwise, I didn't get a lot of plays in the FSU game. I got a few short-yardage plays and was able to help us out on most of those. I did run one counter play where I kind of broke outside for about four yards and then spun back inside and was met by Lawrence Timmons, a senior linebacker, who was drafted by the Steelers the following April. Bad idea. It's not always good to spin back to the inside, because there are a lot of guys coming through that area. We continued to drive down, and Chris hit Dallas Baker on a fade route to the corner of the end zone to win the game. Reggie Nelson dominated the game for us on defense. We won 21–14. Our defense played well, and it was just more of the same story of that year. It wasn't always pretty, but we survived and somehow came away with a win.

With FSU behind us, the next and biggest hurdle came against number eight Arkansas in the SEC Championship Game. Going into the game, we were ranked fourth in the country, but Ohio State (number one) had already finished their season, and USC (number two) was a heavy favorite to beat UCLA that same day to finish their season and earn the right to meet Ohio State in the Bowl Championship Series (BCS) National Championship Game in January of 2007 in Glendale, Arizona.

During warm-ups, we were quite focused, and as the game got underway, we jumped on them early in the second quarter. Chris scored on a called running play, and our defensive scheme was awesome and executed to perfection to shut down Darren McFadden and Felix Jones. We took a 17–7 lead into halftime when Coach Meyer dropped the bombshell news on us: UCLA had just beaten USC, 13–9. If we took care of business, we could very well be playing for the National Championship.

Arkansas, however, had different plans, and in the second half they came back to take the lead from us. After that, the game was back and forth. Clinging to a three-point lead in the fourth quarter, we drove the ball down to Arkansas's five yard line, at which point Coach put me in for a play that we had practiced all that week: I faked a handoff then faked running toward the line of scrimmage, and then pitched it back to Bubba Caldwell, who had circled back from his wide-out position. Bubba then threw a pass to Tate Casey, who was wide open in the end zone, and that put the game away. Our defense did a great job all game—but especially after that. We were able to run the ball, methodically move it, and just manage the clock for rest of the game.

As time remaining wound down, the coaches put me in to run the clock out. I ran a few yards here and there on various plays. Power right, counter left, counter right, power left. Just kept doing that over and over, and in those runs, with great blocking up front, we were able to seal the game. We won the seventh SEC title in Florida history by a score of 38–28.

The next day, we learned that we had leapfrogged number three Michigan and would end up playing undefeated number one Ohio State in the BCS National Championship Game. I don't think anyone can explain the BCS system exactly, but I do know that it worked to our benefit over Michigan that year. And at that moment, I had no complaints about the BCS.

As you would expect, my whole family—except for Katie and her husband, Gannon, who were too close to her due date to travel—went to Glendale, Arizona, for the BCS National Championship Game and had a great time touring and visiting the area, while my time was pretty much occupied by practice and game-related activities.

I wasn't particularly nervous. I was excited, but that energy came from hoping I would play a lot.

Although we felt we were ready, you never know how you will perform after a month without playing a game, and sure enough, the game started with Ted Ginn Jr.'s running the opening kickoff back to the house. Touchdown, Ohio State.

There we were—down 7–0 before we could even catch our breath after warm-ups. Not how we wanted to start after hearing for five weeks about how much better Ohio State was than we were. We were sick of hearing that. We were ready to hit somebody. After watching the film, we didn't think they were very fast, and we were going to gain a speed advantage with guys like Bubba Caldwell and Percy

Harvin. To those who thought they would be more physical than us, we could all remember back to the mat drills and Coach Mick, and we knew we were going to show not just Ohio State but all the pundits and prognosticators just how physical we could be. That was our mentality going in, but the opening kickoff seemed to validate what others had been saying.

But only for about eight seconds.

Instead of folding, we took their kickoff and marched the ball right down the field; then Chris threw a touchdown pass to Dallas Baker to tie the game at seven apiece. That got the momentum on our side. I ran once during that drive and a couple of times on the next possession after our defense forced Ohio State to punt after three plays. We scored on that drive as well to take a 14–7 lead. Our defense was shutting them down. We were blitzing everybody—and often—bringing a bunch of guys at a time. I doubt they had ever seen a defense with that much speed; we were shutting them down from every angle.

We added to our lead, and then with a few minutes left to go in the second quarter, and with us already ahead 27–14, we forced a turnover. Chris then completed a few passes, got down to the one yard line, when they called another one of my plays. It was a play where I motion Bubba Caldwell across, running behind the line, catch the snap, fake a power run, and boot to the left. Marcus Freeman, their outstanding linebacker, was right there and ran into the hole, thinking I was running; then when I pulled up and went to boot outside, I could almost hear him and was sure I could see him mouth, "*Uh oh.*" Bubba was wide open for the pass I threw—another touchdown, and we led 34–14 at the half.

The second half I got to play even more, running the ball to run the clock down. In the meantime, our defense never let Ohio State get into the game. Midway through the fourth quarter we got near the goal line again, and they put me in on a fourth and one. I had lobbied hard to go in. I remember standing in Coach Meyer's line of sight—probably unnecessary given the volume of my voice—yelling, "I'll score! I'll score!" I scored, finishing with one touchdown passing, and one touchdown running.

More important, we won the second National Championship in school history, 41–14. Chris played very well and was named MVP of the BCS National Championship Game. Well deserved. I was happy for him, a senior, ending it on a good note.

That first night after the game, we had a lot of fun, enjoyed just hanging out with everybody. Celebrating a long year's work. We flew back, and those flights are really just the best. I hate flying— imagine those long flights to the Philippines—but after a game like that, you look forward to those flights. There's something about being together, celebrating and reflecting on all you accomplished together, after all the work you put in—you just can't help but enjoy it, whether you like to fly or not. Upon returning to Gainesville, we had the Gator celebration in the Swamp at UF after that, and to be able to watch everything and see the thousands of fans gathered and be with them was remarkable. I remember how familiar it all seemed, because growing up I had a DVD of the 1996 National Champion- ship year, which I watched all the time. I remembered Coach Spurrier had everyone chanting, "*We're number one.*" Now that was us.

And just think, in just three short months from that day in Glen- dale, Arizona, Coach Billy Donovan and our University of Florida men's basketball team would defeat the Ohio State University men's basketball team in the Georgia Dome in Atlanta, Georgia, to again win the National Championship in basketball, and, in doing so, to become the first basketball team in fifteen years to win back-to-back National Championships. That spring, the University of Florida was clearly number one.

Chapter Twelve

STARTING OVER

Be kind to one another, tender-hearted, forgiving each other,
just as God in Christ also has forgiven you.
—EPHESIANS 4:32

Our off-season wasn't all that bright or positive. When we got back to campus in January after the National Championship, the team took a few days off, but soon enough both classes and training for spring practice began. Right away, it seemed like a lot of guys were taking things a little bit for granted, like some were being a bit lazy when it came to getting back to business and defending our National Championship. We had just come off a year where we had all worked so hard during that 2006 season, been recognized nationally for our efforts, and, more important, earned an incredible platform from which to influence kids and others for good. It was something that I believed we should take seriously and build upon. A lot of my teammates agreed and came ready to go. But too many others seemed to have a different attitude.

What some of us saw in them seemed worse than being lazy or being too causal; it seemed more like there was an entitlement atmosphere, an expectation that things and positions should just be theirs because of the previous year, an attitude that led to a lack of commitment. Too many seemed to have an attitude of, "I earned my role last year and am entitled to it and intend to claim it and enjoy it." We did not appear to have the sense of commitment that had helped us win the National Championship.

To me, though, it wasn't about the SEC Championship or another National Championship in 2007. It wasn't about what we would or would not accomplish. It was about coming together and committing ourselves to one another to be the best we could be. It was about building relationships around sacrifice for the team, wanting the best for the other guy, and not caring who got the credit for our mutual success.

Instead, some of the guys weren't going to class or working out individually as hard or purposefully as they should have. Other guys, guys who knew better, simply enabled that kind of behavior and allowed it to continue—when a well-placed word, example, or influence from them might have changed the effort for the better. And some of the new faces on the team liked that they were coming into the Gators' history, but what they didn't all realize was that this history was earned off the sweat and sacrifice of others—not by them.

I may have been particularly sensitive to what I perceived as a drop-off in intensity and commitment that spring because I was entering the year as the starting quarterback. We weren't nearly as talented in 2007, especially on defense, and needed to work really hard.

We simply didn't have enough guys who were workers, committed to the sacrifice it would take. We knew we were going to have some talent returning and new guys coming in as new members of the team, but there were definitely some things missing in the off-season. And, along the way, there were additional struggles with guys who were getting into trouble for a number of different things.

We needed to get to a better place as we began the 2007 season. There were many times we were able to do well, and there were enough of those moments, which allowed us to achieve what we achieved.

But for what purpose? A trophy? A ring? I don't believe so. That's a temporary reward. It won't satisfy. It won't fulfill us for the long haul.

• • •

Complicating matters for me was the fact that I had injured my shoulder during the 2006 season, so during the winter workouts freshman Cam Newton and our other quarterback, Brian Wagner, worked out with our receivers, easing the load on my shoulder as it healed. I headed out with them each day as they threw to our wide receivers, contributing and helping by teaching them the offense and the various routes that we ran.

Cam was naturally gifted, strong, and athletic.

He was similar to me before I got serious with weights in that he is what I've referred to as being "farmer strong," one of those people who is just naturally strong, not from the supplemental process of lifting weights. It was pleasure to work with Cam and have some influence on his life.

With Cam and Brian taking some of the load, I had a chance to heal a bit while still working hard in all other aspects during the off-season. By the time spring practice rolled around, I was feeling physically much better, and overall I had a good spring and spring game. I solidified my position as the starting quarterback heading into the summer, but I was still concerned with our level of preparation during that off-season and the impact it could have on our performance in the fall.

I wanted to do everything I could, however, to make sure I was ready and in a position to be able to do my best, so Coach Mick worked with me individually a number of times. We had done this several times during my freshman spring, and we continued throughout my career. On days when we would only run or have a light workout in the morning, I would go back to him in the afternoon for more work. In the process, he'd try to see how close he could come to breaking me. Actually, for as similar as Coach Mick and I are, he probably wanted to see if he *could* break me.

It might have only lasted for forty-five minutes or an hour, but those workouts with Coach Mick were exhausting. One of the things he loved to do was have me squat with my knees at ninety degrees, my thighs parallel to the floor and my back against the wall. He would then start to stack forty-five-pound plates and sandbags on my thighs and yell, "Don't you move! Hold it! Hold it! I'll tell you when we're done!" I would hold it until my body was shaking and on the verge of collapse, and he'd then—usually—release me.

Other exercises, he would have me do at least fifty repetitions. For instance, he'd put me on the leg- or bench-press station, and then he'd pick a weight slightly lower than my "max," the maximum weight that I could lift. I'd lift it as many times as I could—often seven, based on his starting weight. Once my arms or legs were shaking and I couldn't raise the bar again, he'd take the weight from me and put it back on the rack. Then he'd pick a weight that was slightly less, and I'd pick up with the exercise where I left off: eight, nine, and so on. Once I failed at that weight, he'd take it from me and lower the weight, and we'd pick up again, continuing that process of changing and lowering weights until we reached fifty repetitions. Then he'd take me to the next exercise, for fifty repetitions of that, in a similar fashion of lowering the weights when I reached exhaustion on each one. By the time we'd finish the seated bench press, for instance, I wouldn't be able to feel my arms or hands. I know what you have to be thinking—about Coach Mick. About me.

We'd often do several exercises, such as seated rows, pull ups with weight around my waist, abdominal exercises that we took straight from some of those done by Sylvester Stallone in *Rocky IV*, and a seated bench press to work my shoulders, and he always loved to finish with the leg press. He saved the hardest for last.

The whole routine was as much for improving my mental strength as it was for increasing my physical strength. It built up a lot of confidence in me, but Coach Mick didn't do it with many guys, because some guys would end up quitting in the process, and he knew that wouldn't help their confidence at all. Actually he was afraid that it might dampen it. The Pounceys, Maurkice and Mike, were both good at those workouts as well. Not many others did them. Coach Mick's workouts were based on triggering the sympathetic nervous system—I can vouch for that; there was always a definite moment of "fight or flight" when working out with Coach Mick.

After a Friday workout like that, I wouldn't be able to walk without a limp until at least Sunday. That's why we couldn't do those kinds of workouts during the season; there never was enough recovery time available before we had to be back on the practice field or in a game.

Still it wasn't all work.

During that off-season, I was working on statistics homework in the academic center, when a car pulled up right as I was leaving the building. Phil Trautwein was driving, and Butchie Rowley, David Nelson, and another friend were all there. They told me to jump in, because they were headed to a little place in Gainesville to see Kenny Chesney. I didn't understand why they were coming by to grab me, when they explained that the place only seated about two hundred people—it was a private concert. And since they didn't have tickets, they figured having a quarterback with them was their best chance to get in.

I grew up a pretty big country-music fan, especially in high school. I just really liked it because the lyrics tell stories and I felt it was a lot more real than some other types of music. Obviously it's got its stereotypes about dogs, trucks, beer, and kissing your cousin, but I like the way it sounds. I actually got my dad into it. I put a bunch of songs on my dad's iPod and he listened to them on the way to the Philippines. When he returned, he said his favorites were George Strait, Brad Paisley, and Kenny Chesney. Not a bad trio.

I thought the effort was futile; I didn't think there was a chance we'd get in. Sure enough, we were outside, milling around, unable to get in. After a few moments, a security guard recognized me and said, "Go Gators," and about thirty minutes later, he brought out one of Kenny Chesney's managers and the head of his security. They said Kenny would love for us to come on his bus and chat for a few minutes. The kicker? I could only pick one friend to come. Not a good scene, since they were the ones who initiated the trip. Of course, they started arguing and arguing, and we never could resolve it. Finally, we drove the head of security crazy, so he told us all to come to the bus.

After chatting with Kenny for a few minutes—he's so cool that you'd never know he's a Tennessee fan—we then watched his show for about an hour off to the side, before he decided that he would bring me up onstage and Butchie followed.

We ended up on stage, Kenny asked me to say a few words, and then asked if we knew "She Thinks My Tractor's Sexy." I'm not a singer, so more than anything I did the Gator chomp a few times and swayed side to side. By the end, Kenny put on a UF football helmet; he caught some grief back home for that, but, hey, sooner or later we all end up as Gator fans, right?

Our first game of the season was against Western Kentucky, and for that entire week I was pumped, since it would be my first game as a starter. That moment of coming to the Swamp as the starting quarterback was something I'd looked forward to all off-season—not to mention my whole life.

Things went pretty well, considering. We hit some good passes, made some good runs, and played how we needed to against a team that was clearly overmatched. We didn't take them lightly, though. We competed every down and played hard, and as a result, we won my first start and the first start for a few others as well. With our offense I ended up throwing for exactly three hundred yards. When you play a team like that, you expect them to be scrappy since they may not be as athletically talented. That team, surprisingly, was one of the dirtiest teams I've faced in my career. More than a few times it seemed that they were trying to get their fingers through my face mask while we were in a pile. The only logical reason, it seemed to me, was to get to one of my eyes. Just a guess.

Anyway, Coach pulled me in the fourth quarter, and Cam Newton finished the game, did a solid job, and scored our last touchdown.

That game was unique for another reason: it was called because of lightning midway through the fourth quarter. Our 49–3 lead that we held at the time instantly became the final score.

I know people often criticized the strength (or lack of perceived strength) of our out-of-conference schedule, but our next opponent, Troy, had a solid team. We knew we needed to start out with great intensity and try to get up on them right away by playing well and hard. With their version of the spread offense, that team can put up a lot of points on you before you know it. We started well with intensity and determination and ended up scoring every time we had the ball in the first half, building a lead of 49–7 by halftime. They were playing a soft cover-two defense and letting our receivers get a clean release off the line of scrimmage without bumping them too much, so we were able to take advantage of our "vertical" passing attack by completing deep passes downfield, or in the football vernacular "over the top" of the defense.

In the second half we came out totally unfocused, and they began to chip into our lead. The first-half score and seeing what we were able to do, instead of creating a hunger for us to continue, apparently caused us to lose a bit of our intensity. After Troy quickly scored seventeen unanswered points to start the half, we finally regrouped and regained our focus enough to fend them off, 59–31.

That next week in practice we definitely had a number of things we needed to improve on, especially when it came to making midgame adjustments and learning to not just "pull up" in the middle of the game. This was where the lack of intensity that I'd been so worried about during spring practice was showing itself. With the Tennessee game at home looming large in front of us that week, we had to learn how to finish games and cut down on our penalties.

Though I'd started for the previous two weeks, that did little to stop the butterflies in my stomach as we prepared to take the field against Tennessee. The Swamp was going crazy—it felt like the fans didn't let up from pregame until the game was finally finished—thank goodness. We needed every one of them.

The Vols got the ball first, but our defense stopped them on three plays. They punted to us, and Brandon James was electrifying as he ran the punt back eighty-three yards for a touchdown. The whole stadium was shaking.

It was a lead we would never relinquish. We raced out to a 28–13 halftime lead as I took a shot downfield and hit "Coop" (Riley Cooper) for a touchdown. We ended up doing a lot of different things, spreading them out, and running bootlegs. We passed for a second touchdown, and I ran for one before halftime. To start the second half, we received the opening kickoff and got a great drive going. We marched the ball down the field, deep into their territory, and hoped to put the game away with a speed post down the middle of the field to Coop.

Tennessee's freshman cornerback, Eric Berry, was covering Coop, and Riley was supposed to come in just underneath him. Whatever he did, Coop needed to ensure that he came in flatter than Berry—that is, closer to me and in front of Eric Berry. Riley was young and didn't run the route just right, and I was young and threw it anyway—when I should not have. Then the even-younger Eric Berry came in underneath Coop and picked it. I did all I could to run him down, but I couldn't catch him. Instead I watched his back as he put distance between us, taking it ninety-three yards for a touchdown to put them back into the game. I still remember the play call: "Far Trio Left 60 Houston"—some things you just never forget.

I was frustrated with the interception and frustrated that I didn't catch him. And I took pride in running well for a big guy. I didn't have the same straight-ahead speed, but I have good agility and quickness. During my time at Florida, there were very few guys I couldn't run with. Each year, somebody would challenge a new guy to race me in quickness agility drills—guys like Ahmad Black, David Nelson, and Aaron Hernandez. Aaron was so mad when we raced that year—his freshman year, and my sophomore year. He was sure I couldn't beat him even once. I did. Then I beat him again. And again. We raced over and over, finally quitting with my holding a 34–2 lead in our races. Don't get me wrong—I never broke into the top group with guys like Joe Haden, Percy Harvin, Chris Rainey, and Jeff Demps. But I could run a bit, which was part of why I was annoyed with Berry's touchdown.

It was now 28–20, and they forced us to punt. In their series, their running back, Arian Foster, never got a clean handoff from Tennessee quarterback Erik Ainge, resulting in a fumble. Dustin Doe, one of our linebackers, picked it up in full stride and took it all the way back to the house. With that touchdown, we were up fifteen, and from that point, we proceeded to bury them.

Early in the fourth quarter I hit one of our wideouts, Louis Murphy, on a deep pass, and we scored moments later, this time on the old familiar play: 97 Q Power, our name for a quarterback run up the middle. We ended up changing that name because I'd audibled to it so often, shouting, "Power Power," that people finally figured out what it was. We switched it up and started calling it "Mickey," as a tribute to Coach Mick, who was always so focused on developing power in us.

By the end of the game, we'd gained over five hundred yards of offense on our way to an unexpectedly lopsided 59–20 win. Coach Meyer was proud of us; we kept competing all game long, and guys kept stepping up to make plays when we needed them. To win my first SEC start at quarterback gave me a huge sense of place and purpose. It was a good Tennessee team that we demolished. Thanks to the guys up front on the line and those guys at the receiving end of passes, I ended up with four touchdowns (two in the air and two on the ground). And thanks again to our receivers' catching skills and running with the ball after the catch abilities, we averaged almost twenty yards per completion. Personally, it felt really good, but what felt better was that we'd done it together. It had been a team effort—truly—and a huge win for us.

I was simply relieved that we'd won such a big game and was relaxing with my family that evening when the guys on ESPN started talking about me as a Heisman candidate. Up until then, I was simply thinking about starting and winning our games. It was fun to hear, but I quickly realized that I didn't have time to focus on it—I needed to get back to focusing on preparing to start and our piling up wins.

The good feelings lasted one more week, but we could feel that things weren't exactly right, not yet where they needed to be, even in a win. We beat Ole Miss on the road, in my first start away from the Swamp. We knew they had a pretty good team and they were well coached, but some people still took them too lightly, to the frustration of many of us. We got a lead and played pretty well, but there was an undercurrent of things to come in that game.

I ended up with some surprisingly big numbers for the game, throwing for over 250 yards and rushing 27 times for 168 yards, with two touchdowns passing and two rushing. As a result, I was named the SEC Offensive Player of the Week for the second time that year after our 30–24 win, but the biggest takeaway from that game was how very sore I was following the game. From around the four-minute mark of time remaining in the game, I may have carried the ball every single time as we ran out the clock and kept the ball away from Ole Miss.

I'm not sure why it unfolded that way in 2007, with my running as much as I did, as we had some very talented running backs, but for some reason we struggled to develop a rhythm with our running game, trying to incorporate all our backs into the game.

With that win, we cut Mississippi's all-time series lead over us to one, and with SEC scheduling, we were going to be able to tie the all-time series up with them the next season in Gainesville. To be honest, I don't think any of us thought about that at the time, but one thing is for sure: we weren't paying any attention to Auburn just one week away.

Honestly, Auburn didn't seem like a particularly good team in 2007. They have had great teams before and after, and Auburn and Florida have been known to play some of the most dramatic football games in SEC history. Highlights include Kerwin Bell's leading Florida to eighteen fourth-quarter points to erase a seventeen-point deficit and beat unbeaten number four Auburn, 18–17, in 1986 (note: every Gator fan in the western hemisphere claims to have been at Florida Field for that game—just ask one), or Steve Spurrier clinching the Heisman Trophy with a field goal to beat Auburn in 1966, and plenty of other Auburn–Florida moments as well.

Auburn had started the season ranked as high as number fourteen but lost two early games at home, to Mississippi State and South Florida, and hadn't looked good in the process. However, for the second year in a row against Auburn, right off the bat things didn't go our way. I think we all underestimated them, both coaches and players.

Auburn clearly had more momentum and played with more passion as the game began. They shut us down early. We went three and out on our first possession. In the meantime, they were slowly and methodically moving the ball against our defense. Every time they got the ball, they were holding it for five to seven minutes, chalking up first downs and maintaining possession as they ran the clock down. We weren't taking advantage of our possessions, and they were running the ball trying to shorten the game. They scored twice in the first half, and it was 14–0 at the half.

We tried to rally the troops in the locker room and came back out after the half, and on the first drive we hit a deep post down to the goal line. Down, 14–0, we really needed a touchdown, but Auburn's defense and their defensive coordinator, Will Muschamp—who grew up in Gainesville—rose to the challenge. The first play was 97 Power . . . and a linebacker came straight through and blew me up in the hole. No gain. We couldn't score on second or third down, either, and had to kick a field goal.

Looking back, I think the reason we lost that game was because we didn't put that ball in the end zone to score that first touchdown right after we came out in the second half. It would have been 14–7 and we'd have been right in it while laying claim to that ever slippery momentum. Instead, we kept playing from behind, but we did keep playing. Things weren't going well with our passing game, so they started running me a lot, counter left, counter right. We kept fighting and finally tied it with two touchdowns in the fourth quarter at 17–17.

Our tying touchdown came on an out route that I threw to Cornelius Ingram—whom I played basketball against when I was at Jacksonville Trinity Christian Academy and he was at Hawthorne High School—in the end zone.

With a couple of minutes left in the game, we got the ball in pretty good field position and then called a screen play to Percy. The screen was a good call and Percy tried to turn a good play into a great play as he usually can. But as he was trying to cut to the outside, a defender swiped his leg and tackled him for a seven-yard loss. We were in bad shape, because that hindered our ability to do anything on second and third down. I hit Kestahn Moore on second down, then on third down and long yardage to go, the pass was broken up and we had to punt.

Auburn took the punt and marched the ball down the field and then kicked a game-ending field goal to beat us at home, 20–17.

It was so frustrating because we had the ball with an opportunity to win and I couldn't get it done. Right or wrong, I put the loss squarely on my shoulders. I'd let everyone down. I felt like that T-leaguer again, wishing I had the ball in my hands one more time at the end of the game to try and make things right for us. It was a tough one to take.

I was praying a lot at different times in that game too. Obviously my earlier point about God's not necessarily favoring a particular outcome over another would seem clear. I guess it was an answer to prayer. Just not the answer I wanted.

The next night Coach Meyer and I had a long talk, mostly about handling defeat. His words were quite helpful to me. We went through and read a number of different Bible verses together, focusing on how God won't give us more than we can handle. We spoke about how God has a plan for our lives and our lives together as a team. As we talked, we both realized that we didn't feel we'd played our best. I think it was good for us both that night to be spiritually encouraged in the process. We talked about God's having a plan for everything, even though we don't know what it is. And while we might think we have a lot on both of our plates, we each took comfort in knowing—through God's past faithfulness—that no matter what is on our plates, He will never leave us and will help us handle whatever it is.

Of course, that night with Coach Meyer wasn't all theology; we also talked about the game some. In that last series I felt like I could have helped before we got into second and third down and long yardage.

The competitor in me wanted to say, *"Just give me the ball all three plays and let's see what happens."* Instead, we had a good talk about how we'd handle it the next time and how we'd handle this loss going forward. It was a good opportunity for me and Coach to have that bonding experience and to be able to talk about those things that matter most as well.

I felt really blessed again.

Chapter Thirteen

COMMUNICATION PROBLEMS

Those who wait for the LORD will gain new strength; they will
mount up with wings like eagles, they will run and not
get tired, they will walk and not become weary.
—ISAIAH 40:31

I know I made it to class that next week. I always did. I was well into my major of Family, Youth, and Community Sciences with a minor in Communication. Choosing my major was easy—I knew I wanted to be working with people and youth, possibly in a not-for-profit setting, and figured that zeroing in on that made sense. I never looked back.

But as much as I loved what I was studying, that week was a tough one. There were so many distractions, it's amazing I got anything done. Dealing with that loss was hard enough, but what complicated things even more was the game on the horizon. The following Saturday would be my first trip back to Tiger Stadium in Baton Rouge since Coach Meyer shook his head at me from across the field before that LSU–Florida game when I was in high school. Although we were still in a stunned state of mind that Sunday, a day after the Auburn loss, Louisiana State students took it upon themselves to do their best to make me feel welcome as we prepared for our visit the following weekend.

It started with a few choice voicemails that Sunday afternoon. Not one of them was worth listening to, but sadly they needed to be heard so that appropriate measures and precautions could be taken. Messages coming in like this one: "Hey, Tim Tebow, you'd better tell your family to stay inside because we're going to find your parents tonight and they're going to end up in serious pain." Messages like that—uplifting, positive messages demonstrating good sportsmanship and goodwill toward all.

Of course, everyone on the team had been briefed on what to do if we got messages like that, received intimidating or threatening mail, or were confronted in any way that seemed to jeopardize our safety or that of our families, friends, teammates, or coaches. And so I contacted Coach Meyer and Officer Stacy—Officer Stacy Ettel of the University Police Department was always on hand to keep us safe—to make the coaches aware of what was happening.

By Monday afternoon, the calls were coming in constantly. My cell phone vibrated nonstop, and I had to keep it continually plugged in because the battery was dying every ninety minutes or so, without my ever picking it up at all. Hundreds of calls and text messages were being sent every hour from rabid LSU fans. Crazy, violent, or sexual messages, or all three. Really weird stuff from similarly weird senders. Some of them, but not many, were even literate.

It was such a busy week for me and for us that I simply didn't have the time to deal with getting a new phone with a new number, but I must admit, even though I was no longer taking the calls or listening to the messages, it really got me pumped up to see how much I was in the thoughts of LSU fans. I really was a concern to them and their football team, I guess. In a way it was flattering, but it got old quickly. As best I could figure, someone at LSU or in the surrounding area got my number and gave it out, and I was told that there were announcements at bars around Baton Rouge along the lines of, "This is Tim Tebow's number. Call or text him and give him a hard time."

As we were on the bus that Saturday afternoon heading into the stadium, Jim Tartt, our junior offensive lineman, reached over and grabbed my perpetually buzzing phone. He answered, at random, one of the many calls still coming in and exploded at the caller. It wasn't pretty, but I was glad I had Jim on my side. The caller probably thought it was me letting him have it. Oh well . . .

I appreciated that the guys were defensive of me—we were all in this together, and now we were headed into the unfriendly confines of LSU. When we were just a few miles out from the stadium, it started getting really crazy. The place and its proud fan base were just going nuts. Fans were banging on the side of the bus as we drove by, and as we were getting closer to the stadium, more and more people were banging on the bus. To its credit, the LSU security detail, which was assigned to us, was doing all it could do, trying to pull people away from our bus. We got down under the tunnel, and there were more of them—sitting and hanging from the stands above us, looking down and screaming at us.

I always made it a point to be the last one off the bus. As guys got off, I would stand at the top of the steps, in position to be able to shake all the players' hands as they came by and give each one a hug before they got off the bus. I was standing there hugging people and watching as Coach Meyer and the defense got off the bus. Coach Meyer was already fired up, when one of the fans, from across the ropes beyond which fans weren't allowed to venture, threw a beer on him.

Everything started to escalate after that, and I thought there would be a fight right there around the bus between their fans, our players, and our fans who had also gathered there to welcome us as we exited the bus. In the middle of this ridiculous scene were our parents who were right up there at the front of everything, along with my family, of course. If it wasn't such a potentially explosive and dangerous moment, it would have been laughable—all of this over a football game. Coach Meyer unbuttoned his jacket, dropped his briefcase, and put his hands up in the air to get us, our families, and our friends fired up. Of course, it got the LSU fans going crazy too.

From all the time I'd spent with Coach Miles during recruitment, I knew this whole display would have bothered him as much as it bothered us. It looked like it was going to be a full-fledged pregame brawl. Not exactly the type of warm-up for the game the coaches usually planned—at least for us. It was stunning, some of the things that people were saying to my parents and the parents of other players. Fans were three feet away from them, calmly cursing at them with every four-letter word and more. There were girls who'd come up to my dad and mom and direct vulgarities at them, followed by, "What are you gonna do about it?" For anyone wondering, that is *not* what I'm looking for in a spouse.

We probably used way too much energy too early in dealing with this melee. We all ran into the locker room, still dressed in our suits and much more worked up than we needed to be at this stage in the pregame process. After we got dressed and took the field, the whole pregame was so exciting. Way too exciting. The whole student section was chanting "_____ _____, Tebow," (you can fill in the blanks—but don't think churchy words) for much of the pregame, which got me even more fired up, if that was even possible. If anything, I probably did some stuff to egg it on too. My veins were coursing with adrenaline and anger, and I couldn't wait to take the field and get the game started.

Coming into the game, LSU was ranked number two in the country, but we opened the game playing like the better team, while they were playing cheap. From the outset, Tyson Jackson, Glenn Dorsey, and their other defenders that made up what some say was one of the best defenses ever in college football, were all talking trash to us, and I was loving it. When they were hitting me on an option play to make the stop, they were still trying to hit me while I was already on the ground.

We kicked a field goal on our opening drive and then held them and forced them to punt, after which we drove the length of the field again, down to their two yard line. I faked the run, bootlegged out to the left, looking for Kestahn Moore in the end zone; but he was covered. I kept running all the way to the sideline, looking for someone to come free, then I stopped and backed up for just a moment and momentarily tucked the ball. That's when the three guys around Kestahn finally stepped up for just a split second, thinking I was getting ready to run it in. At that moment Kestahn came open, and I threw it to him—pushed it into the air toward him, is probably more accurate—and he made an amazing grab around his knees for the touchdown, and the kick for the extra point put us up, 10–0.

That was one of my favorite plays of my entire career.

They scored a touchdown, and we tried to put together a drive after taking the ensuing kickoff but ended up having to punt. They had a few very long drives, keeping the chains moving and the clock running down. That was frustrating, but we still led, 10–7. We got the ball, drove to their six yard line, and called a pass play, while also anticipating a heavy blitz. Instead, they dropped back into pass coverage, blanketing our receivers, and so I kept the ball, cutting back left, and then dove into the end zone to stretch our lead to 17–7. I happened to have scored in the end zone designated as the LSU student seating area, and so I took the liberty of celebrating with my teammates right there, all of us jumping around for just a while for the benefit of our mockers. No doubt some of them had placed a call or two that week also.

I may have crossed the line, then, but it had been a long week and a long day already, and all thanks to the antagonistic attitude of the LSU crowd. I jogged over to the corner of that end zone and acted like my hand was a phone and dialed a number and yelled, "Who're you all calling now?"

For some reason, that seemed to get them even more worked up.

We got the ball to start the second half and started marching right down the field on our first few plays. Then, on a play that seemed to sum up the inconsistencies of the 2007 season, I handed off to Kestahn, our most talented running back, who had already made that fantastic touchdown catch, and at the end of a beautiful little ten-yard run he simply tripped, unforced and untouched, and fumbled the football. LSU recovered.

That got the crowd back into it, and we felt the game beginning to change at that point. They drove down the field and scored to make it

17–14 after a fake field goal, when just moments earlier we were look-ing at moving in to take a 24–7 lead. We kept fighting, though. We scored on a thirty-seven-yard pass to CI (Cornelius Ingram) on a well-designed play drawn up by our coaches. They blitzed us, and we read it and beat the blitz for a touchdown to CI, taking our lead to 24–14.

Even after they scored to cut our lead to 24–21, we had chances to put it away, but throw together a couple of drops, an off-target pass, and lining up in a wrong formation a little later, and we were punting again. They converted several fourth-down plays for first downs to keep the drive alive, and in that, their final possession, they marched down the field, scoring with just over a minute to play.

Talk about a frenzied atmosphere.

On our final possession, I ran the ball out to around the fifty, and then on the last play we had time for a Hail Mary, but I overthrew it, just past Coop's hands, and they hung on to win by a heartbreaking score of 28–24.

The game was ultracompetitive, ultraexciting, and one of my favorites to play in because of the atmosphere that surrounded every aspect of it, from the week leading up to it, the bus ride in, the rowdy stands—everything. Annoying as those phone calls were, the LSU fans made it awesome. Really. And we came away with our health, which is why I can probably be so generous with my praise for their totally unacceptable behavior in civil company.

At the same time, the loss was also devastating to me and to all of us, because we felt like we'd played one of our best games up to then. Statistically it didn't look like much—we only scored 24, and we lost—but, still, to do that against a team of their caliber was some-thing. We just needed to find a way to finish it off and win the game. It was crushing for all of us to come so close and do so many things well as a team yet just not do enough to win.

That game reminded me how the little things can change a game. That's why as a team and as the leaders on a team, you can never take the little things for granted. The things that lose games are not necessarily an individual drop or breaking a tackle or something like that—that's going to happen in every game—but what's going to change the game is an error of going the wrong way or not having the ball high and tight. Those are mental errors.

We didn't make big mistakes in that game; it was just a series of little things that tripped us up. That always gets me, because it's not for a lack of talent. It's that I didn't focus quite enough or consistently enough, didn't care enough in my mind to tell myself to do it the right way every time. And that's what was so frustrating— we had so many opportunities on both sides of the ball to do some little thing here or there to win the game. To execute a little better. To make a better block or a better read in pass coverage. On one of those fourth downs, or when they faked the field goal and got a first down, if only we could have read the play sooner and stopped it, we could have won the game. If we had executed better on any of our drives offensively, we could have won it. If we had put it in the end zone just one more time, if Kestahn hadn't fumbled, if CI hadn't gone the wrong way, if I had stepped up and made one more play, seen one more open receiver. There were so many what ifs in that game. And so many things that should never have happened. Things we gave away—they weren't taken away by better play—we just didn't execute fully when we could have.

Maybe, too, the pregame frenzy had sapped just enough of our mental edge by the time all the screaming and voicemails had stopped.

One of the biggest differences between my sophomore and junior years was that we wouldn't tolerate those little mistakes any longer. We used those experiences in 2007, like those we recounted and remembered from the LSU game, to learn and grow and get ready and better for 2008.

As dejected as I was with our inability to perform those little details that could have won the game for us, I walked away from the LSU game feeling really good. To go into a hostile arena like that at LSU, with that pregame atmosphere so thick you could cut it with a knife, to face that kind of adversity and play the way we did—fighting all the way to the end—there was something satisfying in that. And to lose because we just weren't finishing off some of the small things left me feeling confident that, with some adjustments and better attention to some of those little things, we'd be able to handle a lot of challenges from there on out.

We had a bye week before we played Kentucky, and during the bye week, Kentucky beat LSU. Go figure. We headed to Lexington the weekend of the game, and Kentucky was particularly focused on this being their second big game in a row, since it was us and they hadn't beaten the University of Florida in two decades. They were ranked thirteenth in the country at the time, and after that LSU game, we certainly weren't going to take them lightly. Their quarterback, Andre Woodson, had been playing really well for them, and they had other good offensive players and a pretty good defense to boot.

We went three and out to start the game, and then Andre Woodson threw a thirty-three-yard touchdown pass. It was clear we were in for a ballgame. If we hadn't been ready to go up until then, that was a pretty good wake-up call. When we got the ball back after their kickoff, I told Coach Meyer to give me the ball. The first play we threw an option run-pass/stretch play to the right, and I just punctured it by breaking several tackles, gaining about twenty-five yards. From that point on, we really started moving. We drove them backward down the field and closed out the drive when I threw a ten-yard touchdown pass to CI. They couldn't move the ball against our defense, and when we got the ball back, I threw a sixty-six-yard touchdown pass to a wide-open Louis Murphy. It was a lot of fun to be in a game like that with both teams playing well, and scoring. We led 21–10 at the half.

We scored on our first possession of the third quarter to make the score 28–10, and it went back and forth for a while after that. Early in the fourth quarter I carried the ball, and after a gain, I hit one of their players as I continued the run, bouncing off him and throwing me off balance; then when I reached down to put my hand on the ground to brace myself, another player hit me right on my outstretched shoulder. Right away, I could tell that the hit had done some pretty significant damage to my shoulder. I couldn't even lift my right arm. My nonthrowing arm, thank goodness.

I know my body pretty well, and as the game wore on and the pain remained, I knew this was going to nag me the rest of the season. But the pain wasn't disabling, and as we expected, it would require the standard course of treatment as any bad sprain requires.

Kentucky came back to score, cutting our lead to a single score. We needed to mount a drive, and we did. I hit Kestahn Moore in the flat for a big first down. Then we called Trick Left 51 X Pause, and they manned up on Percy Harvin. He beat the guy on an inside fade, and I hit him on the fade at their four yard line.

On the following play, I scored but paid the price again when I lowered my right shoulder to hit a guy to get in there. I remember the agony I was feeling. The sprain didn't get any better with that blow to the shoulder.

But more important, that drive and score sealed the game, as we won a close one, 45–37. The next day I had an MRI on my shoulder, and we found out that it was AC separation (acromioclavicular joint separation) and a sprain. The usual course of treatment for such an injury is icing, anti-inflammatory medication, and physical rehabilitation. I got to work, trying to rehab it and recover as quickly as possible. The problem, of course, was my inability to give either of my shoulders a lot of rest. The activities of daily living were hard enough, but then add football—well, no rest for the weary during the season.

Though I knew this could be a season-lingering injury, I was unwilling to accept that. I expected it to resolve itself and heal within moments of being diagnosed and beginning the required course of treatment. It wasn't to be—at least not as I hoped. By using my shoulder, I wasn't doing anything that would make it worse in the long term. The only issues before me were the pain level I faced and the functionality of the shoulder to be able to execute the plays. That's when I started getting shots before every game and as needed before practice to help with the healing, flexibility, and usability of my shoulder, because it was during this next week that we had to get ready to go play Georgia.

I prayed regularly for my shoulder to heal, a process which was way too slow in coming. I had a few why? moments—not so much "why me?"—but "why not go ahead and heal it now, Lord?" I wondered what lesson I was supposed to be learning through this—I thought I had gotten a bit better at patience. But the truth of the matter was that as much as I loved the scripture verse from Isaiah, I wasn't always real good at embracing it in my life:

> Yet those who wait for the LORD will gain new strength;
> they will mount up with wings like eagles, they will run
> and not get tired, they will walk and not become weary.

I get the "mount up with wings like eagles" part—I have felt His power and protection in the midst of some of the most difficult of moments—in the Philippines, at LSU, in dealing with trouble from others, and making decisions for my future—like the one that led me to the University of Florida. I get the part about "they will run and not get tired, they will walk and not become weary"; I have felt His hand on my back in moments when I didn't understand what was going on and why, and in situations where I wasn't sure I could go one step further.

But I wasn't real good at the "wait for the LORD" part. You would think that when we stop and take a look at all He has done since the beginning of time and throughout the universe—let alone in my life—it would be easy to "wait." It would be easy to understand that His timing should be our timing and that ultimately everything He does is for our benefit and our good—even though at the time it may not seem so and we may not understand. For example, my life, from fetus stage to my birth, if left to the "wisdom" of some doctor sitting before my mom and dad, would never have happened. God's timing, God's will. In my better moments I knew that.

I wasn't there yet, but in my heart I wanted to be, and day-by-day I was working and praying to get there, with Him and for Him.

The LSU and Kentucky games continued to reinforce my place in the Heisman Trophy discussion, because we had put up some big numbers against good teams. Part of the big numbers we were posting reflected all the talent around me. Another part of them may have been due to our inability to get our running backs on track, resulting in my carrying more of the running load than the coaches had originally anticipated. As the season progressed, though, it had been getting harder for me to keep up the running load, because more and more defenses were keying on me. And with my shoulder a bit dinged, it became another personal and team challenge for us to overcome.

As we were getting ready for Georgia, it was clear that my impinged shoulder had become a bit more than a slight problem. I could no longer raise my right arm above my head. The coaches wanted to try to game plan where I didn't have to run, but since without me our running game wasn't solid, that wasn't going to work. We had some good passes and play action in the game plan, so we felt confident that I wouldn't have to do too much in the way of running. Even though I wasn't close to 100 percent, it was exciting to go back to Jacksonville—my home—for the annual battle between Florida and Georgia.

We fumbled on our opening drive, and they took it down the field, scoring easily. That's when a fight broke out on the goal line, or at least that's what it initially looked like to us. We saw Georgia's players on the sideline racing onto the field as if there was a fight, but then we realized they were jumping up and down and celebrating, merely acting like Pee Wee League players. Except that I couldn't remember ever seeing any little kids actually doing that. They were celebrating, dancing all over the field and making gestures to us, the stands, and, I suppose, the national-television-viewing audience.

If we'd have been a more mature team, I think we would have handled that moment differently than we did. Instead we took it as an affront. That was frustrating to me because instead of merely taking it out on them on the field, we had some guys who wanted to go out there and respond to their goal line antics by engaging them in a fight.

It all settled down quickly enough, thanks to the referees and coaches from both teams. We took the ensuing kickoff and drove the ball right down the field, closing the drive when I hit Louis Murphy for a touchdown. Tied, 7–7. Unfortunately, Georgia had a great game plan for us on offense, which we watched throughout the afternoon as Knowshon Moreno emerged as a top college running back with 188 yards and three touchdowns. On defense, they knew I was hindered by the injury to my shoulder and couldn't be myself, so they started dropping more and more people into coverage, believing I wouldn't run very often, if at all. Eventually I started to run the ball a little, even with my shoulder, and I ended up running in one for a touchdown to finish a drive. My shoulder was killing me. It was tough. We had other guys out there for us playing with their own dings and sprains and at less than full speed or strength and with some pain. It was simply something we had to do—the only difference being that my injury was more noticeable and, as such, was highlighted more frequently by opposing coaches, players, and the media.

By halftime, I could barely lift my right shoulder at all. Toward the end of the first half I had been catching snaps with basically just my left hand. We were trying to fight and bounce back. A lot of things weren't going our way, but we were battling, and we were still right there in the game, at least for a while.

The second half produced one of the worst plays of my college career. We had a tight end post route with another player running an under route, coming underneath the post route. Their defense bit on the underneath route, so I had Cornelius Ingram wide open on the deep post. I missed him. Threw it about three yards over his head. Had I been accurate, it would have gone for at least fifty or sixty yards, if not a touchdown. Instead, we got nothing on that drive. My fault. It didn't help with turning the momentum either.

We just didn't have all we needed to make a strong statement on the field that day. We struggled to stop them on defense, with their running, primarily Knowshon Moreno, for big chunks of yardage, taking time off the clock. And also scoring at the end of the drives. We had guys who came to realize, through that game, that they were out of shape and not as disciplined as they needed to be. Unfortunately, for every guy like Louis Murphy or the Pouncey brothers, who made sure they prepared themselves and took care of themselves during the week in preparation for the game, we had some other "leaders" who didn't and who, worse, were a little too eager to stay out on Thursday nights and as a result ran out of steam in the fourth quarter. And in the end, it cost the team. Those concerns, which showed up early in the year as we headed into spring practice, were still with us. We were talented, but we had some really soft spots within the team that showed up in that game. We struggled to find what we needed and to fight through the difficult moments.

That night after the Florida–Georgia game, I stayed at home on the farm in Jacksonville with my family, and we went out to eat. I take losing hard, but being around my family has always helped put things into the right perspective. Even so, I wasn't very hungry. The next day I drove back to Gainesville with my brother Peter. It was one of the worst drives back ever for two reasons: I still couldn't get rid of the sickening feeling I had about the result of the game, how it had happened, and how frustrating it was to endure that 42–30 loss. And then there was my shoulder, which I had reinjured during the game. On both fronts I was upset and concerned. Things seemed to be heading in the wrong direction for us.

It's funny. I'm not sure that we weren't as close-knit as that 2006 team or as well prepared, but the 2006 team had mature leaders. We gutted it out, though, and turned our frustrations toward our next opponent.

Chapter Fourteen

THE HEISMAN

You are the light of the world. A city set on a hill cannot be hidden.
—MATTHEW 5:14

The following week we played Vanderbilt, who made the mistake of showing up that day. The coaches had helped us to mentally and emotionally turn the page on the previous week and had also prepared a good game plan for us. We were able to spread the ball out more to others; because of the possibility that Percy Harvin might not play, the coaches had to game plan for that possibility. Even with as great a player as Percy was for us, the tendency is to key on one person too much, which doesn't always make that person or the team better. We managed the ball very well in the Vanderbilt game, in both the turnover category and in making the necessary plays when we had to. Those are the things we needed to continue to do better as an offense.

My coaching career, if I ever have one, started that day. We had a third down and three yards to go for a first down early in the game and deep in Vandy's end of the field. As we huddled on the sidelines, they called the play, but I didn't really like the call.

"How about if we run a naked bootleg and then pass to (wide out) Jarred Fayson?" I suggested. Coach Meyer wasn't sure it would work, but he said he trusted me and to go ahead and go for it. They came out in exactly the coverage I'd had a hunch they were going to run. Fayson was wide open, made the catch, and walked into the end zone for a touchdown. Coach and I laughed about it afterward, and I gave him a hard time, telling him, "This coaching stuff isn't that hard. I like this gig. Maybe there's a coaching job for me at Florida one day."

But whether you're talking about being a coach or being a player—the thing that's hard is leadership. In the past, I have worked at casting a vision and modeling appropriate behavior, but this season, I was faced with the challenge of getting through to guys who were wired differently than I was. I had to keep finding new ways to motivate others.

South Carolina was up next. They were a good team with talented players, and we had the distraction of Percy Harvin all week. Will he play or won't he? He was having migraine headaches, and the coaches were putting together two game plans again. South Carolina had almost beaten us each of the previous two years, and we definitely weren't going to take them lightly. They had a good defense, and they could score points—especially if the "Old Ball Coach" had anything to say about it.

Speculation surrounded us all week. How bad was Percy's illness? It went right up to the last minute. We flew to Columbia without him, but there was still a hope that he could either be on another flight or someone was going to drive him up later in time to play. The coaches were concerned with not only his health, but with having to develop an alternate game plan without him, simply because he was such an explosive player.

As for me, I told Coach during our usual Friday-night talk—he and I always sat down every Friday night at the hotel to discuss the upcoming game—that we'd be fine, we'd spread the ball around more to others, and that whoever we had with us in Columbia would be sufficient to win this game.

After our talk, I got treatment on my right shoulder that night from AP—Anthony Pass, our head trainer. It was getting better, the inflammation was going down, and AP was doing ultrasound on my shoulder. He had applied the ultrasound cream to my shoulder and then had draped a towel over it while he was working on it. I wasn't paying any attention to what was happening with my shoulder, but instead I was looking away and talking to other guys who were in our training area. After a while, my shoulder started tingling and then hurting. I was surprised at how effective the ultrasound felt that night. AP pulled the towel back and looked stricken when he saw my shoulder. He just started saying, "I'm so sorry," over and over.

At that point, I saw it. There was a bad burn on my shoulder—it looked like some skin had melted away. It really started hurting about then, but I could tell AP felt terrible about it, so I said, "It's all right, man; it's not a big deal." But I knew when I put the shoulder pads on the next night it was going to be a rough night.

I certainly have made sure to remind him over the years what he did to my shoulder that night in Columbia and how dressing and playing the next day with the "sunburn" he'd laid on me was no picnic. And whenever I had the chance, I would make sure that any-one and everyone within listening distance heard the story about the "trainer-inflicted sunburn." He did so much to keep me healthy and on the field for my career that it was fun to give him grief over this accident.

In the end, Percy wasn't able to play. It was an ESPN Saturday-night game. We always loved Saturday-night television games, except this one turned out to be one of the coldest games I ever played in my college career: somewhere around game time, it was freezing. Other than the temperature, there was a really good atmosphere, a little bit like the Louisiana State game but not quite as intense or personally vindictive. Still, their fans knew that without our team's blocking a field goal at the end of the previous year's game, they would have kept us from winning the National Championship. They were giving me a hard time during pregame and I loved it. Being hassled always gets my competitive juices flowing. Some guys prefer home games, and I do love a home crowd too. However, there's something about quieting a noisy road crowd that gets me going. I had a great feeling about that game, and I had a lot of friends and family who made the trip up to support us.

On the opening drive, I scored on a third-down play, plowing into the end zone through another good-size hole our line had opened up and then ending the run on a pretty big collision too. It was one of my favorite plays that game, in no small part because my shoulder held up, despite both the separation and the burn. We went up quickly, 7–0. On their possession, they turned the ball over, and I threw a touchdown pass to Jarred Fayson, a fade route into the corner of the end zone that made the score 14–0.

From that point on, the game turned into a pretty good little shoot-out, with each of us scoring in turn. Aaron Hernandez had his coming-out party that night by having his biggest game of his freshman season. We had a chance to build a bigger lead on them but couldn't do it and instead fumbled the ball and kept them in the game.

We went into the locker room at halftime up 27–14, but they were still in the game. In the second half we stayed with our game plan and kept executing. I was so into what we were doing as a unit that I wasn't paying much attention to the score. In the fourth quarter we needed a separation score to seal the win. On fourth down and goal to go, I ran it, smashed into two guys on the goal line, and piled over them to get it into the end zone for the touchdown. We knew we had it wrapped up. Finally, we added another touchdown on a pass that I threw to Bubba Caldwell for a 51–31 win.

It was a good night for all of us. I later reminded Coach that I'd told him we'd step up even without Percy. I think it was a good growing experience for us as a team to be on the road without one of our best players against a very good team and to win. Not to mention they also had Coach Spurrier on the other sideline, who always seems to figure out a way to beat people. Their best receiver, Kenny McKinley, had a big night in receptions and yards gained, but our defense stepped up and we were fortunate to keep him out of the end zone.

After the game, a reporter asked me how it felt to score all those touchdowns. I knew we'd had a big night but didn't realize I'd had a hand in seven touchdowns—five rushing and two passing. South Carolina was the game that probably did as much to influence the Heisman voters as any game we played that year, but I didn't realize it at the time. People were talking about it, but it really didn't enter my mind. I didn't have any control over it, so I stayed focused on the next game. South Carolina was quite a game for all of us and, thanks to the rest of the guys on the team, for me personally.

The next week we continued on a roll as cohesive units on both offense and defense and beat Florida Atlantic in a game that was a tune-up for the Florida State Seminoles' visit to our place the next week. One interesting note from the FAU game is that both starting quarterbacks—Rusty Smith and I—attend First Baptist of Jacksonville. They played us tough but in the end, we won the game. Percy missed the game again.

But Percy was back for the next one, and FSU was talking their usual brand of trash all week. Of course, I was always ready to play Florida State, but having their senior weak-side linebacker, Geno Hayes, quoted as saying, "Tim Tebow is going down. We can go out there and shatter his dream," helped fuel the fire for all of us. My dream, really, was to beat FSU—badly.

For as much as they were trash talking, we forgot that they were coming in at 7–4, having finished in the middle of the pack in the Atlantic Coast Conference standings. By the time of the pregame warm-ups, they were dancing around. At least they never danced on the *F* in the center of our field—there were several of us watching for that, especially after Georgia's shenanigans on the goal line after their first score a month earlier.

On our very first drive, the referee called a false start, but we had already started the play, so I continued and rolled out to my left before they blew the whistle. After they blew it, Geno Hayes slapped me in the facemask, and then head-butted me after we had all clearly stopped, and was in my face, talking trash, with spit flying everywhere.

Not a good idea. At all. I had started out irritated with them and him, and now I was playing angry. The next play was a third down and sixteen. It was supposed to be a pass play, but nobody was open when I looked around, so I tucked the ball under my arm and ran for a long gain and a first down. Oh, and by the way, during the run I made FSU's trash talking, face-mask slapping, and head-butting linebacker, Geno Hayes, miss.

As much as I would never find myself rooting for FSU, that university and its football program have turned out some fine players and people through the years. People like running back Warrick Dunn and linebacker Derrick Brooks, both of whom I have the utmost respect for and have looked to as role models for how to live life. Warrick Dunn bought houses for families who needed them but couldn't afford them. Derrick Brooks helped children, in so many ways, to be the best they could be and took them on trips to stimulate their thirst for learning. It's hard for me to imagine either Derrick Brooks or Warrick Dunn saying or doing some of the things we experienced that day from some of those FSU players.

Although the score was still 0–0, the game was over at that point. Trust me—we knew it was over. We just kept playing for the fun of it.

We were driving, and on a play-action pass from their twenty-two yard line, I stood up after faking the handoff and saw that their defensive end had come free (unblocked) and had me in his sights. I saw him at the very last second and ducked, taking a quick look at him as he flew over my back, and then I spun out and ran it in for a touchdown. I vividly remember running right and then cutting back to the center of the field at the ten just to run over one of their defenders who was there. I did and finished the run into the end zone.

It's not often that I shy away from contact, and there are some games where I just like to go right at people. This was one of those games, and as I scored, I thought, *This is going to be a great day*.

On defense, we were flying around and hitting people. We stopped them, got the ball back, and drove down the field. I hit Louis Murphy in stride in the back-right corner of the end zone—he did a great job getting a foot down and in the end zone for the score. That was probably one of my best passes that year—and Louis was a big part of that. We went up 14–3. Then it was a bit of a back-and-forth battle, except that our defense was keeping them out of the end zone, making their only option a string of field-goal attempts.

On the next drive, I threw an out pass to Murphy, and although the ball got away from me a little, Murph made a slick, reaching, one-handed catch. We finished the drive and went up by a score of 21–6.

In the second quarter we drove down the field again and ran a Mickey (our renamed Power) up the middle from the five yard line, and while I was stiff-arming one guy in the facemask at the one yard line, and with my right hand pressed against his facemask, another guy missed me and hit my right hand, pinning it between his and the other's helmet. I felt something crack but only as I was getting up and celebrating a new lead: 28–6. I celebrated with the team but didn't tell anyone about my hand.

While we were on defense, AP came over to me, grabbed my hand, and saw my reaction. He wanted to examine my hand further, but he knew I wasn't coming out of the game anyway, so instead he sprayed a cooling spray on it. That stuff was great—the marvels of modern medicine—as it kept me comfortable and able to stay in the game. Every time I'd come over to the sideline, AP would spray it again to give me relief. Percy and I were able to do whatever we wanted to on offense, and Louis Murphy, Bubba Caldwell, and our backs had good games as well. It was really cool. When I threw a touchdown pass to Bubba Caldwell to make it 38–12, Bubba threw the ball up into the crowd—farther it seemed than I had thrown it to him. I was able to finish the game, and we dominated it in all aspects, ending up scoring some more and eventually winning, 45–12.

The last four minutes on the field, as we were running the clock out, the stands were full as the whole crowd was still there in full force and doing their thing—going just a little bit crazy. There were guys there dressed in Heisman shirts and carrying Heisman signs. The buzz seemed to be increasing about that award with each passing game. And the Florida State game was a big game to be able to play really well as a team and individually, as so many of us did—it was a wonderful feeling and night to enjoy.

After the game we went to get an X-ray of my hand and found out that it was, in fact, a complete break. I asked AP what the stuff was that he'd been spraying on it and learned that it was some sort of antiseptic, like Bactine or something.

"But what about what it did for the . . ."

AP grinned. "Nope. No medical value for breaks at all." And then he laughed.

He laughed way too long as far as I was concerned. He really enjoyed that story—I suppose it was a bit of payback for my telling the trainer-induced sunburn story so many times.

They threw a tiny wrap over my hand to keep the outside world from knowing it was broken. When they were done, we hopped into my dad's Altima and drove over to the UF track where we had our traditional family tailgate gathering with the Heavener family, good friends of my parents from their college days. My family figured out that something was not right, however, and asked what happened to my hand; they were surprised to hear that I'd broken it in the second quarter.

And so I had a night hanging out with friends and family. They kept asking if I'd rather go out and see what was going on in Gainesville that night and celebrate the big win. I preferred a quiet evening. For that quiet evening, we ended up hanging out in my buddies' apartment, playing Catch Phrase until late, watching the West Coast college football games.

The next morning a group of us headed to the Cracker Barrel at the intersection near I-75 and Archer Road in Gainesville for breakfast. There were probably eight of us—my two brothers, along with Robby's friend Angel from Miami, a couple of other buddies, and me. The hostess was kind enough to seat us in the back, but before long, someone spotted us. I enjoy interacting with folks a bunch, but sometimes a little privacy is good, because otherwise it gets hard to do just simple things—like eat and talk with family and friends. This was one of those times, as people started coming up one at a time to get my autograph.

People were bringing over napkins and whatever they could find. Then people started heading out into the gift area of the restaurant and coming back into the dining room with their bags of goodies and getting in the line that had now formed in that area of the restaurant. We spent the rest of breakfast signing.

And by "we," I mean all of us. It was funny actually. After a few minutes, somebody mistook Robby for our tight end, Tate Casey, and somebody else thought Angel was our punter, Eric Wilbur. For some reason, we never corrected the mistake, and before long, the other seven were signing as Gator players—that they weren't.

So . . . if you've got a signed University of Florida Cracker Barrel mug from three days after Thanksgiving 2007, I apologize. At least my signature on the mug is real.

When the store sold out all their Gators stuff, the manager excitedly came over to tell me. The crowd died down, and we went to pay for our meal. But the manager pointed to a man in the parking lot and told us that he'd taken care of it.

I ran out to him and thanked him and asked if he wanted anything signed. He didn't—he just wanted to give something to us. He was very gracious and said it was his way of thanking us for being good role models for his grandchildren who were attending the University of Florida. I asked if he wouldn't mind calling my father and telling him that, since it would earn me a dollar. My dad refused to pay me, saying that the character-compliment payment program of earlier in our lives had long ago expired. The character thing though—well, he fully expected that to continue.

In fact, I had to run back inside and pay for my meal, even though it had already been paid for. I'm glad I realized that, otherwise, I was going to have Jeremy Foley, Florida's athletic director, or Jamie McCloskey, UF's associate athletic director for compliance, at my door for taking "improper benefits."

That was the first game that I remember being in a whirlwind of media interest for a lot of different reasons. It was, of course, the last game of the season before our bowl game. Postseason awards were now on everyone's agenda in college football, and I was blessed to have been included in the consideration for a number of them. I had to go to Orlando for the Home Depot College Football Awards ceremony, and then on to New York the following day for the Heisman Trophy award ceremony.

As I was flying around to different places for those events and also to do things for the university, Tennessee was preparing to play in the SEC Championship Game in Atlanta—the same Tennessee team we'd beaten 59–20. That was a bit frustrating to watch, as getting to the SEC Championship Game was our primary team goal every single year, and with a 5–3 conference record—with losses to Auburn, LSU, and Georgia—that wasn't going to happen that year.

The Heisman Trophy Award ceremony was unlike anything I'd experienced before. I'd never been to New York City, and, of course, our whole family went. We received the invitation on Wednesday, had to go to Orlando on Thursday for the Home Depot College Football Awards ceremony that day, and then the Heisman ceremony was on Saturday. I was excited that my parents, Robby, Peter, Katie and Gannon, and their daughter Abby would all be able to make it, but with that late notice, it didn't look as though my sister Christy and her husband, Joey, would be able to attend since they were missionaries in Southeast Asia. Uncle Bill Heavener, who, I'm told, is not really my uncle, helped arrange extra tickets for the ceremony, and once he had them, he called Christy and Joey at 4:30 in the morning on Friday, asking if they'd like to come. There were only three flights per week from where they were, and the last one left at 7:30 that morning. Three hours off. There were two seats left on the flight, so Christy and Joey made it, along with Claire, their daughter, who was small enough to sit on their laps. Ironically, they beat my parents to New York.

We had a great time there as a family. Immediately after arriving, we gathered and Dad prayed that we would be able to let our light shine during the ceremony and throughout the weekend, win or lose. It wouldn't have been the same without my entire family, including Christy and Joey. Coach Howard and Coach Mick were there and Coach Meyer, too, who had brought his entire family. I certainly view them as part of my family as well. Our loud, gregarious group enjoyed our time with Colt Brennan, Darren McFadden, Chase Daniel, and their families—they were great.

At one point on Saturday night at a reception before the presentation ceremony, we were at the Nokia Theater with twenty-seven prior Heisman Trophy winners. We were pinching ourselves; my dad turned to me and said, "Can you believe that we're even here? And that these guys are actually talking . . . to us?"

We had so much fun, and right before the ceremony started, Danny Wuerffel, who was there as a prior winner grabbed me, took me into a room in the back, and prayed with me. It was a calming, very special moment with someone I respected, someone who had taken an interest in me since I was in high school.

It was a thrill for me—for all of us—to win. I'd spent a great deal of time thinking about what I wanted to say, about my family, my university, and my coaches and team, and my relationship with God. I received some positive comments afterward from a number of those in attendance about my acceptance speech—I don't think they realized how long I'd been practicing, from my time sharing Christ as a youngster in the Philippines to that first public speaking class with Professor Webster at the University of Florida.

That's also the time when more details of the matters surrounding my birth began to come out. Until then, Mom and Dad would simply say that it was a tough pregnancy and that they, the family, and lots of friends were praying that she would give birth to a healthy son that they would raise as a preacher. In a piece that was to air on ESPN during the Heisman Trophy ceremony, the producer kept asking me questions about the circumstances surrounding my birth, and I told her all I knew—that my parents were told to terminate the pregnancy. She was fascinated with that bit of information, and that detail made it into the Heisman show. As it turned out, a huge viewing audience saw that show, and so the story of my birth ended up generating a great deal of additional interest. It provided a platform on national television for a pro-life message, and now it provides my mom with opportunities to speak to a variety of groups all over the country.

The next morning, our group of family members who had gathered in New York to share in this moment, headed to the Tavern on the Green restaurant in Central Park on the Upper West Side of Manhattan, for brunch. We've seen over the years that, in a group setting, people always call on the minister who might be with them to pray, even though the Lord is thrilled to hear from any of us who call on Him. It's like he or she becomes the designated pray-er, the expert.

Our family's approach is different. If we're with a group, we always look for the person most likely to be uncomfortable praying in public and ask that person to pray for us. This time, it was my brother-in-law, Gannon Shepherd, who is married to my sister, Katie. Compared to us, he's simply a newer Christian, so we tried to catch him off guard. Strange sense of family humor, I know. Gannon offered a nice prayer, and it was clear he knew he was not talking to us but to God, but when he asked that the Lord "let blessings rain down," my brothers and I cracked up and spent the rest of the weekend calling out to him or in his presence, "Let it rain!" We were merciless.

Maybe not our finest moment, but what are brothers-in-law for, anyway?

Later that day, I was asked to sign memorabilia, along with the other Heisman winners who were in New York City for that weekend of festivities surrounding the Heisman Trophy Award ceremony. We found ourselves alone with Herschel Walker, the University of Georgia's great running back. That was one of the most memorable times of my college career, spending time and listening to him reminisce about how he came to attend Georgia and describe some of the highlights of his long and spectacular college and professional football career.

It was even more special for us because my dad had always held Herschel out as the weight-free model for me to aspire to be like in my exercise and weight-training programs, when I was still too young to lift weights: "Remember, Herschel Walker became the best player in America by doing push-ups and sit-ups, just like you are . . ." I can still hear him today.

I'd heard people say that we had beaten Ohio State the year before because Troy Smith, their quarterback who had won the Heisman, had gained fifteen pounds on the banquet-speaking circuit afterward. I don't know if that was true or not, but if it was, I was very motivated to not let anything like that happen to me even though it was very easy to see how it could. I had to take the eating easy, because my exercise regimen declined considerably with my travel. I ended up only practicing a little bit for the University of Michigan, the team we would face in the Capital One Bowl in Orlando, because of my broken hand. But I was still catching balls with my left hand and throwing them back with the same hand, of course, in practice.

I was also doing the banquet circuit, however. I was a Walter Camp All-American, won the O'Brien Award (where we got to hang out with Troy Aikman), the Maxwell Award, the first of two ESPYs, and won the Sullivan Award as the best amateur athlete, which hadn't been won by a football player since Peyton Manning ten years earlier. All were terrifically fun, and we made some great friendships. The Barbosas, who administered the Walter Camp Award, stayed in touch and ended up coming down to Gainesville for games the next season.

We also received a letter from a family who said that their son had accepted Christ after watching my Heisman acceptance speech. That made all the hectic pace of the travel worth every minute.

When we arrived in Orlando for the Capital One Bowl against Michigan, we had a pretty full schedule of events and appearances. Bowl games can be a lot of fun, but they also can wear you out, because the bowl organizers ask for so many appearances. Some days are so tightly scheduled that you go from one appearance to another to another. Mix in a little practice and then wonder why at the end of the day you collapse exhausted in bed. And I still was having trouble practicing. Being hurt and not at full strength was frustrating.

That year, the Bowl organizers had arranged for our entire team to go to a theme park two nights before the game, but I wasn't going to go. I still get dizzy on roller coasters, so I figured it was a good night to stay in my room and get some much needed rest. Right before they left, though, Officer Stacy called me in my room and said that the head of the amusement park had been calling for the last hour trying to get me there. Officer Stacy didn't want to put any pressure on me but was simply passing along their request.

"They just want to meet you," Stacy said. "They also want you to come in so they can actually advertise to the world and say that you're there—that's it."

I have a really hard time turning people down, which, depending on the situation, can either be a good or bad quality. And so I quickly got dressed and went to meet them, but I knew that if they asked me to get on a ride, I'd tell them I get motion sickness. Once I arrived, they were so excited that I was there that—you guessed it—they asked me to please try out their new ride, that it was awesome. I looked to Officer Stacy for help, and he tried, but I finally agreed to go for a ride on it. The head of security and the guy managing the ride that night went with me, and we skipped past all those waiting in line and ended up at the front of the line at the new roller coaster.

Even worse was that because of being able to get to the front of the line, we were on the front row of the front car of the new roller coaster—all of which I feared was bound to bring on one of my dizzy spells.

I knew this was going to be bad. Very bad. As we took off, I was gripping the bar tightly as the roller coaster began by not only taking us up, but also rolling around and around as it climbed. Over and over, around and around the new—and I'm sure fabulous—ride went for what had to be the longest roller-coaster ride ever. When we finally pulled in after enduring the ride, standing there was an array of folks sporting cameras, taking pictures, and shouting "Tebow . . . Tebow . . . Tebow."

I said, anxiously yet as calmly as I could, "Officer Stacy, I'm going to throw up everywhere. The faster you can get me out of here, the better chance the theme-park folks don't see me throwing up all over the place after a trip on their new ride."

As we walked out, I was throwing up behind my clenched teeth until we got around the corner. I couldn't hold it any longer. I got past the end of the line of people and just took off and sprinted about twenty yards until I got behind the nearest building where I began to throw up. I was trying to catch my breath, and my head was spinning like crazy. We stood there for about twenty more minutes, and Officer Stacy kept people away from that corner because I'd been throwing up the whole time. It was horrible. The management people came by and apologized for putting me through that, and I politely said, "No, it's okay. It's an unbelievable ride."

They poured cold water over me. My shirt was soaked; I was a wreck. I threw up all the way back in the police car. Officer Stacy finally got me back to my hotel room, put me into my bed, and turned out the lights. It was one of the most horrible nights of my life. I just can't do roller coasters, or Ferris wheels, or the like. I can barely do bumper cars.

Meanwhile, my whole family was there for the Capital One Bowl game, and they all had a great time while I was off at appearances and practice. As for the game, it was a strange one. Michigan had a good game plan. They rolled up over five hundred yards of offense with Chad Henne at quarterback in what was Coach Carr's last game, and the 41–35 loss we suffered was a disappointing way to end our season.

With an ending like that, there was no denying that we had work to do. It had been an up-and-down season in which we beat two of our three archrivals (Tennessee and Florida State), had some great games, and won some great awards, but overall there was a little bit of emptiness and regret because we knew we could have done much better. We knew we left some wins on the field. And it left a lot of reasons for all of us to move into the next off-season with a brand-new motivation to be the best that we could possibly be.

Personally, even though it had been a thrill to win the Heisman and the other awards, our not having a better season as a team diminished the luster. I would continue to work hard, as always, and continue to cast a vision for the other guys. And I was hoping it would connect with the guys in 2008 in a way it hadn't in 2007.

Chapter Fifteen

DOING THE RIGHT THING

Since we have so great a cloud of witnesses surrounding us, let us also lay aside every encumbrance and the sin which so easily entangles us, and let us run with endurance the race that is set before us, fixing our eyes on Jesus, the author and perfecter of faith, who for the joy set before Him endured the cross, despising the shame, and has sat down at the right hand of the throne of God.

—HEBREWS 12:1–2

I had been thinking about it for a while, but the first time I mentioned it to anyone else was at a small diner off Times Square. We were in New York for the Heisman awards ceremony in December of 2007, which was a couple of days off. After an official dinner, Zack Higbee and I headed out for more to eat.

"I want to use my profile to raise money to help children," I told Zack. He didn't seem surprised. I told him I thought I could use the platform God had given me to raise some money in and around the Gainesville area because of all the folks who knew me there. I was constantly asked to make appearances and sign autographs, and maybe there was a way to leverage that notoriety to raise money to support the orphanage we started in the Philippines.

When faced with the opportunity to make a difference, I know that those who become involved in positive ways in orphans' lives are themselves blessed. And from that involvement, the kids begin to understand how important they are. Once they begin to be helped, fed, clothed, educated, nurtured, cared for, and loved, they start to become the children and eventually adults that God intended them to be when He created them.

I truly believe that the God who loves me also looks at orphans as extremely special. Over and over, my parents showed us how the Bible talks about taking care of widows and orphans. God created each one unique, with gifts and abilities like no one else, for His purposes in this world. Being able to explain that to orphans is an amazing experience, to tell them God's story, like: "The best dad out there—God—loves you so much and wants to adopt you into His family." I've always found this to be the best, most encouraging thing you can tell an orphan, that we're all adopted into the family of God. Follow it up with a long hug, and then a lifetime of caring and commitment so that they have a chance to become all that God created them to be.

Not long after our bowl game against Michigan, Zack and I sat down with Jamie McCloskey, Florida's senior associate athletic director of compliance, to make sure we were allowed to do what I was hoping to do. The University of Florida and Jamie were a great to help me. They did not have to help me, and yet they spent countless hours working through the NCAA rules about what an athlete can do to raise money. There are a ton of rules even if it is for something worthwhile like a charity. We ended up partnering with the sororities on campus to put on a Powder Puff Football Tournament to raise funds for both Uncle Dick's Home in the Philippines as well as a number of local charities. We wanted the students to feel a real connection to their efforts, and we decided that raising some of the money for identifiable local charities would give them that connection.

We called it First and 15, and the tournament was scheduled to follow the Orange and Blue football game in April. We prayed that it wouldn't rain . . . but it did. Still, we had a tremendous time, raising over $13,000 for the designated charities. We were pleased, considering it was our first effort. Ryan Moseley, Florida's student-body president, and David Sinopoli, a marketing guru, headed the group that was making it all happen. The three of us met with all the sororities on campus to encourage them to partner together and with us for this worthwhile effort.

At a fancy banquet, the sorority that raised the most money and brought the most girls had the first selection of a Florida football player to be their coach. Percy Harvin went first, while the Pounceys went together to the second sorority. As for me, I couldn't be chosen since I was the head.

As a result of a number of things we learned, and by getting others on campus involved, we were better positioned for an even more financially successful event the next year. Not only had we been through it once, but the TriDelt that single-handedly carried her team to victory, Beth, was so excited about First and 15 that she volunteered to head it up for 2009.

Back on the football field, the team that was getting ready for the 2008 season looked a lot different than the 2007 team. Our workouts were crazier, and the internal competitions were far more intense. In fact, the previous year didn't even begin to compare to what the team was doing in 2008. Not even close. We knew we had a different team.

Simply put, we seemed to have a better, more committed bunch of guys. When you've got a core group that believes in the cause, shares the values and vision of the team, and is dying to win a championship, then you have the right chemistry to go all the way. Strong leaders encourage you to do things for your own benefit, not just theirs. And with the right kind of encouraging, equipping, and passionate and visionary leadership, the people who are still sitting on the fence will eventually get off and start working hard, going to class, putting forth an effort, and watching film. Or they will quit. Either way the result is good for the team. That's because the team is now left only with members who are all pulling together in the same direction, believing in the vision, and willing to do what it takes to achieve it.

Along the way, they also have a positive influence on one another. They indeed begin to do the right thing.

We had more of that, and more team members who were leading by example. This time around, when it got hard, guys weren't quitting or doing stupid stuff. That made a big difference, especially on the defensive side of the ball. Brandon Spikes became a leader others were willing to emulate. He always loved to play football, to hit people, but he wasn't a big fan of everything else—all the stuff it took to be even better than you naturally were: lifting, running, and training. Although Spikes was gifted enough that he could get away without doing all of that, all those other guys couldn't. They naturally couldn't play like he could. When the coaches got Spikes to buy into being a leader, work even harder, and realize that others on the team were watching, that was an important breakthrough for the 2008 team. That's when Brandon began to realize his God-given potential—not just to be good but to be the best he could be—and that's when we began to see the potential in that 2008 football team.

Once a week for the entire season, Coach Mick had a leadership group meeting during which he'd share a story or tell how we could do something to improve the team. He was also looking for input into ways we felt we could make the team better. Throughout the season, the leadership group meetings set out and defined a lot of things that the team ended up doing that year—from preparing for games to interacting with one another to growing into being the best we could be. The group also encouraged guys to take a step of faith and move up in the leadership role. Spikes was initially a reluctant leader, but he stepped forward, learned, and grew into it; as a result, he helped others become better on and off the field. The Pounceys were natural leaders and were so encouraging and caring that others just naturally wanted to follow their example of hard work and striving toward excellence.

The whole team began to bond and was working extremely hard individually and together. The Saint Valentine's Day Massacre—as it was affectionately called—was such a hard workout conducted, of course, in February, that it became a thing of legend and an immediate bonding experience. It was so difficult that Omarius Hines had his knee swell up and the trainers and medical staff had to cut into his leg to drain the fluid that had accumulated. It was a big deal. And throughout it all, people were saying, *"We're not going to lose in the fourth quarter."* You could see a change in the team that was tangible and inspirational. Months later, when we converted on fourth down on offense, or stopped them on third down on defense, we had actually already assured that achievement during our off-season workouts many months earlier.

We did Midnight Lifts in the summer that were particularly rigorous. And, of course, at midnight. We had the Saint Valentine's Day Massacre, the Harley Davidson Workout, and a few other Friday workouts that were particularly hard. The Friday workouts in the off-season were usually the hardest. We also held an annual strength competition that I made sure to win, including my freshman year over Brandon Siler.

Some of the workouts screamed accountability while also working our bodies to the point of exhaustion. We'd each have a partner, and our exercises and the length and intensity of them would be linked to how our partner performed. For instance, Coach Mick would make one guy of a particular partnership push a forty-five-pound plate, flat on the floor, around the perimeter of our weight room. And it's a big weight room. Very big. Because the guy pushing the weight around was bent at the waist, it was working his legs, as well as his shoulders and back, among many other areas.

He was always working on his speed, too, because when he began, his partner was doing a seated wall squat with a sandbag on his thighs. The partner pushing the forty-five-pound plate around the floor of the weight room, therefore, wanted to go as fast as he could so his partner holding the sandbag on his thighs, in an excruciating wall squat, could get some relief as soon as possible. And he couldn't move from that squat until his partner returned from pushing the weight around the room.

Accountability. That would carry over onto the field throughout this season, which at the moment was beginning to have all the earmarks of being very special.

Coach Mick loved those sorts of workouts.

Other workouts would take place when just Coach Mick and I were working on our own and he'd be naming off other quarterbacks in college football, saying, "Do one for him . . . do one for him. Do one more for Stafford. Do one more for Bradford. And one more for McCoy."

Those workouts always gave me more confidence, because they consisted of things I either wouldn't do on my own or wouldn't even consider doing because they hurt so badly. But I would do it for Coach Mick. And in the process of going beyond where I thought I could go, I started to develop more confidence in my ability and the stamina to handle whatever I might face—be it in a game, a classroom, or any other setting. There's no way I would have accomplished the things I have in my career if I hadn't trained like that and always pushed myself to do something beyond what I'd done before.

It wasn't all work during the spring preparation for the 2008 season. I also had classes, of course, and other stuff. One weekend in the spring, Robby got a call from one of the guys with Rascal Flatts, telling him they'd be in Tampa with Darius Rucker and asking if we'd like to come. We had met them on a prior trip they'd made to Jacksonville for a concert, and we had become friends with them.

I could hear the guy, Gary LeVox, as Robby was talking with him, and I was yelling, "Tell him yes! Darius Rucker is awesome!" In the meantime, Gary was telling Robby that Darius was a fan of mine and was hoping to meet us; so we headed down there to play golf—me, Robby, and Bryan Craun, a friend from Jacksonville—and meet up with Darius Rucker and Rascal Flatts.

As it turns out, Darius is very competitive on the golf course and was more than willing to pop off about his alma mater, the University of South Carolina. We had a good time on a beautiful day, with views looking out over Tampa Bay. That night we went to the concert and sat on the edge of the stage. Darius pulled me out at one point to join him on a song—anybody who heard me sing "I'm Still a Guy" onstage with Brad Paisley knows that I prefer staying in the background at concerts, but as always, we had a fun night.

Chapter Sixteen

AN INAUSPICIOUS START

From everyone who has been given much, much will be required; and
to whom they entrusted much, of him they will ask all the more.
—LUKE 12:48

All summer, I kept the workouts going—even when I traveled for a combination of mission trips and vacations for a total of three weeks that off-season. I was able to do it because my brothers helped me with the workouts at every stop on the trip; I was not about to lose the edge I'd built up with my teammates in the spring. And so I trained in London, Croatia, Bosnia, Thailand, the Philippines, and in the airport terminal in Frankfurt, Germany. Seven countries in three weeks, if you include the United States. Our workouts consisted of exercises with whatever equipment we could find: stairs, chin-up bars, or rough mountain roads. The materials for the workouts didn't matter; what mattered was making sure that I got them in.

Even more important than training is having the mind-set to want to do it. Coach Mick let me borrow a book called *The Edge.* He keeps reminding me to give it back—I'm sure I will . . . one of these days. The book is full of great motivational quotes, like "The Man in the Glass." During a workout, Coach Mick would say, "Are you going to regret what you see in the mirror tonight?" I worked harder.

Coach Mick and I had a really unique relationship. You might think that because I won the Heisman I could do most anything I wanted. Instead, I found that if everyone else worked out a certain way and for a certain time and number of reps, I felt as though, to be worthy as a leader, I would have to double their efforts. Coach Mick encouraged that side of me, but then he'd take it even further because that's just the way he'd push me. If I ever made an excuse that I'd already done more than anybody else, he'd respond with, "Oh, so you only want to be as good as everybody else."

It was hard to tell which one of us was more obsessive than the other.

Working like that gives you such a confidence to be able to overcome anything you face. You really are overpreparing and readying yourself for any eventuality. You don't care how hard you get hit, because you've already faced harder situations over and over while working out or practicing. By overcoming all those, I knew I was more prepared to overcome whatever I faced. Coach Mick often preached to me about a quote from Michael Jordan, and being willing to take a risk:

> *I've missed more than nine thousand shots in my career. I've lost almost three hundred games. Twenty-six times, I've been trusted to take the game-winning shot and missed. I've failed over and over and over again in my life. And that is why I succeed.*

As this chapter's opening scripture says, to whom much is given much is expected. I've heard that scripture since I was a young boy. There's a spiritual aspect to that, of course, which we read about in the story of the talents in Matthew 25:14–30. The basic lesson of the parable for me is that if God gave us specific talents (abilities), He wants us to maximize our talents and not bury or waste them. He wants us to go out there and double them. I think part of that is to go out there and continue to work—regardless of whether anyone is watching. This isn't just about when we're out there with cameras rolling and pointed in our faces. I may say I'm playing for my Lord and Savior, Jesus Christ. True. But it's not just that. It's about going out every day, in every setting, and working hard. It's about being dedicated and playing hard because I honestly believe that God receives joy when He sees me doing that with the skills he blessed me with. When you, too, do that, He sees you living the life He has given you and loving and respecting the abilities He's given you by working as hard as you possibly can to improve them.

In middle school, my mom assigned me to do a report on Eric Liddell, of *Chariots of Fire* fame. I was impressed by his courage of convictions, and I really identified with his statement, "I believe God made me for a purpose, but he also made me fast. And when I run I feel His pleasure." I always thought since God gave these gifts to me, my role in that exchange was to play as hard as I could and continue giving Him the honor and glory for it. To me that would be the very best way of thanking Him for the ability. If I didn't work as hard as I knew I could, then I think it would be a little bit like saying, *"God, thanks for giving me this ability, but I don't really care about it. I'm going to do something else, and I'm not going to work quite as hard."*

As you can probably guess, my view leads to constantly evaluating my performance and the performances of those I count on. I was two things to this team: a leader and a Christian. As a leader, I needed to be in front and set an example. As a Christian, I needed to lead in a manner that was pleasing to Christ. This ethic can lead to conflict if those around me do not agree.

A good example of this conflict came when I was a freshman. The team was running the stadium steps one morning around six o'clock. We always began our workout when it was still dark in the Swamp. I was determined to finish first; however, to make it more meaningful, I wanted to start in the back. As I would pass each player going up the stadium steps, I would encourage them to push harder. One teammate was offended by my comments. He gave me a real bad look and said he was doing what he thought was right. I kept going and finished a long time before he did. In the locker room, and well after everyone else had gone, I asked why he was not running any harder.

To my surprise, he used God in his explanation. He said, "God told me this morning to stay back and run with this guy because I needed to encourage him."

To be honest, I was livid. Here was a very talented athlete, a team leader, and an outspoken Christian believing God wanted him to be a bad example to the team. You can see the conflict in our thinking.

I may have overstepped, but as a leader and fellow Christian, I felt I needed to confront him. I told him that he was being extremely lazy and inappropriately using God as an excuse. "If you want to bring God and spirituality into this, then you need to obey the authorities that God has put into your life. Coach Mick and Coach Meyer are your authorities, and to not work hard after they specifically told everyone to do so, and called you out about your low effort, is wrong. Because they told you that, it is not acceptable to say that God told you to stay back and run with someone to influence or encourage him."

After pausing to let all this sink in, I added, "Maybe if you ran harder, you would influence that person to run harder himself. You are not being a good leader to anyone by being lazy, and using God as an excuse is unacceptable."

If this incident on the stadium steps was the only example of this attitude, I would not have mentioned it. Though it sounds harsh to say, I feel this guy's public walk was not matching his talk at all. He was always inviting guys to go to church but as a couple of us would tell him, "We need you to go to class because there are many guys here who will follow the example you set and do what you do, or don't do. So if you begin to do the right thing, they, in turn, will begin to do the right thing by following you." He would sleep in and arrive late to meetings or miss class and use the excuse that he was up late at a Christian meeting on campus. Then, his entire running group on the football team would have to run extra as punishment because he missed class. Everyone in the group knew the truth, and having to run for his lack of commitment and his lack of integrity did not sit well with them.

We had several talks after that incident on the stadium steps, but he never changed his attitude, and I never viewed his lackadaisical approach or religious excuses as acceptable.

Similarly, we'd be in the weight room and Coach Mick would tell us to do fifteen reps. I'd stand behind this guy, and he'd do twelve, then stop; I'd ask if he did them all, and he'd say, "Yeah."

In general, I don't care for cheaters and liars, but I have a much higher standard for people who profess to be Christians. This guy was a particular challenge for me. Part of leadership is understanding those we are trying to lead—what makes them tick, what will help them share the vision—and I simply never got to that position where I understood him. To me, our Christian witness matters, and it's what people see when they are watching us. When we think we can do less than our best, when we think others are not watching, we're cheating ourselves and the God who created us.

To me, the best example for being tough and bold and being a Christian is, of course, demonstrated by my Savior, Jesus Christ. It's important to stand behind what you believe in, and sometimes there are some judgment calls to be made—I understand that. Growing up, there were always those people who didn't think that my parents should let me play sports because I sometimes missed Sunday-night church when I was in a championship game, or I would go to Wednesday-night football practice instead of Wednesday-night church service. But no matter where I was physically, my parents were always working on my heart and trying to balance that with the right amount of fellowship and growth.

This team member became a burden on my heart that never really changed. Coach Meyer could never get through to him, either, and I know it weighed on him too. So much potential wasted. As you can tell by now, this guy's attitude was driving me crazy, and if it had been up to me, you can imagine he probably wouldn't have been on our team if he hadn't changed his ways.

In the meantime, however, we had other guys who were learning about matters of faith and growing in that faith. They were going to be accountable to do what was right, to do their best, because they cared about the persons next to them. I know that is a lot of what Jesus would have talked about and actually did talk about.

When I was growing up, my parents knew how competitive I was and how I always wanted to win, so they tried to point out that truth within the teachings of Christianity as well. They challenged me to win rewards in heaven and to compete for those, so God will say, "Well done, My good and faithful servant." Whatever you do, do it with all your heart.

From the time we were very young, Mom and Dad would talk to us about sticking up for someone who was being bullied, talking to someone whom no one else would talk to, or befriending a kid who wasn't popular at church. My parents would see us trying to do those things and would reinforce those behaviors by telling us that God will honor that action of showing His love to others as much as anything else we might do for Him. I think we should hear a lot more of that in church, or perhaps we do and I missed those times. Things like encouraging the guys who are down after practice, or talking to a kid who's sick, or making friends with the kids who aren't cool, even though it's not your first reaction. Most of the time you end up having better relationships with those kids and you find out they really are cool.

In spending time talking to sick kids, I find that I get more joy in those moments than I could have imagined. Usually, you kind of go in because you think it's right and assume they will be better for the time you spent with them. But then when you leave, you find yourself thinking, *That wasn't the right thing just for* him, *it was the right thing for* me. And you leave better and blessed.

I also have a heart for people who can't defend themselves or are not really good in sports. They tend to be taken advantage of and mistreated—bullied even. I try to stand up for them as I've always thought that's the right thing to do. If God has given me the strength and the courage to play sports, the least I can do is stand up for the people who don't have others to do it for them. That applies to any setting—whether it's a Sunday-school class or a sports team, the worst player on the team or the best player having a bad day. That's what my dad always said to us: try to make others feel how important they are, and find a way to make them feel involved in whatever you and your friends are doing. The message to us in living life was always about simply doing the right thing. That honored God.

And doing all those things that your coach or your parents or others in authority had asked you to do would also be honoring God. Doing what is right and doing what others in authority ask you to do demonstrates a way of treating other people the way you want to be treated.

By the time fall was upon us, all our preparation was paying off in the confidence we had in our strength, stamina, and ability. We were ready to start the season—hungrier than we'd been all of last year. We opened the season with Hawaii, but unfortunately, it was a home game. Talk about a missed opportunity.

Last year, leading up to the Heisman, June Jones, their head coach, was trying to pay a compliment to his quarterback, Colt Brennan, but in the process, he singled me out and not necessarily in a complimentary way. On ESPN one day I heard Coach Jones say that I was just a "system quarterback." I wasn't sure why he felt the need to label me and diminish my play, but he later said that wasn't what he was trying to do at all. In any event, I was looking forward to playing against his team. Unfortunately, he took the head job at Southern Methodist University before we had the chance to play Hawaii.

It was probably for the best.

We didn't play particularly well against the Warriors from the Islands, but we still won, 56–10. Interestingly, most teams talk trash—at least a little. Not these guys—not one word. We were a little concerned because we were playing Miami the next weekend. We weren't quite there in our execution: my timing with the receivers, my accuracy, or our connection. Fortunately, the defense played very well.

I did suffer a setback, however. Early in the game when I went to throw a block, a guy ducked as I lunged to hit him. I'm not sure how it all unfolded, but I rolled over him onto the ground, and he then ran over my right shoulder, the same one I'd hurt against Kentucky, and as a result I reaggravated the injury. I was so mad at myself. I had an AC sprain again, starting from the third play in the 2008 season.

I knew God had a plan for it, but it was a little bit frustrating to be going through this again, especially on such a freak play. It was irritating to start the year hurt on a block, of all things.

Still, I tried to look past the injury and just focus on our next game: Miami. Both teams were fired up for this game, and during the pregame warm-up I used so much energy that I had to regroup and regather myself to get a second wind. Maybe it was because of this excitement or maybe it was just the mood I was in; Miami was the first time I ever wrote a Bible verse beneath my eyes. I was getting ready to put on eye black before the game and trying to decide whether to wear the black paint stuff or the black patches that are like stickers. I thought maybe I could use a Sharpie to write a Bible verse on the eye black if I used the patches—I figured that black paint would just make a total mess.

I wasn't even sure if people would be able to see it, but I thought if they could, it might be a really simple way to share a great Bible verse with some folks in the television-viewing audience. And if somebody noticed and asked me about it, I'd have a chance to talk about things of real significance beyond football.

The first verse that came to mind was one of my favorites, Philippians 4:13: "I can do all things through Christ who strengthens me." That was perfect to summarize my approach to football, and it seemed like a good verse to go with the first time out of the box. Paul's point is that Christ gives us the ability to be content with a little or a lot.

I wrote it on the eye-black patches and wore the patches into the game. I don't remember that it got a lot of attention, and I really hadn't given any thought to whether I would do it again. As I recall, a few reporters asked me about it after the game. And so I continued to write Philippians 4:13 on the eye-black patches all through the rest of the season. Actually, I wrote PHIL under my right eye and 4:13 under my left—occasionally I'd have someone ask who Phil was and what that number had to do with him. And even that question gave me a chance to talk about things of eternal significance.

On the opening drive against Miami we made some good plays to move the ball down the field, and I eventually hit Aaron Hernandez in the corner of the end zone for a touchdown. But it was all uphill from there, a tough game. They made some big plays and kept it somewhat close, but we played pretty well and managed to stay ahead, largely due to Aaron Hernandez who had a great game.

Because it was early in the season, we were still getting used to who was doing what. In the off-season, we never fully know who our playmakers will be and who will emerge as focal points of the team. The year before, Louis Murphy had a good year, but he had been more of a Z receiver, while Bubba Caldwell, who was a senior, was the X receiver. The Z receiver is the one who lines up on the same side of the offensive line as the tight end (called the strong side of the line). The X receiver is the receiver who lines up on the other side of the offensive line—or on the weak side. The Y receiver is, in fact, the tight end himself. This year, with Bubba no longer on the team, Murph was going to slide into the X position, and the real question was: will Murph be able to handle the X position? He ended up being tremendous. We knew that Percy Harvin would continue to be great again this season, but we didn't know who else would step up.

The next question was: who was going to be the primary running back? Jeff Demps, Emmanuel Moody or Chris Rainey? The Miami game also gave us an opportunity to see who was going to step up, especially when we had the game somewhat under control. Murph stepped up and made some big plays from the wide-out position and put the game out of reach in the end. He scored on a corner pattern, which came right after a fifty-yard touchdown that was called back for an illegal man downfield. The play was a good response by our offense to the penalty.

As for Murph, he'd been very good my sophomore year, but in that Miami game you could see he really was staking a claim to being the go-to guy in the 2008 season. His leadership and passion and, more than anything else, his competitive excellence would end up making a mark throughout that season. Miami was a big win for us and my only time to play against them, so I certainly didn't want to miss this opportunity to come out on top. I wanted to make certain we did everything we needed to do to end up with a victory. I already had an 0–2 record against Auburn; I didn't need any more winless records against rivals. The defense played well once again, holding them to only three points and 140 yards of total offense. Our 26–3 win was a total team effort—we scored early and finished up by scoring late.

The next week we played Tennessee in Knoxville. The year before we'd beaten them pretty badly in the Swamp, so we knew they were going to come in motivated to turn that around. At the same time, they were the ones who won the SEC East Division the previous year, not us. We drove down the field and scored on our first possession of the game on a pass to Aaron Hernandez. We led 20–0 at the half, and Tennessee's only points against our defense came on a Jonathan Crompton one-yard run in the second half, as we eased to a 30–6 win. It's always good to win an SEC game, but it's particularly big when you can go to Neyland Stadium in Knoxville with their 110,000 fans and come away with a big win.

We had gotten through a tough early stretch and thankfully had a bit of a breather ahead, with Ole Miss coming into the Swamp.

Chapter Seventeen

THE PROMISE

*Consider it all joy, my brethren, when you encounter various trials,
knowing that the testing of your faith produces endurance.
And let endurance have its perfect result, so that you
may be perfect and complete, lacking in nothing.*
—JAMES 1:2–4

We trailed in the overall series with Ole Miss by one game and would
even it with a win. But more important than any history, we'd move
to 2–0 in the conference for 2008. We were starting to play pretty
well on offense, and we were looking to match the defense's continuing high level of play in this week's game.

However, for some reason, we seemed to be in a funk the whole
game. It's hard to even explain. We started out fine—moved the ball
fairly well, scored some points, and went up 17–7 at halftime. Not
a great half for us in what we anticipated would be a game that
we controlled much more, but we were still leading. Usually there'd
be a point in the second quarter where the internal switches would
flip to On and we'd automatically feel some additional drive, get
the momentum, and score a touchdown, or the defense would stop

them, and then we'd begin to go about dominating them. But in the Ole Miss game we never felt that click or anything similar. Several times I thought we'd start blowing them out, because we really were better than they were. It was easy playing against them. Maybe that was the problem.

Honestly, it's hard to even explain some of the things that happened in that game.

In the second quarter, we ran a shovel pass that turned out to be a great call by the coaches. It caught Ole Miss off guard. After his catch and run for a thirty-yard gain, Aaron Hernandez fumbled—our first turnover of the year. In the third quarter, on a read play, I was supposed to read the defensive end and the guy he commits to defend (me or the running back) to determine whether to hand the ball to the running back or fake the handoff and keep it. Brandon James and I both let go of the ball, and it fell to the ground. The defensive end—who himself had a read on everything that was happening—recovered our miscue on our own eighteen yard line. That was the only time I fumbled on a handoff exchange in my entire career at Florida.

We knew we were so much better than they were, but we weren't playing like it. Usually we found a way to win, but we struggled to find one that day. Near the end of the game they scored on a long touchdown pass thrown by Jevan Snead to go up 31–24. The Swamp was silent.

We got the ball back, and I felt that there was no chance they would stop us now—we were going to will the ball down the field. I was right. We drove the ball right down the field for the tying touchdown, but the extra point that we needed for the tie was blocked. The score was 31–30.

We got the ball back again with only a little bit of time left. Again, we felt like we could move the ball. We hit a few passes, things seemed to be going great, but then we missed a couple of passes. Then on a third-down play to the left that I pitched out on at the last second, I thought for certain we'd have the first down. Instead, we came up just short, and it was fourth and one from their thirty-two yard line.

It was the ballgame at that moment. Instead of trying a long field goal—it would have been a forty-nine-yard attempt—Coach called my number on a short yardage play, and Ole Miss made a great call. They slanted the defensive front right side of the line into our play call, blitzed the linebackers right into it, and blitzed the cornerback off the edge of the defense.

There might have been three or four times in my four years that I was stopped on a short-yardage play. Unfortunately, that was one of them.

To this day, I still don't think that team should've beaten us or taken our undefeated season from us. And certainly not at home in the Swamp.

Some fluke things occurred that you have to attribute to our ineffective execution—like my fumbled handoff to Brandon. And Mississippi did a nice job taking advantage of the opportunities as they arose. But going into that game, we felt like we controlled our destiny, and we did, but when we arrived, we could tell that for whatever reasons we simply weren't mentally or emotionally prepared—any of us. I can't explain it, but I can tell you this: from my position and role on the team, I felt largely responsible for our falling short in the outcome.

Walking off the field, I couldn't believe we'd lost. Our only stated goal from the coaches was to win the SEC East and play in the SEC Championship Game, but for us players . . . we also wanted an undefeated season, which had never happened at Florida. That was now gone—the end result of a game we should have won. We might still be able to win the SEC East, or even the National Championship, but we had a loss.

Coach Meyer's comments to us afterward were positive, but I was struggling with the loss. The players got dressed.

I sat alone in my locker for about forty-five minutes, replaying the game over and over in my head. This wasn't supposed to have happened. We had spent countless hours over the summer on our own, and then with the coaches in the August heat, to accomplish something that no Florida team had ever accomplished: a perfect season. Now, with an awful second half against a determined, opportunistic Ole Miss team, that undefeated season wasn't going to happen.

Our Sports Information Department folks kept coming in to ask if I was ready to face the media. Coach Meyer sat right in front of me with his back to me and leaned back against my knee. We sat quietly for quite a while and barely spoke. I knew the media was waiting, but Zack Higbee knew what was going on and was buying extra time for me. I was still crying off and on, and when I thought that I'd finally pulled myself together enough to face the press, I broke down again. I sat there while Coach gave me a hug, doing his best to console me.

Frustrated doesn't begin to capture how I felt, although that was part of it. I probably went through the five stages of grief a few times in that short period of time: denial, anger, bargaining, depression, and acceptance. Initially in what must have been the denial and anger stages, I felt betrayed, that my teammates hadn't risen to the level we needed. That we hadn't brought a level of competitiveness, with a work ethic and game-day focus to match, to the contest that day.

The more I reflected on it, however, the feeling of betrayal faded. The problem lay with me, not them. They had all played hard, but it hadn't been enough. The only thing I could ever control was me and my effort, and I decided that I had been the one who let us down. I took a few minutes to gather my thoughts, and then I got up and began to head out of the locker room with Coach Meyer and Zack to face the media.

In my mind I wasn't going to make a big deal about this press conference. I simply felt embarrassed and ashamed because I felt I'd personally let the Gator Nation down. I simply wanted to make a little apology to the fans and not make a big deal out of this press conference. So I thought about how I wanted to apologize for the lack of enough effort on my part and to promise that they would see a better effort from me for the rest of the year. Finally, when Coach had calmed me down enough to go to the press conference, my parents walked into the locker room and I got emotional again . . . so we had to start the process over while Zack updated the patiently awaiting questioners that it would just be . . . another . . . minute or two.

Finally I was all set, not that I wanted to face the press or anyone else after that particular game, mind you.

As I started to apologize, I started to get a bit emotional in my remarks, and then I got fired up, because that's how I tend to get when I'm speaking. Very passionate. What I said was from the heart;

I had given it some thought in the locker room, but it was still pretty much off the cuff and right from the heart:

> To the fans and everybody in Gator Nation, I'm sorry. I'm extremely sorry. We were hoping for an undefeated season. That was my goal, something Florida has never done here.
> I promise you one thing, a lot of good will come out of this. You will never see any player in the entire country play as hard as I will play the rest of the season. You will never see someone push the rest of the team as hard as I will push everybody the rest of the season.
> You will never see a team play harder than we will the rest of the season. God bless.

It wasn't long before they started playing my speech on ESPN *SportsCenter*. My family told me it was fine. It was good—it was me down deep inside. I do remember having a few of the reporters looking at me like I was crazy. My family and I got in the elevator to go to Coach Meyer's office, and I was covered up in the back of the elevator, hiding, because I didn't want to be noticed in public anymore that day.

One reporter in the front of the elevator turned to another writer next to him and said, "Holy cow. How about that? I know he's for real, but I wonder how the public's going to take that. I think the public will kill him for that."

Those were the first comments I heard, and I cringed listening to them.

By that night, however, the feedback I was getting was all positive. I think that people agreed with the reporter's assessment: I was being sincere. I received a lot of calls and texts that night from people to say they appreciated it and they're supporting me. I have always appreciated the Gator Nation; I certainly did that night. They came through again when I—and my teammates—seemed to need it most.

My comments weren't all that big of a deal immediately afterward. I had apologized to Gator fans, and then I got more impassioned as I continued speaking. But then it started to take on a life of its own.

I couldn't go anywhere without seeing it posted somewhere or on a television screen.

I was uncomfortable watching shows where people were critiquing it. It wasn't really meant to stand on its own for all time; it was simply an apology, and a heartfelt moment about having dedicated so much to a cause and then falling short. At some level people understood that, but I can't say that for the next few days I enjoyed seeing it all that much.

The next day, Coach let me address the team. My comments to my teammates were similar but more intense and personal. In essence I told them I wasn't asking them to do anything that I wasn't also going to ask myself to do: simply, that I would be the hardest worker in the country the rest of the season and our team would be as well, if they were willing. Nothing was over. We still had a shot to go on and win and accomplish everything else we had set our sights on.

Coach Meyer changed our schedule from that point forward. In the past, we had always had a light day on Sunday and practice on Monday. He flipped it. We had an unbelievable, passionate practice that Sunday. We could all tell that this was going to be a lot different. We also scheduled a worship service each Sunday afternoon for the team and family members who could attend.

Coach Meyer later told me that receiver David Nelson went to his office after that meeting and told him that he wanted to do whatever he could to get on every special team, play on the offense, and contribute to this team in any way he could.

David and I weren't the only ones; that loss affected everyone in different ways. But in general, afterward, without it being said, I could see that there was a fire in everybody's eyes and that things would definitely be different. The next few teams we played were going to have to suffer some wrath. It gave you the feeling that, whoever we were playing, it was as if they had said the wrong thing to your mom. It brought everybody together and created a level of unity I had not seen before. I felt, after that, that everyone was now united with one mission and one goal, not to win the conference or the next game, but rather to win the next play. Then the next. If someone stood in our way, he was going to be overcome—physically and through our preparation, execution, and passion—and we were going to dominate our opponents every step of the game.

From that point forward, as a team, we weren't thinking in terms of being a great offense or defense, but rather our focus was to exert our planning, ability, determination, and unified will on whoever stood before us—one play at a time. We were going to do what we wanted to do offensively and defensively, and woe to anyone who stood in our way.

As always, our signs in the locker room still read, Get to Atlanta. 47 days to Atlanta. Each day the sign was updated: 46 days to Atlanta . . .

We had a great week of practice to get ready for Arkansas on the road and started off the game that day in Fayetteville with a great first drive to quiet the crowd down a little. By halftime, we had a comfortable, if not overly impressive, 14–0 lead.

In the second half, leading 17–7, we called a play where we have one receiver run a post route (a route in which he angles toward the goalpost) and another run a wheel route (a route in which the receiver runs an out pattern toward the sideline, then curves the route further up field), Trick Right 50 Z Drive Bullet Alert Zero. (Who thinks up these names?) I dropped back and as I read the coverage, I should have thrown to the receiver running the post route down the middle, but I hesitated and tried to reset myself and throw to the receiver—Percy Harvin—running the wheel route. Not only did I throw it too late and behind Percy, and right into the hands of the Arkansas linebacker who made the interception, but I stepped back as I released the ball and somehow hyperextended my right knee.

By the time I got back to the sideline, I was hurting and furious with myself, and the coaches and everybody knew it. We got the ball back, and several plays later I hit Percy Harvin on a post for a touchdown. It might have been one of the hardest passes I threw my whole life. I stuck it right on his chest, across the goal line—I probably needed to get my emotions in check a bit—but still Percy made the grab effortlessly, putting us ahead, 24–7.

Still, I was so angry and mad at myself that I turned and walked off the field. I could see Coach Meyer watching me with a look of combined frustration and disappointment, because he could see my angry attitude. He was looking at me with his hands in the air, as if he was trying to pump up the Florida fans who had made the trip to Fayetteville. But as he did it, he was mouthing stuff to me like, "Let's go!" and, "Get excited!"

I tried to do what he said, and so I went over to him and chest bumped him to try and see if that might work to snap me out of it, but I hit him too hard. And worse yet, I hit him in the mouth with my shoulder pads and chipped his tooth.

Now it was worse; we were like two little kids; he was mad at me even more now, walked away, and wouldn't talk to me for the next ten minutes, while I tried to apologize, but I was still mad from the way that I was playing. If you knew what was going on—you could only laugh.

Finally he came over to me and apologized and said he loved me. I said the same thing to him. He smiled—you could see the chipped tooth. They checked out my knee, and no one was the wiser when they slipped a brace on it. First time that I'd ever worn one.

In the end, we won the game, and while I was still angry with myself, the win did help to calm me down some. But I knew that if I was going to be true to what I'd said that day after the Ole Miss game, I would have to be better.

We had a good week of practice preparing to host LSU in Gainesville, during which I worked in some rehab on my knee. Coach Meyer got his tooth taken care of. We had a good game plan, which wasn't going to rely so much on my running. The Gator Walk— the walk from the buses through the crowd and into the stadium—was even more exciting than usual that day. I was amped all day before the game, and the atmosphere in the Swamp helped to keep me fired up all day.

On the third play of the game we were facing a third down with still ten yards to go. I think the play call was for a Far Strong Right Waggle Left Cross, in which Percy Harvin ran a deep crossing route across the middle of the field. The defensive back had pretty good coverage with inside position on Percy—between me and Percy—and so I tried to throw it over the top of the defender to Percy. The defensive back jumped, and as it went right over his hand, he tipped it just slightly and right into Percy's arms, who made the catch and ran it in for the touchdown. Seventy yards. A perfect way to start the game.

From that point on, the whole game went well. They turned the ball over quite a bit, and we were able to take advantage of a lot of those giveaways and continue to execute flawlessly during the whole game. Percy and Jeff Demps each had a good game. Demps was definitely not playing like the freshman he was. From the standpoint of making good decisions and throwing accurate balls, making a lot of correct audible checks, I felt that was one of my better games in college. I still was able to make some plays with my speed and athletic ability, but, again, the coaches tried to limit that because of my hyperextended knee.

At the end of the day, I was still myself on the field, with the aid of a knee brace: I still scrambled for a touchdown and had some good runs, but I tried to stay in the pocket more than usual. We won the matchup of the last two national champions (we had won it all in 2006, and they won it in 2007), 51–21. That was a big win for us after losing to them the year before, especially since they still had some of those good players they'd won it all with as well as others they'd added. It kept us on track and added a lot of momentum and confidence to our promise to one another.

The LSU game demonstrated that we seemed to be growing together as a team. We were doing many more of the little things right. Fans weren't getting my cell-phone number (always a plus). But perhaps most unexpected of all was the fact that my relationship with Coach Mullen began to change in many positive ways.

For my first two years, we'd gotten along, but it wasn't particularly warm. For whatever reason, his comments and some of our conversations didn't seem particularly open to matters of faith, which made it harder for us to find a connection. I'm not sure what changed going into my junior year. Maybe his faith changed, or maybe he saw my sincerity about my faith in a new light. Or maybe it was me and my attitude to the whole relationship. Maybe it was something altogether different, but he began spending time on the practice field before practice with some of the visitors who would come by to watch, and he began talking more about matters of faith. I guess God was continuing to work in our lives to grow us closer.

The week after LSU was our homecoming with the University of Kentucky, which turned out to be a special game. For our special teams, that is. We blocked their first two punts and scored after both, then scored again, and then blocked a field-goal attempt—and scored again. It was 28–0 at the end of the first quarter.

We were surprised that the score got away from them like it did. After all, we'd had the shoot-out with them just the year before. Once again, we were focused on winning every play, and we won most of them that day. I came out of the game in the second half, and Johnny Brantley finished the game at quarterback, throwing a touchdown to David Nelson, David's first catch of the year. Final score, 63–5.

We had now played three games after the Ole Miss game and had won all three handily. Clearly, our focus was good. We didn't set out to score that many against Kentucky, but the score really unraveled. We have never set out to embarrass an opponent—well, in all honesty, we may very well have thought about doing that as we prepared for the next opponent during the week following that Kentucky game.

I was probably more nervous about the 2008 Georgia game than I had been in any other game that year. While I wanted to win every game, that feeling before Georgia was particularly intense. I was focused on winning to atone for the embarrassing loss of the year before and make it up to the entire Florida fan base and our team. More than anything, I wanted to win it for Coach Meyer, because I knew how hurt he had been the year before when Georgia had embarrassed us—from their goal-line antics after their first score to the result—and how Coach had taken that. I wasn't going to let that happen again. Not to him, not to our team, not to Gator fans.

All week the players and coaches were asking Coach Meyer what we were going to do for payback. Over and over, he was asked, and every time he said the same thing: "Nothing." After all, Georgia was really good, with Matthew Stafford, Knowshon Moreno, and others, and they were ranked number eight in the country. We just needed to find a way to win, not worry about payback.

It started close. We took a 7–0 lead, then after they kicked a field goal, they tried an onside kick, which we recovered. We took it in for a touchdown and were up 14–3. The game continued in that fashion, with us winning every aspect. We played with focus and passion. We were more physical and simply outplayed them. A couple of our defensive players came off the field saying they thought some of the Georgia offensive guys were ready for the game to end. It appeared that some of them were physically intimidated.

In the middle of the fourth quarter, we were beating them badly. Coach Meyer came up to me and said, "Timmy, I had a dream this week. I dreamt that we were beating Georgia just like we are, you were in at quarterback, you dropped back, took the ball, and threw it into a sea of red-and-black dressed fans." I'm telling you, he really wasn't sleeping well over the prior Georgia game.

"Sweet. Let's do it!" I said.

Coach Meyer laughed. He wasn't going to do it, and he knew that before he told me about his dream. But he knew I would want to— and would—do it for him. Cooler heads prevailed—his. After a few minutes, we did hatch a different plan that didn't involve anything illegal or to cheat the game or to make us look bad . . . or that might have started a brawl. We simply played within the rules and used our time-outs.

We were ahead 49–10, with very little time left in the game. I had already taken a curtain call, as Coach had taken me out a little bit before that. I usually didn't like doing something like that, but I was more than happy to do it this time, because I was still so fired up—it was Georgia—and it gave me a chance to run straight to our fans in the corner of the field and celebrate with them.

I was pretty emotional, which fired up the fans even more. The stadium, while ordinarily half orange and blue and half red and black, was now mostly orange, blue, and teal (the color of all the empty seats of the Georgia fans who left with the score insurmountably in our favor).

It was one of the most exciting times of my life. Period. There we were, in Jacksonville where I grew up. Georgia had embarrassed us the previous year, but on this day we had physically and in every other respect beaten them up. We were mentally more prepared, emotionally more invested, and obviously wanted it more than they did. All we heard about during the whole off-season was that Georgia was the number one team in the country, they had the best quarterback in the country, their running back, Knowshon Moreno, was going to be up for the Heisman, and so on.

So, up 39 points, we called all our time-outs in the last minute of the game just to extend the time, allowing us all to savor the moment. We were playing well, and it was hard to imagine that we'd actually lost a game. It still sat out there like an open wound that kept driving us to try and dominate every team, every individual, that we played. We didn't know how the year would finish, but one game at a time, we were staking our claim to being the best team in the country.

The next weekend we played in Nashville against Vanderbilt, and it just felt like football weather. It was early November and we were on a roll.

We were also sporting new uniforms—all white with long white socks. The best uniforms we ever had, in my opinion. On the opening drive we got the ball and drove right down the field, and then I threw a touchdown pass to Louis Murphy in the corner of the end zone. It was over from that point on. I probably had my best, most consistent game as a Gator that day.

We were scoring like crazy, but somehow, Percy Harvin hadn't scored, even though he had scored in every game in 2008 leading up to this one, so in the second half, Coach Meyer put Percy in at quarterback, and he ran three times from the one yard line, while I was split out at receiver. On the third play, they ruled that he fumbled even though we thought he had scored. I was disappointed—I was hoping for at least one game in which we scored on every possession. By now you shouldn't be surprised by that.

When we got back to the sideline, Percy told me he'd had enough of goal-line plays at quarterback, that he couldn't believe the collisions on every play. He usually got the ball out in space and was able to use his tremendous speed to gain an advantage. He knew it was violent, trying to rush the ball up the middle, especially at the goal line with twenty-two guys packed into a small space, but it still caught him off guard.

As for the game, after I had a hand in five touchdowns, Coach took me out. Johnny Brantley played the fourth quarter. We clinched the SEC East and a trip to the SEC Championship Game with a 42–14 win that cold night in Nashville.

And Percy did finally get his touchdown in that Vandy game.

In the weeks since the Ole Miss game, we'd stepped up our play in every way. We had one more game where it seemed like we were still figuring it all out as a team—Arkansas. It was the next game after Ole Miss. In the latter part of that Arkansas game, however, things all seemed to begin to click for a lot of guys, and all of a sudden we were on a roll. We were simply dispatching our opponents.

South Carolina was next, and ranked in the top twenty-five, they had a good defense, so we needed to be careful to maintain the same level of preparation and intensity. I went through my usual weekly preparation for classes, meetings, and film work. Every free hour that I had, I headed down to the coaches' offices, often sitting in the offensive staff meetings as the coaches discussed the plans for the game. The more I knew about a given game plan, the better I felt, and this week wasn't any different.

I had done that throughout my time at Florida, meeting individually with Coach Meyer and my position coach and attending whatever game-planning meetings I could. I felt it was important for me to not only understand what the coaches wanted to do in a particular situation, but *why* as well. Plus, the more I was around to hear their thinking and watch film, the better prepared I would be for whatever might happen on Saturday.

I owed that to myself and my teammates. If I was going to lead the way I wanted to lead, I needed to be as ready as possible. Therefore, whenever I could fit it in between classes, studying, and tutoring sessions, I did.

On film, we saw that South Carolina ran a lot of different stunts on defense, using only three down linemen. They had Marvin Sapp, a linebacker I grew up playing with at the Lakeshore Athletic Association's Pop Warner football league in Jacksonville.

Before the game, someone told me that it was the first time a coach who had won a Heisman was facing a player who had won one, and if we hadn't been about to kick off, I might have reflected on that more. That Coach Spurrier and I both won it at the University of Florida was pretty special, but I didn't have time to think about it at that moment.

As it was, we remembered our last close call with South Carolina in Gainesville during the National Championship season of 2006 and knew we needed to stay focused. Instead, we started rather slowly on offense. Our defense scored our first touchdown on an interception return by Brandon Spikes, and Ahmad Black gave us good field position with an interception of his own on South Carolina's next possession.

Ahmad was having a terrific year, and I was happy for him. He had a mind-set that I could relate to. Throughout my life, my brothers and I have always been football junkies—we love watching it and love playing it. Even now, when we end up at home, we'll head out into the yard and play—except that we finally quit playing tackle a couple of years ago. I've never viewed playing football as a job, like some others I've known through the years did, and so everything I did—playing the game, practice, workouts, study—all emanated from my love for the game.

Ahmad and the Pouncey brothers, Maurkice and Mike, seemed to share our love of playing. They'd play anywhere, with anyone. The Pounceys, in fact, were terrific receivers and quarterbacks in pickup games despite their size, which made them naturals to play on the offensive line. There it is again: "playing position by body stereotype." Oh, well.

We fumbled twice in the first half but still led, 28–3, at the halftime break. As always with South Carolina, it was a physical game. I know Coach Spurrier has a reputation with the fans for having passing, finesse teams, but his teams always hit. Hard.

We played better in the second half, and like the rest of our games during that stretch, it wasn't close.

We had one more tune-up, which resulted in a win over The Citadel, and then we faced FSU again. This time, it was in Tallahassee—my *Braveheart* game. I really appreciated the similarities as that's my favorite movie. A pouring rain soaked the field, and I got garnet paint on my uniform and face early in the game. It ended up looking like blood, but that was where the parallels between me and William Wallace ended. On that day, *we* were the ones doing the slaughtering.

We scored early and often, and as in other Florida State games, I was looking to make contact with someone on each of my runs. Early on I ran over their safety, helping to set the tone for our approach to the rest of the game. Our guys didn't need any help, however. Percy scored again, and I threw three touchdown passes and ran for another. I even recovered a fumble.

They had the ball in good field position a couple of times early, but our defense played great, holding them to field goals, while we were scoring touchdowns. We stayed in control all day long.

My one rushing touchdown came after Percy was injured. In every other stadium I've played in, there's silence when a player is injured, whether he plays for the home or visiting team. But when Percy went down in front of their stands, the FSU fans burst into loud cheering and chanting, celebrating his injury. Even while he was being attended to, before anyone knew if he was all right. That only reinforced my long-time and well-established feelings for them.

We had the ball at their four yard line at the time, and I was steamed at the cheering. I jogged over to Coach Meyer.

"Give me the ball."

He nodded.

I hit the line and was stood up by a couple of FSU defenders. In a play that summed up our approach that year, most of my teammates joined the pile and pushed me—and the surrounding FSU players—into the end zone. Touchdown.

I ran over to the section of the stands where our fans were seated and waved my arms, bringing them to a frenzy. Throughout the game, we controlled FSU, scoring on five of the first seven times we had the ball, and we had more than twice as many yards as they did for the game.

Chapter Eighteen

A PROMISE FULFILLED

For God so loved the world, that He gave His only begotten Son,
that whoever believes in Him shall not perish, but have eternal life.

—JOHN 3:16

It was a good thing I loved big games, because the week after the FSU game, we had another big one, as we headed to Atlanta for the Southeastern Conference Championship Game against Alabama.

After the 2007 season, Nick Saban had left the Miami Dolphins to replace Mike Shula, and he had Alabama playing very well. They were undefeated and ranked number one in the nation. We were ranked number two and had that one loss to Ole Miss, of course. It had been two months since we'd lost, however, and we were a very confident group.

After wearing Philippians 4:13 on my eye black all season, I thought about switching it for that game and going with John 3:16. I mulled it over for a while but decided to leave it the same. If we ended up on a bigger stage—the BCS National Championship Game for example—I'd switch.

The atmosphere was electric in the Georgia Dome. Our whole family was there and had all stayed at Katie and Gannon's house. Our defense set the tone for us immediately by stopping Alabama on their opening drive. Even though we were missing Percy Harvin, who had sprained an ankle in that FSU game, our offense drove right down the field on a great drive in which I hit Carl Moore for a touchdown on third and goal. Our coaches did a great job preparing us with the absence of Percy, who up until then had scored in every game that year.

It was one of those well-played games by both teams, where you're happy to be a part of it. We went into halftime leading 17–10, after David Nelson caught a touchdown pass right before the end of the half. After the Ole Miss game, David had stepped up as he said he would, and he had come through at some critical times for us.

Alabama came out strong in the second half, and we didn't score in the third quarter. They tied the score on a touchdown by their freshman running back, Mark Ingram, and then added a field goal to take the lead, 20–17, entering the fourth quarter.

We were both playing for everything—the SEC title and a spot in the National Championship game.

We embarked on an offensive drive that was the biggest drive of the game for us. If we didn't score, we ran the risk of their scoring again and putting the game out of reach. It was a slow, methodical drive where we kept making play after play after play. Great offense vs. great defense.

I looked at the faces in the huddle. "We are going to win this game *right now*." I believed. They believed.

We were able to make some great plays and manage the ball. After I picked up a couple of third downs, we had the ball on their one yard line, and Coach Mullen made a great play call. I'm pretty sure Alabama thought we were going to run it right up the middle, but instead I ran an option with Jeff Demps, in which, after I flipped it to him, he basically walked into the end zone untouched—our guys made some great blocks.

Great call. Great execution.

We now led again, 24–20, and desperately needed to keep the momentum. I ran over and head-butted everybody on the kickoff team, trying to get them all fired up to stop Alabama. I don't really know if the head-butts were the reason or not, but our kickoff team and defense got big stops, and we got the ball back with just a few minutes left to play.

The only way we were going to be safe was if we scored a touchdown. If we kicked a field goal, we would still only be up by seven and they could tie us on a single play. With a touchdown, they would need to score twice.

We systematically moved the ball on runs and with the help of a big Alabama penalty, and then we were able to hit a swing pass to David Nelson—another big catch for him—for ten yards. We kept moving the ball down the field and working time off the clock in the process. Eventually we had a first down from their twenty-one yard line. I connected with Aaron Hernandez on a shovel pass and got the first down. It was a huge call. Great call again, and very well executed by Aaron and the guys.

On first and goal I ran the ball and gained five yards down to the goal line. Second and goal from the one.

Flag. A yellow flag was down on the field. The officials, inexplicably, called a penalty on Coach Meyer for being too far on the field. I've never seen something like that—at least not in a situation like that.

Now we were on the six yard line with second down and goal to go for a touchdown. Jeff Demps gained one on second down, leaving us with third and goal from the five. We desperately needed a touchdown.

Our coaches called "Trick Left 51 X Stutter Bend Cash," in which Riley Cooper ran a stutter slant from the right toward the middle of the field. I anticipated Coach Saban would have Alabama come out in a Cover One (man defense) with certain players having no responsibility other than reading my eyes. After the snap, I immediately looked left to freeze those free defenders—a linebacker and a safety were reading my eyes—and quickly threw right to Coop before they could adjust. I had to throw it down and in front of Coop, because of the defenders. He did the rest. That was one of the biggest plays of Riley's and my career.

That was the game right there. We had so much momentum. Our defense held them again, and we ran out the clock. We were the SEC champions and would be slated to be playing in the National Championship Game in South Florida early in January 2009.

Afterward, Coach Meyer said he thought my performance was the best fourth-quarter performance that he's ever seen from a player. I know he's biased, but it felt good to help the team and get us to the next game. The truth was, a whole lot of us chipped in—both on the field and on the sidelines—to achieve the victory that day and keep the promise we had made to one another.

The next morning, however, my head was killing me. I didn't understand why, but when I looked in the mirror and saw the knots all over my forehead, I realized what I'd done. Those head-butts with the kickoff team? I'd forgotten that I didn't have my helmet on. I'll never do that again.

While we were beginning our practices for Oklahoma in the National Championship Game later that month, the award circuit began again. I was really hopeful about being a two-time winner of the Heisman.

Unfortunately it was not to be, but that merely further fueled my desire. I'd been to the BCS Championship once, and now I was headed back. And I was determined to win.

Game on.

We had a month to prepare. It was a busy month, between finals and the announcement that Coach Mullen would be named the head coach at Mississippi State. Coach Mullen had a particularly tough stretch, as he worked for both schools that month: recruiting for Mississippi State and hiring a staff and putting together a game plan while staying with us through the game.

I have never been more nervous than I was headed into the BCS National Championship Game. The fact that it was my second one didn't change a thing. We were playing Oklahoma, and "Game on" or not, they were really good. They had been scoring at will on good teams all season, winning games by large margins. They were the highest scoring team in college football history and had scored more than *sixty* points five games in a row at one stretch.

But if there was any defense that could handle that and deal with what they had to do to prepare to stop that great Oklahoma offense—it was our defense.

Hands down. And they would be ready.

All week, their defense was talking trash, saying that I would have only been the sixth-best quarterback if I had played in their conference, the Big 12. I found that hurtful and upsetting; I was sure that I would've been at least fifth.

When we're playing a night game, Coach Meyer always gives us about three hours off during the day. When we're playing on a Saturday night during the regular season, this is a good thing. I could sit up in my hotel room, stay off my feet, and watch other college games from around the country.

However, this game was Thursday, January 8, 2009. When you're sitting in Miami, waiting for the final game of the entire football season, with nothing to do but sit around and check out Thursday-afternoon television while trying not to dwell on the game that night . . .

I decided to have an impromptu Bible study and called as many guys as would fit into our room, including Pastor Lindsey (Lindsey Seals), the Ocala minister who served as our team chaplain. I spoke to the guys on Matthew 11:28–30, which says,

> *Come to Me, all who are weary and heavy-laden, and I will give you rest.*
> *Take My yoke upon you and learn from Me, for I am gentle and humble in heart, and you will find rest for your souls. For My yoke is easy and My burden is light.*

I told my teammates gathered that Jesus promises to take on the weight of the world, so that we don't have to. All we needed to do was follow Him—the yoke was used for leading cattle or oxen, plowing or pulling a cart. He would be responsible for the pressures we might have felt.

I then looked around the room and said, "Guys, we are *going* to win the National Championship tonight. And when we do, we are going to give so much honor and glory to Jesus Christ. It is going to be awesome."

Somebody had a guitar, and for the next couple of hours, we just sang hymns and other worship songs. There were a lot of bad voices in that room, but none of us cared. The Bible says to "make a joyful noise to the LORD" (see Psalm 98:4), but it doesn't say anything about a "good" noise—thankfully. You could feel the experience we just went through together, even moments later as we met up again in the lobby, having changed into suits and ties.

I walked up to Coach Meyer and told him that I had prayed about it, and that I was going to change the scripture on my eye black to John 3:16.

"You can't. What are you thinking?" was his immediate response. "Philippians 4:13 is such a *great* verse," he continued. We both knew that it was the same superstitious streak bubbling up in him that caused him to sit on the forty-fifth row at Florida Field when waiting for my announcement as to which university I was going to attend, three years earlier.

I repeated that I was changing it to John 3:16. He looked into my eyes and could tell that I knew it was the right thing to do. He paused. "Yeah, that's a great one, too. Okay, that'll be *great*!" And, excited about it, he bounded onto the bus.

After getting dressed in my uniform, I passed Coach Mullen in the locker room, and he immediately noticed the change.

"What's that verse about?" he asked.

"For God so loved the world, that He gave His only begotten Son, that whoever believes in Him shall not perish, but have eternal life."

His jaw dropped. "Can you do that with *every* verse in the Bible? I just name one, and you quote it?"

I laughed. "Unfortunately, no." Thanks to my parents, I had memorized a lot in my life, but not all of them. Of course, I stacked the deck—I made sure that I knew the ones I was writing under my eyes.

During pregame warm-ups, I walked over to Coach Meyer. He's always so focused, but I figured I'd loosen things up a little.

"Hey, don't you have like a million-dollar bonus if we win?"

He laughed. "Something like that."

"That seems fair. Meanwhile, I think I get an extra orange juice at training table if we win. How 'bout we just split that bonus?"

"I would if they'd let me." He seemed sincere. The NCAA's stance on paying players—or not paying them—seems unfair to me, with the preposterous amounts of money being made by schools, television, coaches, and the like. And the players?

Just a thought.

But a serious one—for serious consideration by serious people.

I love Christmas and gift-giving, but it was a pain to have to scrimp every winter to try to get enough together to buy decent presents for everyone in my family (another reason to not have a girlfriend—I couldn't have afforded even one more Christmas present). In fact, that year, when we had a couple of days off before going to Miami for the National Championship Game, I went home and spent several hours in a pouring rain on Christmas Eve, weeding my mom's garden. She loved that garden, but after years of chicken manure and Mr. Bell's biddies (the young hens), those weeds were hard to keep up with. That was the best present I could afford to give her. And Mom made me feel as though it was the best present she could have received—whether or not it really was.

I guess I didn't do a very good job on closing the deal for a championship-game bonus juice, and moments later, we were under way.

Neither team scored in the first quarter. Both sidelines could attribute it to nerves, but Oklahoma did some really nice things on defense. They had previously run a four-man front (four defensive linemen) during the season but switched to a three-man front for the game. It took us a little while to adjust, and in the meantime, I threw an interception early in the game. I had only thrown two all year, as we had done a really nice job taking care of the ball during the season. This was not a good time to change that.

In the second quarter, we jumped to an early lead, when I connected with Louis Murphy on a twenty yard touchdown pass to make it 7–0. Oklahoma quickly tied the score at 7–7, and then I was picked off again, deep in our territory. Frustrating, but I didn't have time to get down on myself. It was a time to forget what was behind—but learn from it—and press on toward what was ahead.

Our defense made a great fourth-down goal-line stand, and then after our series we punted, and they drove down to our six yard line, at which point we picked off a pass from Sam Bradford. The two teams had led the nation in fewest turnovers during the season and now had combined for three in the first half. It was 7–7 at halftime.

Game on.

Thirty minutes for the rest of our lives.

After all of those hours, days, and months in the weight room, it was time for all of that to pay off. And it did.

I told Coach to give me the ball on a possession early in the third quarter and carried several times as we moved the ball down the field. At the one, I was so exhausted that they took me out and Percy Harvin, who actually turned out to have a hairline fracture and not just a sprain from that FSU game, scored on a direct snap and we led, 14–7.

After Oklahoma tied it, we took the lead with a short field goal, 17–14.

Oklahoma drove down the field looking to take the lead, but Ahmad Black picked off Sam Bradford at our twenty-four yard line. It was the fourth quarter; we needed to put the game away.

We mounted a drive with three critical plays, each with a different guy who had made huge plays for us all year.

On third and twelve, they came out in a perfect defense. I scrambled to my left and Riley Cooper kept moving after he ran his pattern, cutting right, and broke away as I released it across my body. He made the catch between the safeties for a twenty-yard gain. First down.

David Nelson made what may have been the biggest catch of the game on a second down and eleven, down the middle on a post between the safeties who were in a Cover Two (zone defense, with each safety responsible for his half of the field).

On third and six from their ten yard line, I hit Aaron Hernandez on a shovel pass to set up a first and goal.

Finally, I hit David Nelson again, on a jump pass from the four yard line, for the touchdown that put it away, 24–14.

Moments later, we had the ball back. As we were running out the clock, I thought an Oklahoma player gave me an extra shot in the pile, so I scrambled up and directed a Gator Chomp toward him with my arms. The referee appropriately flagged that—not my finest moment—and the only personal foul of my career—but it was worth it.

Game over.

After the final touchdown I walked over to Coach Meyer. He pulled off his headset, opened up his arms, gave me a great big hug, and said, "Atta boy. Great job. You finished. I love you." It was a great feeling to hear him say that, after filling all the roles he had in my life as a coach, a friend, and a father figure.

As great as that was, how much greater will it feel when we get to heaven and Jesus takes off his headset, opens up His arms, gives us a big hug, and says, "Atta boy. Great job. You finished. I love you." I talk to kids about that all the time—finishing strong. It's great for football. You have to finish in football; you have to learn how to finish in the weight room, through the line, finishing a sprint; everything gets hard. Finish. Eventually some people are going to stop, some people are going to quit, and some people are going to start going slower, but the people who can finish and finish at the same pace or stronger than when they started, those are the ones who are going to succeed; those are the ones who are going to be great. Those are the ones who are going to have an impact in this world and on the lives of others around them. How much more so in life to finish strong. For yourself. For the world. For others. For the God who created you.

In addition to living by this motto myself, I talk to prison inmates about it. I started visiting prisons my freshman year and have been to quite a few, even visiting death row. I really enjoy speaking with those guys—they are so hungry for people to interact with them and share anything at all that is encouraging. I tell them that they might have had a bad first, second, or third quarter, but they can still have a great fourth quarter. They can finish strong in life—wherever they are—and it starts by having a personal relationship with Jesus Christ. When a person comes to know Christ, he not only has a home in heaven and is born into God's family as His child, but he can also have hope—hope to salvage his remaining time on earth by finishing strong with purpose. And when they find that relationship, they not only assure themselves a place throughout eternity with their heavenly Father, but they also find that He still has a plan for them to finish life strong right here. Even though they're in prison, even on death row, they can still finish this life stronger and still make a difference for themselves in eternity.

When I leave this world, I want to leave something behind that keeps on making a difference in people's lives. When you finish strong in life and get to heaven, God's going to say, "Well done, good and faithful servant" (Matthew 25:21, NIV).

I see it more in terms of rewards in heaven than just leaving a legacy on earth, because if one is not careful, focusing on a legacy could easily become material or "thing" focused. But a legacy that left eternal fingerprints on the lives of others would be a legacy to be remembered in this world and the next. The legacy God intended each of us to leave has to do with the impact our lives have had on the lives of others whom He calls us to serve. It has to do with the difference our lives make in the world—in our families, with friends, at work, at school, with our coaches and teammates, and all those others around us. Our legacy should be about building in the lives of all those others, doing something for others that will not only last in their lives here, but for eternity. That's why building a school or a play room in a hospital is going to leave a legacy of lasting and eternal consequence, not just a name on a plaque or a stadium.

What I can leave behind: a life that is marked by always trying to do things the right way, building a foundation in others, something that lives beyond me, helps people, and, more important, causes them, in turn, to want to help other people. Finish strong and you help not just yourself; you help others.

• • •

That night we had a celebration party back at the hotel for family and friends. I was so exhausted that I ended up getting sick on the bus coming back from the game as well as at the party.

The next morning, after some rest, we were on the bus to head to the airport and fly back to Gainesville. Even though I was scheduled for surgery—I had been dinged on the third play of the year against Hawaii—I was excited to get back and celebrate with my friends at school. Coach Mullen and I sat together on the bus, reminiscing about all we had been through together and as a team. He was headed off to Mississippi State and would be missed as a coach and a friend.

It was a fun trip home.

And so we were the national champions. All that we had worked for in 2008 came to fruition in that moment, and we enjoyed it for a few days. In all honesty, I wasn't particularly troubled by the BCS system at the time; after all, it worked to our benefit by putting us in the National Championship game. I can, however, certainly see the unfairness in it at times.

As someone who has always pushed for people to evaluate me on my merits and not any preconceived notions, I couldn't help but feel for the kids at Coach Meyer's old school, Utah. What else could they have possibly done? They were 13–0 with a decisive win over Alabama in the Sugar Bowl to close out their season.

Imagine for a moment if the NCAA implemented one of the many calls for including major college football in a playoff system or compensating players. How hard could those be to implement?

Just another thought.

Chapter Nineteen

MATCHING THEIR INTENSITY

Godliness actually is a means of great gain
when accompanied by contentment.
—1 TIMOTHY 6:6

I'm told that ninety-four million people searched for John 3:16 on Google during and immediately following the National Championship Game. I knew that the verse would be seen by a ton of people, but that was beyond anything I would have imagined.

I thought and prayed about my upcoming decision a lot.

I thought I'd have a chance to finish strong in college. Since I'd always preached about finishing strong, I wanted to act on what I'd said. But then again, there were some who thought that maybe I should go pro after my junior year—once a college player has been in college for three years, he can choose to make himself eligible for the NFL draft. By leaving early, I wouldn't risk a debilitating injury in my senior year, but I would risk the chance to be a part of one of the greatest college teams of all time and one of the greatest football recruiting classes of all time, especially if we could win a third National Championship to go with the ones in 2006 and 2008.

Between my dilemma of staying or going and Coach Mullen's leaving Florida for Mississippi State, our celebration after the National Championship was short lived. There were a lot of question marks hanging in the air. I really didn't want to leave Coach Meyer. He and I had become more like brothers than simply coach and player. I would text his children on a regular basis, and he and I had lunch together in his office almost every day during the season, just talking. That relationship was a major factor in my decision.

Although I had thought about it and prayed about it a great deal, Coach Meyer and I hadn't spoken a word about it. We returned from the National Championship game the following day, Friday, and met at a restaurant on Newberry Road in Gainesville, Ballyhoo Grill, on Saturday, just down the street from the university.

It was Coach, my parents, and me. We talked and went through all the pros and cons of the decision. Coach made it clear that he wanted me to stay for selfish reasons, that he liked coaching me and hanging out in his office with me. He also thought that with one more season, my career might go down as one of the best in college history. I wasn't sure about that, but I agreed that I loved my time with Coach and at Florida. Still, Coach Meyer tried to be objective and helpful, even offering to call people he knew in the NFL and try to get an informal gauge on my draft status.

At one point, my dad and Coach Meyer left the table, and my mom reminded me what we'd just heard about the incredible number of Google searches of John 3:16 that week just because I'd worn the verse on my eye black.

"Timmy, I doubt that people follow professional quarterbacks in the same way. Or if they do, there's no guarantee that they'd ever follow you in the pros the way people follow you here."

I nodded.

"Ninety-four million people on Google for John 3:16? Think of the influence you can keep having on kids and others if you stay another year," she said.

Although there are plenty of popular professionals, what she said made sense to me—we were leaning that way anyway. We knew that the platform God had given me as the Florida quarterback was a big one; who knew what it might be next? Bigger? Smaller? I knew God would give me a platform wherever I was—he does that for all of us—but I wanted to make sure I didn't give up the one He had already given, if I could continue to use it for His glory for another year.

There was more, though. For me, it all came back to finishing strong, to practicing what I'd been preaching. The thought that I'd be with Coach Meyer and that I could finish my college career strong, and that we'd make something extremely special out of it—win or lose—was very appealing, and I would graduate this upcoming December. There would be plenty of time to go and pursue my dream of playing quarterback in the NFL, if that's what God had in mind. If not, He'd close that door, anyway.

I was also trying to figure out when I would have shoulder surgery, which I needed. Between workouts and the Combine, that might be challenging to schedule.

For now, I felt that I wanted to finish college strong, to do the best I could, and to be there for my teammates and Coach Meyer. To have a great senior year.

I didn't tell Coach Meyer that yet, though, but asked if I could speak to my family for a bit. He left to drive back to his office, but he did notice that I didn't take him up on his offer to call NFL coaches and scouts. Thirty minutes later, I called to ask him to meet me downstairs in the stadium. I figured that he knew, since he wasn't seated in the stadium on the forty-fifth row, but I told him anyway that I was staying.

He and I celebrated and decided that I would announce it publicly the following day, at the National Championship celebration that the university was holding for us and the Gator Nation at Florida Field.

And Monday I had my shoulder surgery.

Once I'd decided to stay, I turned my attention to the season. After our experience with the 2007 season, we knew that we needed to fight complacency and continue to press on the accelerator to stay where we were while everyone else was chasing us.

While I'd made my decision to stay, not everyone was able to do the same. We lost several good players to graduation and the NFL draft including Percy Harvin and Louis Murphy. Brandon Spikes, however, chose to stay for his senior year, which made me happy.

The remaining players came in and tried to focus to prepare to repeat as national champs, but there were many distractions for a lot of the guys. For the most part, everybody was focused a lot like we were before the 2008 season, but it was always a problem finding just that right edge. You can tend to get complacent with the day in, day out stuff, because, frankly, you know you're a good team and have a lot of good players. I mean, you're the national champions, so you must be fairly talented to begin with, but you have to be on guard all the time so that complacency doesn't begin to set in.

We were digging to find the edge that would keep us on top. That whole off-season all Alabama talked about was how we beat them up in the fourth quarter to win the SEC Championship Game. We knew they were working hard in Tuscaloosa, so we needed to exceed—or at least match—their level.

Somewhere he is out there, training while I am not. One day, when we meet, he will win.

To keep that from happening, we'd either have to fake that motivation or muster it up somehow. Not all people are self-motivated to be the best they can be. If we had lost the big game to end the season—that's something completely different. We could feed off that to motivate us as we began the next season, much as Alabama was using their SEC Championship Game loss and their bowl loss to fuel their off-season work.

We, however, needed another impetus to motivate us. Coach Mick and Coach Meyer worked to give us that through the off-season with a variety of guest speakers, like Tony Dungy, Billy Donovan, and Doc Rivers. The rest of the coaches also worked to motivate us. Because Coach Mullen was at Mississippi State, Coach Meyer moved Steve Addazio into the role of offensive coordinator and hired Scott Loeffler as the quarterback coach. I was pleased, as I really liked Coach Addazio and I had gotten to know Scott when he recruited me to Michigan.

As leaders, we did a pretty good job of staying focused and helping the rest of the team as well to stay focused, knowing what our jobs were. A lot of us talked about it. Brandon Spikes, Brandon James, Riley Cooper, David Nelson, and I talked about how this was something we wanted to accomplish. We didn't shy away from talking about it. Sometimes we'd break the huddle after a workout and shout it: "Best Ever!"

The coaches wouldn't say it, but our goal as the class of 2009 was to become the best team college football had ever seen. That kept us motivated.

Meanwhile, I continued to try and use my success for other purposes. Jamie McCloskey helped me get permission from the NCAA to put on the First and 15 event once again, but this time we made it a weeklong event. We still held the Powder Puff game with the sororities, but we added a number of other events to make it a full week. We added an auction that Coach Meyer and others helped with, and we held something we called a Brighter Day Event. Bill Heavener, my parents' friend and the founder of Full Sail University, brought a couple of RVs up to Gainesville to transport twelve underprivileged kids with us to Disney World for the day with at least one adult per child going along. One of my favorite events of the week was an ice-cream social in the pediatric wing at Shands Hospital, with balloons and ice cream in the kids' party room. For as much as I try to eat well, I've always had a soft spot for ice cream. Couple that with kids, and that's an event I can look forward to, every year, or even more often.

At the auction, we auctioned off my FSU "Braveheart" jersey, splattered in garnet paint—it sold for $250,000. All in all, we raised over $500,000, a nice increase from $13,000 the year before. Part of the money went to add a new children's room at Shands, called Timmy's Playroom, where other players and coaches continue to visit to this day. In fact, we raised the most in one week that any student organization in the country had ever raised.

To me, this event was just as important as school. Classes had become routine and easy by this time. I graduated with a 3.66 GPA, and while I enjoyed Florida, I was also starting to think ahead to my future. I knew that somehow I would be involved in the community once my playing days were over. While that hopefully would not be for quite a while, it made sense to use my status as leverage to broaden that reach. Someday I figured I would be in full-time ministry work in some way, whether with my family or elsewhere. Why not get a jump now? Too many people wait for something to happen or for conditions to be just right, but God has given each of us a platform right where we are, and I was trying to use that as best I could.

Every year in August, before the season begins, college athletic conferences conduct Media Days during which the press has a chance to ask questions of representatives of each school: the head coach and a player or two. I was with Coach Meyer in Birmingham for the Southeastern Conference Media Days. It's a chance for the press to ask each coach what he expects of the upcoming season—about players, other teams, and so forth. A chance for football junkies to get their fill of football. While there, a reporter, Clay Travis, thought it would be newsworthy to go in a totally different direction than the other questioners.

"You've worn your religion on your sleeve . . . and I think that's made you very popular in the South and all over the country, that even if you're beating . . . their teams, they still like you personally. Are you saving yourself for marriage?"

I didn't dodge the question and answered truthfully, "I am." But I didn't understand—and still don't—why it was something that needed to be asked. Since when does anybody else get asked that? Travis later said he knew what my answer would be and thought it would be positive for kids and others to hear it publicly.

The funniest part about it is that the next reporter was too flustered to get his question out. We all had a good laugh.

To his point, athletes seem to be in the news far too much for the negative ways in which they relate to women, all too often with a lack of respect, and horrifyingly, at times, with violence. That distresses me. God wants us to foster healthy relationships in all areas of our lives, and those relationships should never be marked by conquest or putting ourselves or our "needs" ahead of others'. We are called to serve. I may not have thought the question to be appropriate, but thinking about it afterward, I realized that young women and men heard my answer and would continue to hear it going forward. As a result, there was the chance that they might find encouragement in my words and lifestyle to do the same and to wait until they were married to engage in sexual activity.

My attitude toward women has actually always been a decent way for me to talk about my faith. I'm constantly asked in locker rooms why I don't have girls around me all the time. Apparently, some guys think that women find quarterbacks appealing.

Whenever this has come up, I've always responded that our relationships are what matter to God, and that if God wants us to treat strangers well, shouldn't we treat people we know and care for even that much better? I mean, I want to be a certain way when I get married, so shouldn't I treat those that I'm around and interested in that same way?

Another factor is that I have trouble finding girls who really like me for me. Ever since my recruiting experiences, I've kept my guard up because I realized that girls would often tell me whatever it was they thought I wanted to hear. I recognize that we all put our best foot forward when we're meeting new people, but it just seems that I've run into this a great deal, for whatever reason.

Sometimes in college it felt like some girls merely wanted to be seen with me. Meanwhile, I have the opposite dilemma. Because I'm so recognizable, and because I've been trying to stand for something, I try to be careful about who I'm with. I'd prefer to just get to know girls first, anyway. One of these days, maybe, I'll meet the right girl.

Some guys also seem to think that it's impossible to resist temptation. I've found—as in other areas—that if I've already thought through a situation and have a response prepared ahead of time in the event temptation rears its ugly head, it is that much easier to resist. Of course, staying away from situations and questionable areas whenever possible, where I know there may be temptations, is an even better solution.

The question seemed to have a ripple effect, where suddenly my decision to save myself was national news. In a way, I wouldn't have chosen to have him ask that question; sometimes I'd just rather live a private life. Plus, I never want to come across as preachy or thinking I have all the answers, or that I don't make mistakes. I make plenty—I'm far from perfect. At the same time, I didn't shy away from answering, because it's part of my platform, and it got a lot of people talking about it. Even reporters who were sometimes critical of me wrote that in a time when so many athletes were having children out of wedlock, they appreciated my stance. Seeing my words have that kind of impact made me realize that God had a plan for this, too—of course.

In the end, it was a mild distraction. We pushed it aside, because we had work to do, and I just kept my head down and got back to it.

Though I worked hard that summer, training for fall, there were moments to relax. For a few days that summer, we went on a family vacation, and while we were away, I got a call out of the blue from none other than Phil Mickelson, the pro golfer. He'd gotten my number and invited me to play golf at Sawgrass, home of The Players Championship. Under NCAA rules I couldn't play there, but I was allowed to play at Timuquana Country Club, where my dad is a clergy member.

I cut my stay at the beach vacation short to be able to meet him at Timuquana the day before he played in the TPC. I was excited to start off the first three holes playing out of my mind, simply because playing with him was helping me to play better. I usually shoot around ninety, but I just don't play very often, so my short game isn't very good. After those first three holes Phil and I were tied at one under. Maybe this was a career path for me I hadn't even thought about. Certainly the physical abuse on the body is a whole lot less. Eventually, reality set in, and I started to fall apart a little bit, but I still had a good round. Playing from the tips (the longest yardage) with Phil, I shot an 82, which was the best round of my life.

We had a great time talking about life, faith, and things of importance. He was going through some tough times, and I just tried to encourage him. How about that? You never know what God may use you for—no matter your age, place, or position in life.

Interestingly enough, he told me that whenever he comes to a club, he makes it a point to play well, but not too well. You don't want the members to suddenly think that their scores aren't that good. At the same time, you don't want to play badly because then they'll think the course is too hard.

So after a couple of holes, he said, "I'm just going to shoot a 67 and that'll be perfect."

Probably on the fifth or sixth hole, he said, "Man, you can really hit it a long way with your driver." Then he offered me his, telling me that it would be much better than mine. (We're both left-handed.) He was right—the ball went at least thirty yards farther. It was an insane drive.

On the fifteenth hole, a par 5, he handed his driver to me again and said, "Let it rip, man." He told me to tee it up just a little higher and I might get more carry, plus a better roll. So I did. I teed it up higher and hit it as hard as I could. Absolutely crushed it. Except that I got under it a bit too much, and the ball literally went straight up in the air. It may have landed five yards down the course still on the tee box, after going eighty yards straight up.

Even worse than the embarrassment of that shot, it made a crazy sound right when I hit it. I had hit so far under the ball that it had scuffed the top of his driver. I felt terrible and apologized, but he said not to worry about it—he'd told me to do it. Thankfully, I was sure that he had ten of those drivers. Right?

"No, *this* is my driver. It's my baby. I love this club." He looked stricken as he said it but was trying very hard to be nonchalant and gracious, but I still felt terrible. He ended up using his favorite driver all week and played well but didn't win the tournament. Hopefully he doesn't blame me.

We kept playing, and then after a while we were both bragging about our strong throwing arms. Finally, on the last hole, with a crowd gathering at the clubhouse, we challenged each other to a throwing contest. He had somebody bring us a football, and the challenge was that I would throw it from my knees farther than he would throw the ball standing up.

He's got a good arm and probably threw it fifty or fifty-five yards. So I got on my knee, didn't say anything, and just let it fly. It went at least five yards past his.

He wanted a do-over, and I beat him again.

By the way, he shot a 67. Amazing.

Every year at the end of July we'd have a Strong Man competition at Florida for fans. After that we would get a few days off and then start training camp to get ready for the beginning of the season. During that Strong Man competition I was flipping tires end over end down the field with Brandon Spikes, my partner. I hadn't warmed up that great, and I'm not sure what happened—if it slipped from Spikes's grip or whatever—but I tried to pull up with all my might to lift it, and I felt instantly that my lower back gave out. I can be an idiot sometimes because I'm so competitive, and since the competition was still going on, I didn't stop. I kept going through the pain.

Fortunately, I had only strained my lower back, but I ended up having to rest at the beginning of training camp that August. When I finally was able to start practicing, I wasn't allowed to engage in any contact. I was getting better each day until I was carrying out a fake and didn't even have the ball, and not thinking, Carlos Dunlap pushed me from the side and I aggravated my back again and had to sit out even more practices. That loss of practice time due to my back strain bothered me a bit, as did a slight nagging strain during the first half of the season, but it finally cleared up over time.

As a team, we had a good training camp and were well prepared for the season. We knew we still had to find an identity because we'd lost Percy Harvin and Louis Murphy. Of the offensive players that we lost in the off-season, Louis was one of the toughest to replace because he had become my go-to receiver, especially on third downs. Of course, the loss of Percy hurt, too, but in a different way—he was such a playmaker and his explosiveness would always make something special happen on the field.

So we had to find receivers who could take their places. One of those was Riley Cooper, my roommate for two years, who made it clear from the start of camp that he was stepping up his game. Another was Aaron Hernandez, who did a good job catching the ball for us, since his speed at tight end made him a real match-up problem for defenses to cover with a linebacker. But as good as Riley and Aaron were, we didn't have the same deep threats we'd had the year before, which was going to make things more of a struggle offensively.

Similarly, we had two fast running backs with Chris Rainey and Jeff Demps, who would be outside guys with their fantastic speed, but we struggled to find an inside presence who could run the ball up the middle and help us out on short-yardage plays.

One thing we knew was that we had a great defense that we would need to rely on since we lacked the deep threats we had the year before. We knew we could still have a great team—we had a ton of talent—but we would just have to find new ways to get the job done.

From the score of our first game you wouldn't have noticed that anything was different. We opened the year with Charleston Southern and beat them 62–3. But we didn't play great, and we all knew it. In the end we were fine, and that was more than enough to win the game.

Then, for the second time in three years, we played Troy. I don't think that this version of their team was as explosive on offense as their 2007 version, but the rain would have slowed them down anyway. It poured in Gainesville that day, but it didn't make much difference on the field. We were a little sloppy but played a bit better than we had the week before and won, 56–6.

Things seemed to be headed in the right direction, but it was hard to tell. Neither of our first two opponents was as good as the teams that were to follow. You never want to look past teams like that, but I understood when guys did. In fact, maybe the rain helped us focus a bit. For me, it reminded me of games on the farm in the rain; as my dad says, "There's nothing more fun than football in the mud."

Where the weather made a big difference was off of the field. My sister Katie was down from her home in Atlanta for the game. Katie had obviously recovered from her double hernia surgery in the Philippines nicely and was toting my niece, Abby, everywhere, despite being pregnant. The family headed into their regular seats in the stands, but Katie and Abby, a toddler at the time, were headed up to Bill Heavener's box above the west stands in the stadium to stay out of the elements.

At one point, someone on the university staff overheard Katie mention that I was her brother, and because people at Florida have gotten very sensitive to NCAA regulations since the early 1980s, they incorrectly informed Katie that she couldn't stay in the box. Because Uncle Bill had been a college roommate of my father, Katie's presence in the box did not constitute an impermissible benefit to the family, but those words fell on deaf ears. Compounding matters, even beyond the rain, was the fact that Katie realized she no longer had her ticket to her seat in the stands. She couldn't reach any of the family on their cell phones in the packed stands in the pouring rain, so Uncle Bill escorted her down into the stadium and to the seats. That game wasn't as memorable to me, but I know Katie will never forget it.

Lane Kiffin seemed to have a lot to say when he brought the Tennessee Volunteers to play us the following week. In person he's actually very nice, but in the weeks and months leading up to the game, he had way too many things to say to the press about Coach Meyer and the rest of us. At his first press conference right after he was hired, he said he'd stay up all night long singing "Rocky Top" after they beat us in Gainesville that fall. Then, over the summer, he had told Tennessee boosters that Coach Meyer had committed a recruiting violation, so the SEC office got involved; he ended up apologizing to everyone for his statements.

All that talk added up to an emotional game. It was also a frustrating game. Eric Berry got me again early on in the game with an interception on a poorly thrown ball, but aside from that, we did move the ball a bit. We were up 13–6 at the half and then had a chance to separate ourselves in the second half. We were up 23–6, and then I had a really good run down the right sideline, broke a few tackles, and was down around the two yard line where I spun and was stripped of the ball. Fumble. Recovered by Tennessee.

That run would have put the game away, but instead, they drove down and scored, making it 23–13. Later, when they got the ball back, something curious happened. Down by ten in the fourth quarter in a conference game against a bitter rival, Tennessee kept giving the ball to Montario Hardesty, their running back, who was having a big day. There was no sense of urgency, however. They were huddling up and taking their time. I appreciate that our defense intercepted their quarterback, Jonathan Crompton, three times on the day, but it still was curious that they weren't trying to win the game; rather, it appeared that they merely wanted to keep it close.

Whether it was that lack of urgency or our stellar defense, we ended up winning, 23–13. I think they were happier with the score than we were—Coach Meyer even had to try and encourage us in the locker room after the game.

It was turning into a strange season, with the pressure to achieve something special and the expectations we had placed upon ourselves. At this point in 2009, we were 3–0 and had won thirteen straight games over the course of the last two seasons, the longest streak in the country . . . but we were miserable. Simply winning didn't seem to be enough to satisfy us.

I didn't see it at the time, but looking back, I think we maybe should have embraced the 2008 National Championship longer than we did. We immediately applied pressure to ourselves in the off-season, which some guys didn't respond well to. Even those who did find themselves burned out and stressed out early in the season. Certainly we should have worked hard and diligently, but I think we may have overdone it. Despite wins, it simply wasn't a very good situation.

With Kentucky up next, we tried to get past our issues and return to the drive that had fueled us for all of the previous year. Unfortunately, my health turned out to be the story of the next week. Actually make that the next three weeks.

It started on Thursday when I came down with the H1N1 virus, which at the time everyone was calling "swine flu." It came on fast and was awful. I threw up all night and got IVs all day Friday along with several others on our team who'd also gotten it. The doctors kept us away from the rest of the team because the virus was so contagious. That fall, a couple of college and pro teams had it sweep through their entire roster in days. Because we still had symptoms on Friday, the doctors had those of us who had been sick fly separately on Saturday to join the team before the game.

By game time I felt much better, and the game itself started off well enough. As in most of our games against Kentucky over that last two decades, we dominated them. I was having a big day running, even though I had to have fluids administered intravenously throughout the game because of the flu. They used a big—huge really—diameter needle and squeezed the IV bags to force the fluids into our veins that much quicker, so we were able to get back on the field quickly.

I had rushed sixteen times for 123 yards into the third quarter, and we were driving again. We called Trick Left 351 P-Stick Lion, and as we were breaking from the huddle, I remember thinking that we actually should have scored on the play before. I went into my count and caught the snap. I looked for my receiver who was on a slant across the middle. *This* play would be a touchdown.

Darkness.

My parents looked serious, with a low metal ceiling above them.

Darkness.

"It's okay, Timmy," Kyle, our assistant trainer, said. "Just roll over." I couldn't figure out why I was rolling over or what the white metal was around me.

"They're just gonna slide you in there for a CAT scan." I rolled, stayed quiet, and waited for an explanation of why I was there.

As I was waiting for the slant to come open, a Kentucky defender had flown into me, hitting me below the chin. They told me much later that the blow to the chin wasn't what caused my concussion, but rather the back of my head hitting my offensive lineman, Marcus Gilbert, in the knee as I fell backward from the hit. Rather than being apologetic, Marcus pointed out that he was the one who should be hurt and that no one was asking if I'd damaged his knee with my head. (I hadn't.)

My family, sitting and watching this all unfold before them in the stands, were horrified, and as they always do in times good and bad, they started to pray. It was an awful-looking hit, and the chief of neurosurgery at Kentucky later told my dad that he was sure my spinal cord had been damaged.

AP and our training staff, as well as Kentucky's staff, all immediately flew into action, as trainers always do when someone gets badly hurt. And the ones we have, along with Doctor Pete (Indelicato), at the University of Florida are exceptional. I've always appreciated that about sports-medicine professionals—they are a part of the team, but when someone goes down, the team allegiances fall away as they scramble to attend to the player. Any player.

I threw up as I was taken off in a cart—they were good enough to have draped me with a towel so I could at least have a moment of privacy. My parents rode in the back of the ambulance to the hospital, concerned and praying as I was checked out.

Coach Meyer came straight over to the University of Kentucky Medical Center, not far from the stadium, immediately following the game. He told me that my first question when I briefly came to on the field was, "Did I hold on to the ball?" I did. And my second, in the hospital, was, "Did we win?" We did, and John Brantley had filled in nicely for me in the fourth quarter. I found that to be consoling. Of course, I hated that I hadn't finished the game alongside my teammates, but I was pleased they had gone on to win.

Coach started telling me about the game, which my family says was about the time the fog started to lift for me. The medical staff kept me up all night, not letting me fall asleep, and took really good care of me. I checked out fine and returned to Gainesville the next day.

It's noteworthy, for reasons that don't immediately come to mind, that both times I went to Lexington, I came back injured. Those were good games, and I'd love to have them everywhere I played, but I just wish I could have the good games minus the injuries.

Thank goodness we had a bye week following the Kentucky game, because our next game was in Baton Rouge. We were ranked number one, and they were ranked number four, and despite our loss there in 2007, I loved playing in Tiger Stadium.

Florida flew in a concussion specialist from Pittsburgh to look at me. After evaluating me, he determined that one of the most important factors for me to be able to play again was that I be completely free of headaches for a certain number of days. To this end, the prescribed course of treatment was that I had to sit in my darkened apartment for days with no stimulation. No television, no reading. Just dark with no input of any kind whatsoever.

The LSU fans didn't seem to have my new cell-phone number, so that helped keep things quiet too.

I was so worried that I wouldn't get to play that I did everything I could to stay quiet and in the dark. I wasn't worried about playing again. I'd been hit plenty of times—hard—but had always bounced back. I didn't fear playing or being hit. I just prayed that the Lord would allow me to play—quickly. In keeping with my personality, that if a little is good then a lot is better, I stayed totally quiet and dark for the week. It was hard, but I tried to keep my thoughts quiet as well.

After our bye weekend, I was allowed to start to take on some light activities.

There was so much speculation as to whether I would play or not. It seems that everyone in the media had an opinion, which they were more than happy to share. I didn't care. I don't pay attention to all the noise out there, since everyone always seems to have an opinion, whether the person has the facts or not. For me, it was easy. I was going to do everything I could to get out there—by doing what the medical professionals were telling me to do.

The guessing continued right up until game time. Coach Addazio put together two game plans, one for me, and one for Johnny Brantley. I was worried about the flight, since, as with roller coasters, my head doesn't always respond well to flights, but as it turned out, the flight wasn't an issue.

After a number of tests, the doctors cleared me to play the morning of the game, but Coach took me aside before we got on the bus to go to Tiger Stadium.

"I'm not going to let you play," he said. He had tears in his eyes—he knew how much it meant to me.

"I *have* to play," I responded.

He cut me off. "I keep asking myself, if you were Nate, would I let you play? I keep saying, 'No.' I can't let you play." He really wanted to win, but he was unwilling to take a chance with my health.

"But they cleared me, and I haven't had headaches in days," I countered. "There's no reason for me not to play."

"No headaches?"

"No, Coach. No headaches." A headache had been starting to set in, but for all I know, it was from stress or a migraine, not the concussion.

Coach Meyer softened and said that we'd decide after warm-ups. All other things being equal, he would have erred on the side of caution, but I know my desire to play was eating at him.

I was praying in the locker room that the headache, which had been getting worse and worse, would simply go away. It didn't. I could barely see by the end of pregame warm-ups, it was hurting so badly.

Even though I don't recommend for anyone to ever do this, I played.

We started our first drive from our own seven yard line. Coach sent me in, and then, the moment I crossed the wide, white sideline and ran across the twenty-five yard line (Tiger Stadium is the only stadium I ever played in that paints the numbers every five yards instead of merely every ten) toward the end zone, my head completely cleared. No pain. I don't know if it was the adrenaline, the warm wishes from the LSU faithful directed my way, or the Lord's touch, but the pain was gone instantaneously. It never came back.

I only carried a couple of times, anyway, as the coaches didn't want me to take any more blows. We marched eighty-two yards on that first drive and kicked a field goal to take a 3–0 lead, and then they tied it in the second quarter. We really struggled on offense, but our defense stepped up in a big way. Right before halftime, I hit Riley Cooper on a twenty-four-yard touchdown, and our defense made that touchdown stand up. We won, 13–3. It was a great return to Baton Rouge.

We were very happy heading back to Gainesville. Certainly we would have liked to have done more on offense, but we were limited with what we could do because of my injury. So much of our offense was predicated upon the possibility that I would rush the ball, but everyone knew—especially LSU's defense—that wasn't going to happen. Not that night. At the end of the day, that was a good win against a very good team.

We had things to work on that week but were upbeat as we practiced. We had gotten over a major hurdle without being at full strength.

The game against Arkansas was remarkable the following week at our place. My head had been totally fine ever since I stepped onto the field at Louisiana State. Arkansas played well. It was a game to remember, even though our fans seemed less than pleased that it was so close. The whole game consisted of missed opportunities, which kept it close. We had an uncharacteristic number of fumbles and missed tackles, and for a while it felt like the Ole Miss game of 2008 all over again. There was no way I was going to let that happen. No way.

At one point, I hit Chris Rainey, who was wide open on a swing route. There was no one between him and a seven-yard touchdown except for the safety, and Chris totally made the guy miss. As the safety was falling away, he stuck his foot out and kicked the ball, which caused the ball to fly out of Chris's grip, up into the air, and onto the turf. They recovered. No one else was even in the area to tackle Chris, and yet a stray foot caused a turnover. Later on, Aaron Hernandez fumbled after a long reception on which he'd made a great effort, and still later I was stripped of the ball and they recovered the fumble. Just totally bizarre stuff, which was what made it reminiscent of the Ole Miss game from the previous year. Here they were with the worst statistical defense in the conference, and we couldn't put them away. In fact, we were trailing until late in the game.

We tied the game in the fourth quarter at 20 on a great play by Jeff Demps, and then we got the ball back. On that final drive, we were trying to score and leave as little time remaining on the clock as possible. In addition to our four turnovers and numerous dropped passes, our defense had even struggled, surprisingly. After saving us against LSU, they had an off day against a very solid Arkansas offense. Because of that, we didn't want to leave any time for Arkansas's offense to get back on the field.

I felt that it was our turn on offense to step up—I mean we had turned the ball over an unacceptable four times. I told Coach to give me the ball; I was in one of those crazy moods.

I ended up throwing for thirty yards on that drive and rushing for twenty-two more. On a third and ten play, we called time-out and then ran a play to Coop, where if it was man-to-man, one-on-one, he was going to run a stop route and I would put it right on him. The defender would think Coop was running a fade to the end zone, but instead we'd just get the first down.

If they weren't in man, then we'd probably go to Hernandez on an in cut. They gave us man-to-man and blitzed. Coop tripped coming off the line, but he scrambled up and I hit him in the chest for a first down. A huge play. Of course, the pass was at chest level because he was going to the ground again, and he actually made the catch of my low pass while on a knee—an amazing grab.

At the end of our drive, Caleb Sturgis kicked a field goal to win it with nine seconds left. I didn't open my eyes until I heard the crowd roar; 23–20.

Sure, it shouldn't have been that close, but it was a fun game and a gut check for us. We had been confronted with the Ole Miss game, the 2009 version, only this time we'd survived. We had to find a way to win that game, and we did. I was proud of our team.

On the one hand, it was troubling to have struggled with Arkansas. On the other, every team has the occasional game that they simply have to escape. When you're on the field scraping it out, you're not thinking about "style points" or coaches voting or what people on ESPN will say when the highlight reel rolls; you're thinking about winning the game. A win is a win, and we'd gotten exactly that. While there was a mild sense of anxiety over the game itself, we felt that we would have a chance to correct any shortcomings moving forward. We were still undefeated, and that was what mattered.

Chapter Twenty

FINISHING STRONG

*I have fought the good fight, I have finished
the course, and I have kept the faith.*
—2 TIMOTHY 4:7

I knew Mississippi State would be interesting. We were looking forward to seeing Coach Mullen and hoped that our knowing him as well as we did would counter any advantage he might gain by how well he knew our schemes and our personnel.

Therefore, going in, everyone knew that Coach Mullen was going to design some stuff for us because he knew our physical limitations and tendencies, and, man, did he deliver.

The game started off well. In the second quarter, I rushed for a touchdown to tie Herschel Walker for the all-time SEC rushing touchdown record. But things went downhill from there. We were ahead 13–3 right before halftime and were driving against the Mississippi State defense, trying to put the game away. We were inside their ten yard line. Coach Mullen knew exactly what my check was on this certain play, so they showed like they were blitzing but didn't. I threw it up to the corner at the goal line as they anticipated. It was tipped and intercepted by Johnthan Banks, who ran it back one hundred yards for a touchdown, making it 13–10 going into the locker room at halftime.

A bad play by me, and now we were only up three. There was clearly some dissention in the locker room. It was not going well, and making matters worse on the other side of the ball was the fact that Brandon Spikes wasn't playing due to a hurt groin.

Finally, in the fourth quarter, we scored a touchdown on a run by Chris Rainey to put us up by nine and give us some breathing room. On Mississippi State's next possession, Dustin Doe returned an interception for a touchdown to put the game away. I'm thankful that he did, because I then threw another interception that was returned for a touchdown. Coach Mullen definitely had my number that night.

Even before my last interception, it had already been a tough night. A defensive leader had a pointed comment for me on the sidelines, which didn't sit well with any of us on offense. For four years we had always stuck together, with no finger pointing between the offense and defense, regardless of what was happening. I don't know what it was that was bothering him, but the Pounceys responded to him, and things started to heat up on the sidelines. I grabbed the Pounceys and pulled them away, but at the same time I was just as mad about the situation as they were.

We ended up winning, but it wasn't a good feeling for anybody; we were all a bit empty. I was really upset by it all after the game— my interceptions, our poor play, the moment on the sidelines. Afterward my family encircled me, under the stadium, helping me deal with it all.

From the outer edges of our group I could hear somebody asking to get through to me—Dan Mullen. He was great. He took me aside, put his arm around me, and encouraged me with thoughts both football-related and otherwise. It was a moment I'll never forget.

He didn't ask about my eye black, however. It was Ephesians 4:32, which was particularly appropriate for that day—"Be kind to one another, tender-hearted . . ." I'd heard that he had started an optional coaches' Bible study for the Mississippi State staff, which is impressive. It's tough to give up staff-meeting time, but he did. It's simply amazing what God will do with relationships if we allow Him to work in our lives.

When we got back to Gainesville, we had a leadership meeting and a team meeting. The leadership meeting was with Coach Meyer, Coach Mick, the coordinators, and some of the player-leaders. The defensive player sincerely apologized, and we went on our way with that behind us.

Still, there was no denying that it had become a surprisingly tough season. If we weren't winning in perfect fashion, then we were very dissatisfied. That's a tough standard to live with. And I think that because we had such a high standard and such high expectations—Best Ever—we put unnecessary pressure on ourselves at times rather than just going out and playing the game. We'd been looking so hard for a way to motivate ourselves in the off-season, and that title of Best Ever seemed to get everyone motivated and thinking the right things. But in actuality, what we really needed to do was focus on doing whatever we could to get ready to win games. The labels could always come later.

And honestly, we should have relaxed. We were a team stretched tight like a rubber band. We were probably starting to fray at the edges, and that was in no small part because of the pressure that we'd put on ourselves. I wish we had all taken a step back at some point, but charging ahead always seemed like the right thing—keep our focus, keep working harder. We needed to appreciate where we were, where we'd been, and who we were. But in that moment, this was a very tough thing to do.

We pushed ahead and got ready for our annual skirmish in Jacksonville. Even though they had a lot of talent and a lot of good players, Georgia wasn't as good as the year before. Of course, that didn't stop them from talking their usual trash during pregame. They came out wearing these new uniforms with black helmets, and we just went to work on them. I threw two touchdown passes in the first quarter and then rushed for a touchdown in the second, breaking former Georgia Heisman Trophy winner Herschel Walker's all-time SEC rushing touchdown mark. To do that against Georgia, in my hometown, made it that much better. I kept that ball and gave it to my dad for Christmas.

After a first half like that, we knew we were in control, and we went on to beat them handily, 41–17. The only controversy came when Brandon Spikes tried to poke a guy in the eye. Coach Meyer suspended him for the first half of the next game, because what he did was wrong. He shouldn't have done that, without question. Brandon would tell you that too.

At the same time, though, people are so naive about what happens on the field. Spikes said he was retaliating for someone's trying to do the same to him earlier in the game, and I believe him. After all, I had three occasions in that game as well when guys were trying to grab my neck or gouge my eyes. And you do not want to know what happens in piles in every game, with guys trying to grab someone in places that could cause some serious pain. It's awful, but it's not like Spikes invented this stuff.

I agreed with the punishment as a way to hopefully deter this in the future—Spikes himself ended up agreeing to sit out the entire next game because of the outcry—but I think people were singling him out unfairly. Maybe we could get more pictures from piles or maybe get the referees to pay more attention—I'll bet something like that happened to me at least forty times in my college career. A lot of good players that I played against unfortunately engaged in stuff like this.

With Brandon out for our next game at Vandy, our concerns about being without one of our best players on defense were eased by the hope that we could repeat our solid victory over them from the previous year. While we didn't put up the kind of numbers that our offense was used to, our defense had a stellar performance, as we beat them by a score of 27–3.

There was no doubt we were better than they were, but as with some of the earlier games that season, our play was only good, not great. This was especially true on offense where we encountered a carefully designed game plan that they executed well. They had a solid cornerback, Myron Lewis, who stayed on Riley Cooper all game. They gambled that he could stay on Coop without help, and then they had the rest of their guys available to help on Hernandez and the rest of our offensive threats. Lewis played great, and that was a game when we missed some of the receiving talent—Caldwell, Murphy, and Harvin—that we'd lost the last few years to the NFL.

People everywhere were looking for a reason to explain what was off about our offense, and often that reason was Percy Harvin's absence. While there's no doubt that not having Percy's explosive ability hurt us, in my opinion, the person we missed most was Louis Murphy, who I'd always thought was publicly underappreciated. Murph was the guy that we were going to on third downs when we had to have it, because he was going to find a way to get open and beat man coverage and win the play. He and I were always on the same page. I could look at him a certain way and he'd know what I was thinking. He was also the hardest working receiver I'd ever played with. Other guys worked really hard, too, but every single day my freshman through junior years Louis would stay after practice, keep working, and then work more on his own.

His drive was clearly exhibited on a play that year. While we were missing him, he was playing well for the Oakland Raiders. Zach Miller, the Raiders' tight end, caught an eighty-six yard touchdown pass that never would have happened but for Louis's hustle to get out in front of the play and block three different guys at different times. Three. I love that. That's what I mean about Louis Murphy.

As we prepared the next week, we continued to try and refine our offense and make improvements based on what each game was showing us. This was crucial because the next game was at South Carolina, and it was tough, as always. With the sense that we still could be playing better ringing in our ears, I was pleased that we were able to make that game one of the best games of the year. Very early in the game I hit Coop on a skinny post (almost a straight line pattern toward the goal post, almost down the exact center of the field) for a touchdown. Even though we didn't score a lot that day, I did a good job of managing the options and audibles to get us into some good plays. There was even one fourth down and one, at their twenty-five yard line; I audibled to an option to an overload that wasn't even in our game plan for the week. We were able to get the edge, and I pitched to Demps, who scored on it.

In general, the game was going much as we'd hoped it would. Unlike the Vandy game, we were playing more like ourselves, executing better, and maintaining possession. Then, in the third quarter, I was running down the middle, when I cut it inside and tried to side-step someone going low for the tackle and at the same time hurdle him. He hit my leg, and I flipped over him, landing on the back of my head. I got up and started walking toward the wrong sideline, when Coop grabbed me and pulled me back to the huddle. On that next play the offensive guys helped me call the play because I was still gathering myself as to exactly where I was.

AP was always very alert and aware, so when I got to the sidelines after the drive, he asked if I was okay. I was dizzy but didn't let on to him that I was anything but okay. We never told anyone, but Coop and the rest of the offense knew. It went away quickly and I was fine the rest of the game. We won, 24–14.

After dispatching Florida International University, FSU was coming to town for my last game in the Swamp. Senior Day. It was an emotional week, between a wonderful Thanksgiving holiday and the knowledge that my last game was coming. I could see that Coach Meyer was pretty emotional that week, too, so I tried not to think about it too much, but we spoke of it some during the week leading up—our last game together in the Swamp. We talked around it a little, that we wouldn't be able to spend as much time together in the future when I was no longer playing, but neither of us had the heart to bring it up directly.

We had really great practices as a team that week, and the coaches' speeches before the game made for a great atmosphere. It started with Vitamin Addazio. He's one of the best at pregame speeches, any-way, which is why Coach Meyer nicknamed him Vitamin Addazio—because time with him gave us a charge. That day his talk was packed even fuller than usual, as he spoke about the seniors, what the group had accomplished, and our overall level of character. The other coaches spoke as well, and by the end we were all a mixture of being ready to play and never wanting it to end.

By pregame warm-up time, I was throwing the football badly. I wouldn't have said that I was so emotional that it was throwing me off, but I'd never had that happen before. I don't know what happened. I asked David Nelson to come into the locker room so I could throw the ball to him in there to continue to get loose even after pregame.

Eventually they began reading off the names of seniors, and one by one they'd run out onto the field. I hadn't thought much about what I was going to do when they announced my name and I ran out on the field by myself—for that one last game. Other people did stuff when they got called. I figured I would just go out of the tunnel like every other game, give Coach a hug, and go win the game.

When I was waiting in line—I was the last one— I was seeing the other guys go out, and they were getting hugs and everything. It got so emotional, and I really didn't even think I was going to get emotional, but by the time it was my turn and I was up—I was already crying. I took off out of the tunnel, one last time, and reached Coach Meyer, who was also crying.

So many lunches. So many times hanging out at his lake place near Gainesville. So many film sessions. So many discussions. So many Bible studies. So many plays called. Injuries and chipped teeth. So many moments that we would always remember. He would always be there in my life, but it was going to be different. I later heard that fans were getting emotional as well when they saw us—it was impossible for us not to be emotional, too. I'm not sure why I ever thought that I wouldn't.

That was pretty much the end that day for FSU. Game over.

Somehow, the emotion of the moment and the extra throwing with David changed everything—when the game started, I began hitting all my receivers. I played my best game of the year against FSU. Probably because I was playing FSU. We killed them. We had great checks. They were covering our receivers really tight, but our guys were still able to create enough separation that I was able to put it on them. Anything and everything we wanted to do, we were doing on offense.

Behind a great offensive line, I threw three touchdown passes, and ran for two more. I even fumbled late in the game, but for once I didn't beat myself up too much about it. The fumble came at the end of a good play and we were killing them by that point. It still bothered me . . . but it was a really awesome play.

It was good to beat them four times.

After the game, we went to the Hilton, where we'd planned a surprise celebration for my mom's birthday. All her friends and everybody in town were there, about a hundred of us in all, in what proved to be an incredibly happy occasion on an otherwise bittersweet day. As good as it felt to beat FSU and close out the regular season undefeated, it was hard to shake the knowledge that my time was coming to a close. Of course, before that could happen, we had to face the biggest test so far this year.

The next week was the SEC Championship Game against Alabama. Carlos Dunlap got arrested during the week for driving under the influence of alcohol, and Coach Meyer understandably suspended him. I was furious with Carlos.

I don't get why anyone would take substances that would affect their thinking anyway, but how someone could be so reckless and thoughtless, not only toward himself, but also toward both innocent bystanders as well as his teammates as we prepared for such an important game, was beyond me.

His loss really hurt us, both as a distraction during the week and during the game. Not only was he a good run stopper, but he was someone who could have brought pressure on the pass rush against their quarterback, Greg McElroy. As it turns out, we couldn't do that all game. That hurt us.

They started the game off better than we did. We fell behind, but after every lead we came back. Unfortunately, we simply couldn't stop them. We trailed 12–10 in the second quarter and then 19–13 at the half. Looking back, I should have been more unsettled than I was at halftime, but I was certain we would come back to win. They were controlling the line of scrimmage on both sides of the ball, however, and were simply crisper than we were.

As the second half began, they didn't miss a beat, playing solid football that we couldn't counter. They had a good plan for us defensively, by switching up their coverages and bracketing our receivers. On defense, we just couldn't stop them enough. Or even at all, really. We ended up losing on a very long night, 32–13. On that night, they had the passion and focus and were the better team.

After the game, I was, as you probably can imagine, overwhelmed by emotion and could not hold back the tears. This wasn't how this was supposed to go. Things weren't supposed to end here like this. The feeling I was faced with now was different from after our last loss—the Ole Miss game in 2008. Disappointing as that loss was, I knew I could still do everything in my power to change the course of that season, and I did. I'd approached this game the way I'd approached every game since the Ole Miss game: I'm going to do everything in my power to make the future what I want it to be. On this day it hadn't been enough, and it was an incredibly hard thing to swallow. And worse, it was the end. There was no bouncing back, at least not for our National Championship chances.

Before I could take the podium to address the media, Coach Saban came and found me. He was quite gracious. He told my family what a class act I was and how my determination last year had become the focal point for Alabama this season. As it turns out, while we were searching during the off-season for the motivation that would drive us to becoming the Best Ever, Coach Saban was telling his players that they had to match my determination. All year, Alabama was using my drive as their measuring stick. Nothing was going to shake off the pain of that loss, but I appreciated his comments that night more than he probably realized.

That game is one that will always be with me. It'll always hurt like all the St. Augustine losses while at Nease. To lose an SEC Championship Game, and an undefeated season, and a National Championship, all in one fell swoop . . . well that was tough. We believed we were the two best teams in the country and whichever one of us won that day would win the National Championship game.

It ate at me, but that's life. Sometimes it doesn't break your way, yet the Lord has a plan for it all. I'd rather there be fair winds and following seas all the time in my life, but that's not always what God has in mind for us. But either way, we are to honor Him and bring Him glory.

Sometimes, people see more of your witness when you're facing adversity than when everything is going your way. People expect you to be a good winner, but they know how agonizing it is to lose. When you are able to reflect God's light during those times of great disappointment, it can have quite an impact. I try to keep that in mind.

I know that somewhere people may be watching you or me, and how they see us handle the adversity that comes into our lives could make a difference in how they handle something they face in their lives.

The next week, I went to Orlando for the Home Depot College Football Awards ceremony again. There was no pressure that year—I knew I wouldn't win anything. We'd had a good year, but statistically other guys had been better.

There was a function the night before the Home Depot Awards, and as I walked into the ESPN Club at Disney's BoardWalk, I saw her outside the window, looking at us. We sat at our table—the exact same spot in the exact same restaurant from which Uncle Bill (Heavener) had called my sister Christy in 2007 to see if she could come to the Heisman ceremony two days later. This time, however, I was thinking about the girl outside the window. The way she was looking at me, pointing toward me.

My dad tells me that he was trying to get my attention to introduce me to someone "important," as he says it. I don't recall that, because I was focused on someone else important. I asked Robby to go outside and bring the girl and her family through security, and I met her. Kelly Faughnan had been diagnosed with a brain tumor the prior year, and following surgery, she had asked her parents if they could come to Disney, not only for a vacation, but also to hopefully meet me at the Home Depot Awards. I was both flattered and shocked. Then, I had an idea: since I didn't have a date for the following night at the awards ceremony, I asked her if she'd walk the red carpet and attend the event with me.

She agreed, and Uncle Bill also offered to give Kelly and her family a tour of Full Sail University's Orlando campus the next afternoon. It's a fascinating place to see, training people in entertainment, media, and fine arts.

They were late to their tour the next day and, in fact, ended up rescheduling it altogether. Turns out they were busy dress shopping for the event—I hadn't even thought of that.

We had a great night, talking, walking the red carpet together, and enjoying each other's company through the event. The Lord provided everything—we walked the red carpet more slowly than anyone else, because the surgery had left her balance a little off, but at the same time, I enjoyed stopping for everyone who wanted something signed. It was the perfect speed for both.

At the end of the evening, I turned to my mom and said that, sure enough, I didn't win anything.

She paused, and I could tell that I was going to get some of Mom's wisdom.

"You had the best night of all."

Right again, Mom. Right again.

Going to the Heisman that weekend was fun. Although I had won the Campbell Award, the "Academic Heisman," we knew I wouldn't be winning the original Heisman that year. I knew I wasn't going to win, so that took all the pressure off. I'm the only player who has ever been invited to three of them, but I'm still not entirely sure why they even invited me. At the same time, I wasn't going to turn down another one of those fun New York family vacations that we'd gotten used to the past few years.

While we were there, we got a chance to visit with Mark Ingram, and we adopted him into our family, since he'd made the trip by himself. At first he thought we were nuts—we showed him how we were breaking people's hands on the sidewalks of Manhattan. Not literally breaking them, but breaking apart couples. For some reason, starting in 2007, Robby, Peter, and I were trying to see how many couples who were holding hands we could get to unclasp hands. I'm not sure why we did it, but we got some looks, followed by an occasional look of, "Wait. I think that was Tim Tebow who just made us let go . . ."

We would also do spin moves, by simply walking directly at people, then at the last minute, spinning as if they were a defender and walking past them. We got a lot of weird looks on that, too, including one from Mark. After a few minutes, however, he joined in.

So . . . if anyone tells you that Mark Ingram and three other guys made him and his wife unclasp their hands, or put a spin move on him on a New York sidewalk in December of 2009, it's completely true.

On the Heisman night I could tell Mark was so tight and nervous; I asked him if he wanted to pray with me, much like Danny had done for me two years before. I knew how nerve wracking that night can be. I was pulling for him to win, especially after a weekend of spin moves. I encouraged him to handle it with his usual grace and humility and give God the credit. Thankfully, Mark won. What a class act.

In the meantime, I was concerned about Coach Meyer's health. During the SEC Championship Game, he'd experienced chest pains, but with the way we'd played, who wouldn't?

We tried to put it all out of our minds and prepare for Cincinnati. They'd been highly ranked all year, but to be honest, the excitement and energy to play Cincinnati in the Sugar Bowl wasn't there in the same way. It was nothing personal against them—the same would have been true no matter who we faced. The bottom line was that our goal had been to play for the National Championship; anything less than that was a disappointment.

Still we had a pretty decent few weeks of practice. It was important to me that we finish strong. Sometimes in life things don't work out as you'd hoped. You adopt phrases like Best Ever, and yet it doesn't work out with the fairytale ending. How you respond is important. Do you put your tail between your legs, or do you find the next challenge and press on?

I wanted us to press on, to finish strong.

The day after Christmas, we were thrown a curveball: Coach Meyer resigned. I was excited for him to start his next phase of life with his family. It also gave us a renewed focus on the Sugar Bowl. The next day we went out there in shorts, shirts, and helmets and had an unbelievable practice at which Coach got really emotional.

I guess it was hard for him to decide what to do, and he was trying to make a quick yet wise decision. He changed his mind that same day and decided to come back for the Sugar Bowl and then take a leave of absence through the spring and stay as the head coach.

I really wanted the best for him, whichever direction he chose—he is someone who is always trying to do the right thing for his family, for himself, for the school, for his players, and for his coaches. He tried to figure out the best chance for success for his players, not just for football but for their lives. Every Tuesday during my senior year he would bring in people to talk about job opportunities and how you can get jobs, building your resume, etc. Stuff that would help the players when their playing careers were over, and he took away from practice time to do that for us. I think that shows a lot of character too. Really, though, you can't even begin to scratch the surface of the number of lives he has affected and changed because he cares so much.

We finished strong, by the way. Cincinnati was ranked number four in the country, while we had fallen to number five after our loss to Alabama. They were undefeated and disappointed that they wouldn't be playing for the National Championship. We, of course, were disappointed as well. We took out our disappointment on them.

I completed my first twelve passes, and we scored on our first five possessions, racing out to a big lead. I completed twenty of my first twenty-three passes for 320 yards and three touchdowns by halftime, and by early in the third quarter we led, 30–3.

We won, 51–24, and I passed for the most yards in my college career, 482, completing thirty-one of my thirty-five attempts. I ended up with 533 yards of total offense, the most in the history of any BCS game. It was a tremendous way to finish, both for me as well as for our senior class. In doing so, we became the first school to win thirteen games in back-to-back seasons.

Some think we showed that we were, in fact, the Best Ever.

And when I was finished with my eligibility, Nancy Scarborough, Coach Meyer's assistant who is such a good friend—who I hung out with every day with Coach Meyer—called and said that I had a package there to pick up. Phil Mickelson remembered how bad my driver was when we played, so he sent me two drivers.

Coach was coming back to the University of Florida, but I was not. I was headed out into the unknown, again.

I was finished here, and like so many of the guys I was privileged to play with and the coaches who coached us, I did the best I could, trying to always finish strong.

Chapter Twenty-One

THE DRAFT, DENVER, AND AN ETERNAL DIRECTION

Brethren, I do not regard myself as having laid hold of it yet;
but one thing I do: forgetting what lies behind and reaching forward
to what lies ahead, I press on toward the goal for the prize of the
upward call of God in Christ Jesus.
—Philippians 3:13–14

I was finished with my college eligibility. I had also graduated with honors from the University of Florida with a bachelor's degree in family, youth, and community sciences. I don't think I could've squeezed many more experiences out of those years than I did.

By then I had selected an agent for the next phase in my life, a potential professional career in football—the NFL. Florida has a panel to help screen agents, and after interviewing a number of them, my family decided that Jimmy Sexton from Memphis, Tennessee, was the best fit for us.

Jimmy suggested that I attend the Senior Bowl in Mobile, Alabama, in late January, to work out for the NFL scouts who would be there en masse. Unfortunately, when I arrived in Mobile, I was coming down with strep throat. I pushed through the infection, not letting anyone know that I was sick. It wasn't easy—I felt terrible and didn't eat for two days—but I didn't want to skip anything. Jimmy, instead, began telling people that I was ill, which I hated because I didn't want to use an excuse. I did, however, actually have esophagitis, and I lost sixteen pounds that week.

He probably had to, because once again, as has happened every time I moved on to the next challenge, the critics were out in full force. And if I wasn't able to practice and play at my full speed and ability because of an illness, it would be much better for those evaluating my performance to know that any shortfall in performance wasn't the result of lack of effort but instead because of strep. Much like the writers who said that my style would never work in the SEC, now the prognosticators were saying that my throwing motion—thanks, Dad!—would never allow me to be successful in the NFL. My draft status was speculated to be anywhere from the first round to well down in the draft order.

At one point in Mobile, I was in my hotel room signing autographs, and my brothers were there with me, joking around and always helping to keep the atmosphere light and bring a little perspective to the moment. Suddenly, an ESPN commentator came on the television screen and opined, "Tim Tebow is probably the fifth or sixth best quarterback in the 2010 draft." I guess that's a step up—based on what Oklahoma said, I thought I was only fifth or sixth best in the Big 12. The room was instantly still and quiet, but I kept signing autographs. Robby noted that the commentator wasn't in charge of any club's draft and never had been. "You know how many guys he'll be choosing at the draft? Zero."

I didn't care. Really. I'd heard that before. I was already working as hard as I could; some comments by someone I didn't know weren't going to change my approach or how I saw myself. I kept signing, and then we went to the weight room for a workout.

Somewhere he is out there . . .

As Jimmy kept reminding me, we didn't need to convince all thirty-two teams to value me enough to pick me, only one. My Senior Bowl stay and performance was adequate and gave me a baseline from which I could improve. Adequate, though, has never been a measure I have aspired to reach, and so I was looking forward to improving in all the areas I needed to for the next level. Those improvements started immediately, as I began working out in Nashville at a facility called D1 Sports Training.

I ran, I threw, I lifted, and I did a variety of drills to improve my body. I also continued watching film and looked for ways to improve the mental part of my game. Anything I could do to make myself better, I did. I threw thousands of passes of all distances, arcs, spin speeds, touches, and routes.

Even as we were thinking about what possibilities my next platform that God had in store might bring, another opportunity arose. In conjunction with Bill Heavener and Focus on the Family, we decided to create an advertisement to be played during the Super Bowl. We were very fortunate that Focus on the Family had donors step up to fund the ad.

Mom and I were the main actors in the ad and had a lot of fun shooting the commercial. But we didn't let the subject matter of the script get out, and as soon as word got out that we were doing an ad with Focus on the Family, it instantly created a huge swirl of attention—with both supporters and detractors trying to figure out what the ad was all about. It was fun to see the speculation on every front as to the message the ad would convey. Because of the story surrounding the circumstances of my birth, everybody on both sides of the issue immediately assumed that it was a pro-life message. So many columnists took me to task for something they assumed was going to be in the ad, but wasn't.

Ultimately, the ad was a celebration of life and about the importance of family, showing me and my mom laughing and just being together. At one point in the ad, I tackled my mom, and she popped back up and warned me to be careful—"You're not nearly as tough as I am." Considering that she raised five homeschooled kids, she was right.

People seemed to enjoy the ad, and it really captured my mom and me and our relationship perfectly. Fun, lighthearted, enjoying life together. Focus on the Family's website did contain a message about the circumstances of my birth, and they received a number of stories from people who altered their outlook on the issue based on my birth story. A survey by the Barna Group showed that five and a half million people indicated that they had cause to rethink their position on abortion. All in all, it was a great experience.

By late February, it was time for the NFL Combine, gathering together the projected top college football players, in Indianapolis, Indiana. The NFL teams, through their representatives and club scouts, take physical examinations; test your strength, speed, and agility; work you out in football drills; and interview you. I was pleased with my performance—I even had the fastest three-cone time of all the quarterbacks at the Combine and third or fourth-fastest overall, a test of quickness and agility.

And then after the Combine, back to my regimen—more lifting, more running, more throwing.

There were a ton of NFL folks at the Pro Day hosted by the University of Florida on March 17. That was understandable, because we had a lot of really good players who were entering the draft: Joe Haden, Brandon Spikes, Aaron Hernandez, Riley Cooper, David Nelson, and others. The scouts and coaches were also curious to see me and how I threw; I had chosen not to work on any passing drills at the Combine because I wanted to continue working on my throwing motion.

Pro Day went well, I thought, but at the end of the day, the measure by which all quarterbacks are evaluated is winning and losing. Drew Brees is too short, they said. He's turned out to be a pretty good quarterback. Meanwhile, other guys with great mechanics couldn't lead. I just needed someone who believed in me and my abilities and who I was inside.

I didn't have to get *every* team to want to take me . . . just that *one*.

We stayed in Jacksonville for the NFL draft. I was invited by the NFL to attend the draft in New York, but given the relative uncertainty of the round in which I was going to be selected, as well as the desire to stay at home with family and friends who had watched and been a part of this long journey with me, I decided to stay back in Jacksonville.

We actually had a big party, with family and friends. Jeremy Schaap of ESPN was there, as was Scott Hanson of the NFL Network. Bryan Craun, our longtime friend, was gracious enough to host it at his home—watching the draft at his house had become an annual event for my brothers and me. It was the first time that we were listening for my name, however.

Jimmy predicted that Denver would take me somewhere toward the end of the first round. However, Denver used their first-round pick on a wide receiver near the end of the first round, so it didn't look like that would be the case.

In the meantime, the Draft had been going on for hours—pick after pick, name after name. The excitement was still there, but people were nervous and tired. Would I be taken that night, or would I have to wait for the second round the next day—or later?

The phone rang. I looked down and saw a 303 area code. Denver.

I turned to Jimmy. "It's from 303. Should I answer it?" I knew who it was, but I didn't let my expression give it away.

Jimmy almost fell out of the chair, scrambling to his feet. "It's Denver! Answer it! Answer it! It's them!"

We still laugh about that.

It was Josh McDaniels, the head coach of the Denver Broncos, who told me that they were trading picks to move back into the first round and were selecting me.

I've heard rumors that the Minnesota Vikings and Jacksonville Jaguars were also trying to trade up to take me. However, neither did, and I was a Denver Bronco.

A few days later, on Mother's Day, I spoke at a church in Memphis and shared briefly about my mother's refusal to abort me. After the service, a young woman waited to speak with me. "I have an abortion scheduled for tomorrow morning at 9 A.M.," she cried, "and now I will not go through with it."

Amazing what God does when we simply plant seeds.

I rented a house with my brothers in Denver and began spending as much time as I could there, participating in every team activity.

Robby helps handle my off-field activities and Peter's in graduate school there. Although I had hoped to compete for the starting job from the beginning, the coaches made it clear that they didn't want to rush it, but would rather allow me to get acclimated to the NFL. They had traded for Kyle Orton the prior season, and he was still the starter.

I started the Tim Tebow Foundation to carry on the work that we began with First and 15, to bring faith, hope, and love to those needing a brighter day in their darkest hour of need.

I kept working hard, learning as much as I could the best that I could. It's a challenge, being a backup in the NFL. You get very few repetitions in practice during the week, but you need to be sharp and ready in case you play. As for me, I didn't play much at all for most of the year.

In our opening game, a loss to the Jaguars in Jacksonville, I rushed twice for two yards and didn't play again for five weeks. Then, against the New York Jets, I rushed six times for twenty-three yards, including my first NFL touchdown. The following week, I ran for another touchdown against the 49ers in a game that we played at Wembley Stadium in London. Two weeks later, I threw my first NFL touchdown pass and ran for another, against the Chiefs.

I was playing primarily in goal-line situations, and while I was pleased to be contributing, it was hard to watch from the sidelines while Kyle was quarterbacking. I hoped to have my role expand, of course. I don't know anyone who is successful who didn't believe that he could do something well if given a chance—I am no exception.

As the season progressed, we struggled to win games. After week 13 of the season, we were 3–9 (having already had our bye week), and Josh McDaniels was fired. His firing was distressing, in that Josh believed in me enough to draft me. It was also a strange situation once I arrived, because despite his belief, he didn't play me much. It's not like we were having such success that it would have been an unreasonable risk. But I also realized that the NFL is different, and Josh, the coaches, and management wanted to give me every opportunity to learn and grow to give me every likelihood of being successful. And so I continued to learn, work hard, and support Kyle and the team and, occasionally when I got in the game, do whatever I could do to help make us successful.

After Josh was let go, the uncertainty seemed to focus on me as much as on anyone. Speculation began immediately that I might not remain in Denver for long, because Coach McDaniels, my biggest supporter, was gone.

I didn't have time to focus on that. Instead, I dealt with the uncertainty the way that I've always tried to: I don't know what the future holds, but I know who holds my future. That's what gives me hope and peace and is what I lean on, because each day is going to have enough trouble of its own. That's why we don't need to look to tomorrow; we need to worry about today and look to Him as He guides and directs our day. What can we do today that will have eternal consequences not only then but now; how can we affect people in a positive way today; what are the right decisions we can make today? I know that no matter what happens, there's a plan for it, and even though we don't always understand it all and why things happen the way they do, I know that one day it will all make sense as part of God's eternal plan for all of our lives. Even if it doesn't turn out the way that I hope, it will be disappointing but I'll be all right, because God never stops loving me, or you. And God will use every one of those things—some of which may seem good and some bad to you at the time—in His overall plan for your life and mine.

Just because something bad happens doesn't mean that He stopped caring about you or that He stopped being sovereign. Those things are simply part of His plan that we'll never understand here on earth, like trying to understand the Trinity—the truth of God's existing in three persons: Father, Son, and Holy Spirit. I'm just never going to fully understand it. That's where faith comes in. It's not knowing about tomorrow, but it's knowing that I have a God who loves me and is going to keep me in His plans and safe in His hands through those coming days without my even knowing what's going to happen. It gives me great comfort to know that God is not only with me and carrying me when I need to be carried but, already waiting for me in my tomorrow. Now what is there for me to worry about with God already there to care and lay out His plan for me?

Sure, the emotions of the moment can weigh on me, but I try to quickly get myself refocused on the Lord. One way I do it is through prayer, and another way is by giving everything to the Lord. That's something my mom taught me when I was young, and she still says it to me today.

"Did you give your disappointments to the Lord?"

"Did you give your victories to the Lord?"

I've learned that even more important than the victories are the disappointments. So many times we can hold on to them and build a grudge and be frustrated at other people and at God, wondering why something happened, instead of giving it to the Lord.

I work as hard as I can but give the result, whatever it is, to the Lord, letting Him keep me humble in success and victory and lift me in disappointment or defeat.

I can't even remember how many times in high school Mom had to tell me to give my disappointments and losing to St. Augustine to the Lord. And also about losing to Alabama—to give it to the Lord. And about not starting at quarterback, giving that to the Lord. Just giving it to the Lord emotionally and spiritually and saying, "Lord, I know it's Your plan. I'm giving it to You, and You're going to handle this stress, because You're the one who is plowing the field, and You take this yoke from me. You're going to be the one pulling this yoke, and therefore I don't have any of the pressure. I'm just trying to live as best I can, but all the weight is on you."

Praying that prayer eases the burden, and that eases the pain of disappointment, heartache, and defeat we all face at times. Knowing that He has the plan for your life and also helps you in everything to give thanks, knowing it is all God's will in Christ Jesus. That's something else we heard a lot about as children, because all those bad things that happen to you, they happened for a reason. We might not always know what that reason is, but there is a plan. As competitive as I am and as mad as I can get on the football field and then with all those things that happen on and off the field, I still have to be able to give it to the Lord, even, and especially, all my disappointments. Because without giving it all to the Lord, I wouldn't have the same joy in my life or the same peace. I have had too many defeats and discouragements to not give them all to the Lord to be able to have a joyful life.

My parents have been a great nurturing mix for me. While my mom was helping me hand my disappointments to the Lord, my dad was always encouraging me, telling me, "You're going to be great. You are great. Just wait until they give you a chance."

Mom encouraged me, too, of course, and Dad also told us to wait upon the Lord. But in some ways, being who they naturally were, they made for a great pairing to raise us—optimistic and focused on God and His plan for our lives. All those things paid off, because they became ingrained in my heart and my life.

"You're going to be great, but give it all to the Lord."

Finally, in week 15, at the Oakland Raiders, I started my first NFL game. The plan had been for Eric Studesville, our interim head coach, to start me for the final two games, both home games, but Kyle had bruised his ribs the prior week and couldn't practice for the Oakland game, and so I started game 14 as well.

It was a challenge for all of us, because Kyle and I have very different styles, and the offense had been installed with his talents in mind. The coaches tried to tweak it in the game plan, but since they were monitoring his injury status, it still had many plays that were better suited for him.

I wanted to write a scripture verse somewhere for that game, but couldn't use my eye black because that was against NFL rules. Instead, I wrote it on my wristband, under my plays, and tweeted it that morning to my Twitter followers.

Given that we were playing in the Oakland Coliseum, which is known for its crazy, hostile crowds, the verse I chose seemed particularly appropriate:

*Even though I walk through the valley of the shadow of
   death,
I fear no evil, for You are with me;
Your rod and Your staff, they comfort me.*

PSALM 23:4

It was rainy and muddy. Fun football conditions.

In the first quarter, I made a mistake. On a third down and twenty-four play, they called for a "tailback draw," but instead I heard "quarterback draw." I don't know why—maybe my subconscious knew that I wanted to run the ball.

I held on to it and ran for a forty-yard touchdown. On the play, I stiff-armed their safety, Michael Huff, just before reaching the end zone, and the photos that resulted after the game were really cool, because "Psalm 23:4" was very clearly readable along my wrist. Later that quarter I threw a touchdown pass on a fantastic catch by Brandon Lloyd, and in so doing, I accomplished something that only two other players in NFL history had ever done: throw a touchdown pass of thirty or more yards and run for a touchdown of forty or more yards in the same game.

Unfortunately, we lost the game, dropping us to 3–11. I'd never been on a team with a losing record. Ever. It was tough and not anything that I want to experience again.

The next week we were facing the Houston Texans at home. Their quarterback, Matt Schaub, is very good, and we were looking forward to the challenge. The coaches had a week to prepare a game plan specifically for me, and we started off great. I was so excited to hear the Denver crowd react as we came onto the field for our first offensive possession. The cheers were so loud that I had to signal the crowd to quiet down so we could hear our snap count. That never happens at a home game.

We drove right down the field, with me completing my first two passing attempts, until I misjudged the angle on a one-on-one situation that our receiver had in the end zone, and the pass was intercepted.

We didn't do anything else of note during the first half and went into the locker room at halftime trailing, 17–0. In the second half, we decided to open up the offense, attacking downfield more than we had in the first half. Early in the half, I hit Jabar Gaffney on a fifty-yard pass that led to our first touchdown. We exchanged field goals, and then they added another, closing out the third quarter down 23–10.

Early in the fourth quarter, I threw a touchdown pass to Correll Buckhalter, and we trailed only 23–17. We got the ball back and began driving.

We reached their six yard line, and the coaches called for a pop pass on second down and goal. It was a fake quarterback draw to the right, and our receiver, Eddie Royal, was supposed to fake like he was blocking and then release to the goalpost for the pass.

The coaches made it clear that the play could be run against any defense except Cover 1, which consists of man-to-man coverage on the outside with the free safety in the middle of the field. I looked out and could see that Houston was in a Cover 1 alignment—good call by them, but not good for us. I sent the running back into motion, who is supposed to go into motion to the left, giving us three receivers to the right and two to the left.

He went right instead. That resulted in four receivers to the right, with only one to the left. With the play clock running down, we had to snap it and improvise. I took the snap and faked the quarterback draw, then began backing up, buying time. I hoped that a defender would leave his man to come after me, giving me an open receiver to throw to. No one did, and instead, I was able to beat the left end to the outside; and because the defensive back covering Brandon Lloyd on that side of the field didn't turn around, I was able to slip into the end zone.

The fans were going crazy in the stands, and we were too. We kicked the extra point and led 24–23. Minutes later Syd'Quan Thompson ended Houston's final drive by intercepting Schaub, and we had our fourth win of the season. In the process, I threw for over three hundred yards. All in all, it was a good day.

It was even more special because my entire family was there, including my nieces and nephew. Getting there was no small feat because the Atlanta airport closed, causing some to re-route, and Katie and Gannon to catch the last flight before it shut down. We had all planned on being together that week, because Christmas was the day before the game. Because I had to stay in the team hotel on Christmas, we actually celebrated two days after the game, on Tuesday the 28th.

A very merry Christmas for our family.

Our season finale was at home against the San Diego Chargers. My confidence was high, and it seemed that the coaches' and players' confidence in me had grown as well. I was particularly excited to face the Chargers, since Philip Rivers is widely recognized as one of the best quarterbacks in the NFL.

We didn't get off to a great start. A receiver dropped a long pass on our opening drive, and then I followed that up by throwing an interception on the next play. Even so, Brandon Lloyd and I connected on a touchdown in the first quarter, and we took an early 7–0 lead. However, by the third quarter, we trailed 23–7, and then 33–14 midway through the fourth.

On the ensuing kickoff, Cassius Vaughn scored for us on a ninety-seven-yard return, and then with twenty-six seconds left, I scored on a run, bringing it to 33–28.

We recovered the onside kick. The crowd was frantic, hoping for another miraculous finish. So were we. We ended up with two chances to win it. I threw two Hail Mary passes into the end zone from our own forty-six yard line, but both were knocked down by the Chargers. We lost, but had fought to the very end.

It's not often that a 4–12 team gets cheered as it leaves the field for the final time for the season—on a loss, no less—but that's exactly what happened. I think they appreciated the heart that the team showed in the loss.

Afterword

*Just as it is written, "Things which eye has not seen and ear has
not heard, and which have not entered the heart of man, all
that God has prepared for those who love Him."*
— 1 CORINTHIANS 2:9

The months since the end of the football season have been as busy and
exciting as ever. In addition to preparing for the upcoming football
season, I've been doing all I can to grow my Foundation, starting
with the hiring of executive director Erik Dellenback. Although the
Foundation is just getting underway, through the support of many
generous people that donate through timtebowfoundation.org, we
are already fulfilling the dreams of children with life threatening ill-
nesses, partnering with deserving children's organizations throughout the U.S., and supporting over 600 orphans worldwide. There is
no question that God has blessed me with a heart for children and I
fully intend to spend my free time working to bring faith, hope and
love to those in need.

As for football, the Broncos began their search for a new head
coach, and though everyone seemed to want to talk about where

I'd fit in with any new coach, I did my best to tune out all that chatter. If there's one thing I learned early on playing football, it was that I couldn't live my life if I was constantly concerned about what other people were saying about me. There have always been people saying that I couldn't do something, starting with that Mindanao doctor who said that I couldn't be born, but through it all, there's only been one voice that mattered. And I could hear Him loud and clear.

In the meantime, all I could do was tune out the white noise, keep working, and wait for the Broncos to make their decision. After speaking with a number of candidates, they hired John Fox, the former head coach of the Carolina Panthers. There were a number of candidates interviewed whom I would have been delighted to play for, and Coach Fox was one of them; I was pleased with the selection. When I was coming out of Florida, I had visited with Coach Fox on a number of occasions, but we both knew that there was a good chance I wouldn't be going to Carolina, since they didn't have a first-round pick, having traded theirs away. Even though we had to wait a year, we finally ended up together, and Coach Fox and I began working together this year.

His selection left me invigorated about the coming season and everything that it will bring. I've been working hard, training, pushing myself, trying to build up and improve upon the base that I created during my first season in the NFL. In many ways, the things motivating me now are the same as they were back when I was playing Pop Warner. Even today I find myself thinking constantly about the person out there who could be working harder than I am. I push myself to be the best I can be, and I listen to the voice that tells me to keep going.

As I've said before, I don't know what my future holds, but I do know who holds my future. With that in mind, I'm pressing on toward the upward call of Christ Jesus, seeking to continue living in the way that always brings glory to Him.

I hope it's on the football field, at least for now. But I know that He knows my platform and holds my future in His hands, and it's up to me to use it as best I can wherever He has me planted. God's Word will not return void. Football has always been my passion, and in one way or another, it always will be my passion.

I simply pray that I will continue to have the humbling privilege to touch others and lift them up through His Word—all for His glory.

Acknowledgments

First and foremost, I want to thank my Lord and Savior, Jesus Christ, for once again blessing me with a platform to share my story, which hopefully will influence others positively.

To Dad, because of your courage, you have inspired me to never settle and always press on.

To Mom, words cannot express how much you mean to me; you are a true example of a godly woman.

To my sisters and brothers-in-law:

Christy and Joey—thank you for teaching me the importance of sacrificing for God's work. You lead by example.

Katie and Gannon—I always have a brighter day when I'm with y'all. You always put a smile on my face.

To my brothers:

Robby—thank you for always looking out for and protecting me, you are so much more than a big brother to me. I couldn't do it without you.

Peter—thank you for being real and always reminding me to keep God first in my life.

To Uncle Bill, thank you for always being there for me, providing me with godly wisdom, and being like my second dad.

To Angel Gonzalez, I truly cherish our friendship. Thank you for your great ideas throughout this process, including coming up with the title, and your dedication to see the book through to completion.

To Coach Meyer, for believing in me and giving me a chance. I will forever treasure you and your family—y'all mean the world to me. Thank you for taking me in as a son. We had a great run.

To Kevin Albers, my best friend. Thanks for the memories. I'll always have your back—love you, Brother.

To Bryan Craun, thank you for your kindness, friendship, and unwavering support over the years. Make sure to keep that neck warm! Love you, CD5.

To Nathan Whitaker, thank you for everything. What I enjoyed the most was the transition from initially just being my co-author to becoming my friend. I am also very grateful for the assistance of Nathan's mother, Lynda Whitaker, who transcribed our many hours of conversations, and his father, Scott Whitaker, who worked alongside him to craft the manuscript and make my words a reality in print.

To Matt Johnson, Wendy Kirk, DJ Snell, and Greg Suess, thank you for your expertise in guiding us through the logistics of creating a book.

To Lisa Sharkey, Matt Harper, and the rest of the team at Harper-Collins, thank you for your patience and professionalism in making this a book of which I'm proud.